Praise for

'With her usual rigour, Tracey Spicer ———————— its clear biases and range of equalit————————— hensible.' **Faith Agugu, founder of Silve.** ————

'*Man-Made* is just the book we need as we grapple with how ——— will ch——— lives and our world . . . This is a book for everyone. Starting with an explana——— of how AI is already invading every facet of our everyday lives, Spicer delves into the questions we are all asking – and those we haven't even thought about. As the story of AI unfolds in *Man-Made*, the sense of urgency escalates, making this an exhilarating read. Spicer deserves our gratitude for throwing a light into dark places, and giving us the knowledge, tools and power to begin to understand the future.' **Dame Quentin Bryce, AD CVO**

'Tracey's brilliance in providing us with hard hitting realities, is perfectly coupled with her quick wit and humour, bringing forth invaluable history of our female tech, science, mathematics and medicine contributors and creators. Tracey manages to elicit anger, outrage and full-body laughter at the outrageous happenings of the past, all whilst providing a much needed history lesson on how we've managed to rub out female contributions, discoveries and innovation in the evolution of the digital age.' **Iyari Cevellos, Chair of Women in Technology (WiT)**

'I have felt concerned for some time about the power of algorithms, personal data collection, AI, virtual assistants, deepfakes, the invasion of my personal conversations that creates advertisements on my phone and the invisible digital filters that have been created with clear gender, anti-women and ethnic biases, but after reading Tracey Spicer's deep exploration of the truth, I am now really terrified about the future of humanity.' **Maggie Dent, author, educator and host of award-winning podcast** *Parental as Anything*

'*Man-Made* is a fascinating read that transforms something wholly inaccessible, elitist and terrifying into a real, tangible and suddenly very alive state of play. With her conversational tone and penchant for pop culture/real-world references, Spicer invites us all to take a seat at the table and have our eyes opened. Using humour, wit and an honestly jaw-dropping amount of research, I found myself yelling out loud in parts, blown away by just how deeply bias and bigoted coding runs. A must-read for anyone who relies on AI to help them succeed which, according to this book, is all of us. Run, don't walk.' **Hannah Diviney, writer, actress and advocate**

'Spicer's acutely observed dystopia about our AI future reminds us that actively tackling sexism in every part of our lives is a fierce battle that has barely started. With unrelenting detail and analysis, Spicer shows how a male default is woven through every part of our lives and will shape a disastrous AI future unless we act now. This call to arms for women's fundamental inclusion as AI shapes our world will stun many and should trigger a revolution.' **Catherine Fox AM, author of** *Stop Fixing Women*

'There's plenty of books by AI academics which succeed when it comes to explaining the technology but they are less robust at foreseeing the implications. This is where Tracey Spicer's book *Man-Made* truly excels. The Walkley Award-winning journalist brilliantly paints the picture of how AI and machine learning works and what it means for us right now and importantly how it will impact our future. Tracey highlights how AI is predisposed towards "misogyny, racism, ableism, homophobia and ageism" and as she reminds us, it "replicates at speed". Her book helps you understand the real issues at stake particularly when it comes to unconscious bias in AI. We all need to speak up about the very issues that will impact our future and this book will inform and embolden you to do that.' **Robyn Foyster, Editor,** *Women Love Tech*

'In *Man-Made*, journalist and author Tracey Spicer pulls back the curtain on the threats that AI poses to a future of equality and equal opportunity for all. Her six years of research, including the theories of academia, is presented in a way that is easy to digest, equal parts entertaining and frightening, but always compelling to read . . . I couldn't put *Man-Made* down.' **Marina Go, Independent Chair, Non-executive Director and author of** *Break Through: 20 success strategies for female leaders*

'This book will have you enlightened, educated and enraged all at the same time, while feeling hopeful for the future, because of women like Tracey Spicer shedding light on an area most of us felt too complex to challenge openly . . . but not anymore!' **Shivani Gopal, Founder and CEO, ELLADEX**

'AI is everywhere. But society's terror about it seems fixated on the wrong questions: will it help kids cheat on exams? Will robots be built smarter than humans and eventually overthrow our domination? But these are wrong questions. In her book, *Man-Made*, Tracey Spicer uses incisive journalism and impeccable research coupled with fierce curiosity and humour to peel back the layers of what it means for the future if machines are embedded with human bigotry such as misogyny, racism and homophobia. Far from technology being neutral, Tracey asks the question: What if an algorithm is actually a tool that persistently reinforces inequalities? . . . This fascinating, alarming, intelligent, compelling and ultimately hopeful read is for anyone who uses tech (yep, that's all of us!).' **Ginger Gorman, author of** *Troll Hunting: Inside the world of online hate and its human fallout*

'A defiantly funny and informative read – what should be bleak, Spicer makes inspiring. Both a correction of history and a warning for the future, *Man-Made* is a must read for those seeking a fairer future.' **Corinne Grant, lawyer, comedian and television presenter**

'Gripping. Compelling. Do yourself a favour and read this cautionary tale. We all need to read this, and learn from it. Tracey Spicer's storytelling methodically unpeels the biases that technology is wrapping around daily life and empowers women to stand up against a future designed by men to disadvantage them. Compulsory reading if you care about the future and its entrenchment of existing power structures.' **Madonna King, author of** *Ten-Ager*

'As eye-opening as it is entertaining, *Man-Made* is full of truths about the gendered impacts of AI that are uncomfortable to learn but crucial to act on.' **Antoinette Lattouf, author of** *How To Lose Friends and Influence White People*

'Coinciding with the re-emergence of artificial intelligence as a hot topic in mainstream Australia, Tracey Spicer's book is exquisitely well timed. Filled with illuminating and entertaining case studies, data and anecdotes, *Man-Made* exposes just how much of our seemingly brave new world is in fact shaped by a not-so-brave old guard. A wake-up call for anyone assuming the ChatGPT future will not be designed largely for – and by – the boys' club.' **Sarrah Le Marquand, editor-in-chief of** *Stellar* **and media commentator**

'Alexa not Alex, Siri not Sir. A brilliantly researched, and slightly terrifying look at how gender bias is as much a part of technology as . . . well, motherboards.' **Dee Madigan, Creative Director Campaign Edge, author and media commentator**

'*Man-Made* is not just engaging, it's important. In a world that is right now being invisibly shaped by powerful algorithms and AIs, Spicer shines a journalistic light into places that have remained too dark for too long.' **Darren Menachemson, Head of Digital Societies, Chief Ethicist and Global Partner, ThinkPlace**

'Far from creating a perfect world, Spicer reveals AI's unwieldy capacity to replicate existing patterns of inequality. In reckoning with its potential, she forces us to consider how our past is being programmed into our future. The sincerity of this book is nothing short of heroic.' **Vivian Pham, author of** *The Coconut Children*

'Thank God it's funny. If it wasn't, I'd be too scared to sleep. Tracey brings her sparkling wit and journalist's critical eye to this Frankenstein's tale for the digital generation. Meticulously researched, hilarious and shocking. Read this book before it's too late.' **Juanita Phillips, ABC TV News anchor and author of** *A Pressure Cooker Saved My Life*

'Tracey Spicer whips away the curtain to reveal the biases behind the technology we use every day. This is a fascinating, frightening, and important book that will change the way you see the modern world.' **Kerri Sackville, author of** *The Secret Life of You*

'In this brave new world of artificial intelligence, we are carried along by vast oceans of data. The services we receive, the news served to us, even the quality of our healthcare are increasingly shaped by how AI churns through data about us and everyone in our community. Just as the real ocean currents shift the water beneath us while remaining invisible and out of our control, so too is AI. Tracey Spicer's brilliant and sometimes terrifying book makes these hidden phenomena visible. She shows how AI can result in more injustice and unfairness, but there's hope. By better understanding this world, we're better equipped to survive and even thrive amid the data ocean's most terrifying tempests.' **Ed Santow, Co-Director of the Human Technology Institute and former Australian Human Rights Commissioner**

'AI is rapidly transforming our lives, and this important book highlights the stark challenges we are facing – that bias and inequity is deeply embedded at every turn. Tracey offers a compelling call to action for more accountable, equitable and ethical AI that properly reflects the diverse world we live in.' **Carol Schwartz AO, Chair of the Women's Leadership Institute Australia**

'The new world may be brave, but not as brave as Tracey Spicer. This book isn't just a warning to every government, business and human being on earth, it's also a cracking read that moves at fibre optical speed with wit, compassion, and intelligence of the non-artificial variety.' **Justin Smith, journalist and author of** *Cooper Not Out*

'Tracey Spicer uses her unmistakably human voice to warn us all about the deeply sexist Frankenstein's Monster that is modern AI. Humanity's potential overthrow and replacement by those without morals, without heart and without soul is real – and marching toward us right now.' **Yumi Stynes, author and broadcaster**

'Finally, a book on AI that is accessible to all people. In *Man-Made* Tracey Spicer, in a fabulously conversational style, delves into the history and development of artificial intelligence and maps out the absolute lack of consideration of women and minorities in the design and development of the machines that are running our world. *Man-Made* will put fire in the bellies of women and girls and will surely cause the tech men-folk to sit up and review the role they play. Essential reading for all people interested in the future of humanity.' **Dr Catriona Wallace, Responsible AI expert, Founder of the Responsible Metaverse Alliance and Adj. Professor**

'Brilliance! Artificial intelligence has been thrust upon us by the tech bros, in their own image and – terrifyingly – with Silicon Valley vested interests. No one consulted us; the ethics and existential risks have not been thought through. Tracey Spicer bravely leads us through this conversation, the biggest of our era . . . and one we need to have fast!' **Sarah Wilson, author of** *This One Wild and Precious Life* **and** *First, We Make the Beast Beautiful*

MAN-MADE

MAN-MADE

HOW THE BIAS OF THE PAST IS BEING BUILT INTO THE FUTURE

TRACEY SPICER

SIMON & SCHUSTER

London · New York · Sydney · Toronto · New Delhi

The cover image for *Man-Made* was created using Midjourney, an AI art generator that produced original images based on text prompts submitted by the cover designer, Meng Koach. AI generators use algorithms or 'neural networks' to analyse hundreds of millions of images online and compose all-new material based on the machine's understanding of the text. This process is evidently open to bias, and raises ethical questions about authorship, as discussed in *Man-Made*.

MAN-MADE: How the bias of the past is being built into the future
First published in Australia in 2023 by
Simon & Schuster (Australia) Pty Limited
Suite 19A, Level 1, Building C, 450 Miller Street, Cammeray, NSW 2062

10 9 8 7 6 5 4 3 2 1

Sydney New York London Toronto New Delhi
Visit our website at www.simonandschuster.com.au

© Tracey Spicer 2023

All rights reserved. No part of this publication may be reproduced, stored in a retrieval system, or transmitted in any form or by any means, electronic, mechanical, photocopying, recording or otherwise, without prior permission of the publisher.

 A catalogue record for this book is available from the National Library of Australia

ISBN: 9781761106378

Cover design: Meng Koach
Cover image: Meng Koach via Midjourney
Author photograph credit: Tāne Coffin
Typeset by Midland Typesetters, Australia
Printed and bound in Australia by Griffin Press

For Jase, Taj and Grace

CONTENTS

INTRODUCTION   1

1. The Founding Fathers   13
2. The Mother of Invention   21
3. Ghosts in the Machine   29
4. A Stable of Secretaries   37
5. Man-Made   45
6. Down the Rabbit Hole   55
7. Algorithmic Injustice   65
8. Black Mirror   75
9. Sounds of Silence   81
10. Robot Slaves   89
11. Domestic Bliss   99
12. Killer Fridges   107
13. Coercive Control   115
14. Virtual Rape   123
15. Sexbots   131
16. Deepfakes   141
17. Childcare Robots   151
18. Computer Says No   159
19. Frankenstein Datasets   167
20. Fair Game   179
21. Reality Check   187
22. Road to Nowhere   195
23. Military Intelligence?   205

24.	Worker Bees	215
25.	Cracking the Code	227
26.	Embracing Equity	237
27.	The Existential Threat	245
28.	Dystopia?	253
29.	Utopia?	261

EPILOGUE: Rage Against the Machine   269
GLOSSARY   277
ENDNOTES   281
ACKNOWLEDGEMENTS   289
ABOUT THE AUTHOR   291

INTRODUCTION

'Mum, I want a robot slave!'

It's 7.47 am on a Monday in 2016, and I'm wiping sleep from my eyes. Frankly, it's too early for an existential discussion with my 11 year old about the intersection between technology and human rights. Against our better judgement, Taj has been watching an episode of the adult cartoon series *South Park* in which Cartman – a very naughty boy – gets an Amazon Alexa. Like a colonial overlord, the 'toon hoon proceeds to order around Alexa in language replete with insults, abuse and sexual innuendo.

This is a lightbulb moment. Instead of moving towards a utopian future based on equity, we're reinforcing stereotypes around women and girls being the ones to fetch the tea and scones. I have form in this area: my memoir, *The Good Girl Stripped Bare*, rails against this demeaning treatment. We see this trope time and again in the mass media, local communities and even under our own roofs. And it has a wider significance.

Now, I'm no spring chicken, having worked as a journalist since – well, roughly – the early Cro-Magnon era. Much of my work is centred on the inequities faced by women and people from marginalised communities. I write newspaper columns and work on documentaries about everything from the Me Too movement to domestic violence in Uganda and gendercide in India.

It's heartening to see courageous communities around the world rising up and fighting back. Witness the Woman, Life, Freedom protests in Iran in response to the death in custody of Mahsa Amini, arrested for not wearing the hijab properly. Or the brave women in Afghanistan, taking to the streets after the Taliban banned girls and women from going to secondary schools and universities. The worldwide Women's March in 2017, and the Black Lives Matter movement.

I've always been a glass half-full kinda gal. At the end of speeches, I've often quoted the great Martin Luther King Jr: 'The arc of the moral universe is long, but it bends toward justice.' Nowadays, however, I'm not so sure that justice will prevail. My 'spidey senses' are tingling. I have a premonition of a fifth Horseman of the Apocalypse accompanying War, Conquest, Famine and Death. New technologies have the potential to worsen existing inequalities, sending us back to the Dark Ages.

After issuing Taj with a stern 'No', I walk him to the school bus stop. But I can't stop thinking about the implications of misogyny being embedded into these machines. Does this mean they're beset with other types of bigotry? Are racist, homophobic, ableist, transphobic and ageist attitudes also evident in the chatbots populating our homes?

So begins six years of research that almost kills me. From my keyboard in Australia I virtually traverse the continents from the Americas to Africa, tracing the constellation of technologies known as artificial intelligence. Put simply, AI is an umbrella term for machines which simulate human intelligence. Ultimately I'm on a mission to identify the villains: an antipodean Miss Marple, from the famed Agatha Christie novels. Minus the racism, of course.

Any fan of crime fiction wants to know 'whodunnit'. It's the same with AI. Who's building this beast? What can we do to mitigate its damage? And which organisations will be held to account? Actually, will anyone be held to account? At least in Mary Shelley's classic work of horror, Frankenstein realises the error of his ways before dying while fleeing from his monster. A related question is whether we, too, are culpable. After all, we're feeding this creature with our never-ending list of wants and needs.

INTRODUCTION

This issue is wildly complex. As a 55-year-old woman, I'm far from being a 'digital native' – more like a digital newbie – so it's like learning an entirely new language. Once we translate the tech-speak, we need to look back to antiquity, and ahead into the realms of science fiction. Writing this book is a labour of love: for the sake of our daughters, our sons, and humanity itself. No-one wants girls facing a future where they're considered inferior to boys; nor is it desirable to stereotype boys into rigid gender roles. And where do gender diverse children fit into this picture?

What I learn during my six-year odyssey changes my feminism forever. I begin by focusing on service bots in a feminised form. Over time, I discover automated soap dispensers that only work for white hands; so-called 'smart homes' trapping people with disabilities inside; and over-50s being refused medical help because, 'Computer says no'. I finish with the strong conviction that intersectional bias is being built into the machines running our futures. Consequently, our activism must be focused at the confluence of technology, race, gender, age, sexuality and disability.

Two-thirds of the way through the writing process, I'm struck down with long COVID. My health hangs by a thread. Attending back-to-back medical appointments for a year deepens my experience of bias within this 'fraternity': every single specialist I encounter is a white man. I'm certainly not blaming them individually. Some are extremely skilled and knowledgeable. But we view illness and treatment through different lenses.

Long COVID is experienced by twice as many women as men, according to the largest study of the condition to date.[1] Some of its symptoms are similar to myalgic encephalomyelitis, also known as chronic fatigue syndrome. ME/CFS was dismissed for decades as being 'all in your head, little lady!' or just some form of 'yuppie flu'. To think of historical medical bias being exacerbated by technology at scale is terrifying.

Conversely, artificial intelligence could save millions of lives. Machine learning, which is a subset of AI, can screen medical images, predict cancer and triage patients in emergency departments. Here's a personal example: more than 20 years ago, my beloved mother, Marcia, died from pancreatic cancer. The same disease later killed her father, my grandad 'Gunga'. It was a privilege to care for each of them towards the end of their lives.

Nowadays, my sister and I can take a simple genetic test to determine whether we carry this gene. In fact, I'm scheduled to do this next month. The test results will be crunched by an algorithm. If I carry the gene, I'll be able to modify lifestyle factors to reduce the risk. This might mean giving up the grog, more's the pity.

However, if bias is within the datasets or algorithm, the results will be tainted. The fact is this: all technology is biased because all humans are biased. Stereotypes comfort us in an ever-changing world. They allow our brains to make decisions quickly. This is incredibly helpful on the savannah while being chased by a tiger; it's not so helpful in the modern workplace.

People in tech – from the designers to the programmers and the billionaires running the show – insert their beliefs, attitudes and bigotry into their creations. Much like Frankenstein does into his creature. These innovations are supposed to make our lives easier. Spoiler alert: they don't. Instead, they're reinforcing the mistakes of the past. Actually, it's worse. They're amplifying inequity. Bias is a little like the COVID-19 virus: without interventions to flatten its trajectory, it replicates at speed. There are no masks, vaccines or ventilation to curb the spread of the bias bug.

This becomes obvious during a dinner to celebrate the *Australian Financial Review* 100 Women of Influence Awards at Sydney Town Hall. I bump into Dr Nicky Ringland, a fellow category winner. Dr Ringland has a brain the size of a small planet and is easy to spot with her shock of blue hair. I feel like an imposter being here: Nicky is

INTRODUCTION

an entrepreneur and a computational linguist who conducts outreach programs for kids. She's a Superstar of STEM – part of an initiative by Science & Technology Australia to smash gender assumptions in science, technology, engineering and mathematics, and provide role models for the next generation.

Fortunately, Nicky's also wonderfully down-to-earth, bouncing on her heels as she explains the challenges with 'big data'. Full disclosure: until this point, I've pretended to know what this expression means. For a long time, I've dropped it into discussions to sound more intelligent. (I rarely succeed.) Nicky is now a technology product manager, and – in her snippets of spare time – works on Tech Inc, a not-for-profit organisation teaching and mentoring people from underrepresented groups.

'The tech companies are all using texts from the 70s and 80s,' she tells me.

'What do you mean by texts?' I ask. 'Like books?'

It's a relief Nicky is adept at describing these concepts to children. 'Exactly right,' she replies. 'To train robots they feed them data, like words, images and videos. This is how they learn about the world. The problem is that in books from that era, every doctor is a "he" and every nurse is a "she".'

I'm having an epiphany. The baby bias, which is born in the algorithm created by the programmer, becomes a troublesome teenager through what's called 'machine learning'. It seems old-school bigotry is new again. Over time, the robots become increasingly biased, like white supremacists going down the rabbit hole of conspiracy theory websites.

Around this time, I'm asked to facilitate a most unusual discussion in the glorious grounds of one of Sydney's historic mansions. The topic centres on the ethics of sex with robots. To be honest, this isn't something I've given much thought to, aside from while watching Ryan Gosling in *Blade Runner 2049*.

In the real world, the overwhelming majority of bots are built in the female form, an extension of the madonna–whore dichotomy: either servile voice assistants or full-bodied sex toys. The great institutions of society – the justice system and governments – can't keep up with legislation to regulate the use of this technology, which raises salient questions. Is it rape if the robot doesn't consent? Can it be called sexual assault if the bot merely *represents* the female form? Or is there a place for automatons that can improve the quality of life for people who are elderly or living with disabilities? After all, sex is one of our basic physiological needs.

These ideas might appear esoteric. They certainly do to me, before these eye-opening conversations. But pernicious algorithms – and androids of all shapes and sizes – surround you from the moment you wake up in the morning to the time your head hits the pillow at night. As unsuspecting humans, we're propelled by forces beyond our control.

This doesn't mean that artificial intelligence is inherently evil. But it's still capable of killing us all. Even Elon Musk is scared. AI could be used to create 'an immortal dictator from which we could never escape', the tech billionaire says in the 2018 documentary, *Do You Trust This Computer?* 'If AI has a goal and humanity just happens to be in the way, it will destroy humanity as a matter of course without even thinking about it.'

It's time for a short and sharp review of the past few hundred years. From the late eighteenth century, successive industrial revolutions alter the course of history. The first Industrial Revolution, from the mid-1700s, introduces steam power. Beginning in 1870, the second sees the mass production of electricity. One hundred years later, electronics and information technology herald the start of the third Industrial Revolution. Artificial intelligence and data are the main drivers of the fourth.

The broad adoption of AI is as revolutionary as the invention of electricity. That's why I'm not anti-tech, per se. In fact, saying you're

INTRODUCTION

anti-tech is like saying you're anti-air, anti-water or anti-housing. We can't survive without it. Technology now has a place in Maslow's hierarchy of needs, the psychological theory explaining what motivates human behaviour. Nor do I have a set against artificial intelligence or machine learning. This specific technology, which will guide our future, could create a utopia with more leisure time, a healthier population and a fairer society. It might even reduce and perhaps reverse the devastating impacts of climate change.

But if you believe it's all 'sweetness and light', I have a lovely opera house in Sydney to sell you. There's a clear and present danger that we're heading towards a dystopia marked by authoritarian governments, mass unemployment and poverty, and digitally entrenched inequality.

Like cigarettes in the past, technology is touted as a cure-all, must-have prestige product, which should be firmly attached to your hand. How often do you see people sitting alone with their thoughts these days? Pondering the wonders of the universe? Daydreaming about their desires, hopes and fears? Instead, we're always hunched over our electronic toys. Imagine these masses of metal, plastic and wires becoming sentient. This is occurring through artificial intelligence, as our expensive playthings morph into our masters.

So what do the experts think? Well, to say they're worried is an understatement. In the words of Ghanaian-American-Canadian computer scientist Dr Joy Buolamwini, the founder of the Algorithmic Justice League: 'By the time we wake up, it's almost too late.'

I hope this book will join the canon of works identifying upcoming catastrophes and providing meaningful solutions. These include *Invisible Women: Exposing Data Bias in a World Designed for Men* by Caroline Criado Perez; *The Smart Wife: Why Siri, Alexa, and Other Smart Home Devices Need a Feminist Reboot* by Yolande Strengers and Jenny Kennedy; and *Sex, Race and Robots – How to Be Human in the Age of AI* by Ayanna Howard. In the interests of transparency, I don't

MAN-MADE

consider myself to be in the same *universe* as these luminaries. The majority of books in this area are written by academics and technologists. As a journo from the typewriter days, I'm merely a conduit between the dense research and what it means for you.

However, before we try to tackle the problem, we must understand where artificial intelligence exists in the everyday. We encounter AI every time we search for a product using Google or ride a 'smart elevator' in a city building. To explain how it's invading our lives, a group of ethical artificial intelligence experts in Australia has developed a timeline based on a single parent named Emmanuelle. This is from the group's website, aptly called SurvivAI:

6.00 am: Emmanuelle wakes up to an alarm using sleep performance metrics. I wear a Garmin watch to check my overnight health stats. But it seems sleep is considered 'performative' these days.

6.05 am: She turns off Mubert, a music platform created by artificial intelligence to enhance sleep. Believe it or not, lullabies created by machines are often technically better than those crafted by composers.

6.30 am: Time to do some stretches to prepare for the day. Emmanuelle does a 20-minute workout based on a yoga app that records her stats against fellow practitioners. Yoga is supposed to be non-competitive, but who am I to judge?

6.50 am: Emmanuelle checks her work emails using Spark, an app that automatically organises her inbox into sections such as Personal, News, Notifications and Seen. Didn't we used to be able to sort this ourselves? Or am I sounding like a curmudgeon?

7.00 am: The kids are woken by A.I. Awake, an alarm clock with a conversational robot. I imagine it whispers stuff like, 'I'm coming

INTRODUCTION

to kill you in your sleep'. Yes, I read far too many dystopian future novels.

7.10 am: Emmanuelle starts to make school lunches. The fridge notifies her which supplies are low. Seriously, fridges should have an alarm that blares when a teenager puts an empty milk container back in the door. Again.

7.20 am: She checks the forecast for the day using a weather app, then seeks clothing recommendations from Style by Alexa. Are humans losing the ability to dress for the weather conditions?

7.30 am: One of the kids checks how late the school bus is running via a real-time app. This, I like. Thank you, robot overlords.

8.15 am: Arriving at work, the car notes telematics from the journey. This is a digital blueprint covering every aspect of the car's functionality. Artificial intelligence is revolutionising the automotive industry; soon, we won't need to drive at all.

8.30 am–5.00 pm: Every day is saturated with exposure to artificial intelligence, from video conferencing to shared work platforms and smartphones. Even the office coffee machine is monitored by an app to optimise its operation.

5.30 pm: Emmanuelle sends a video to a group of girlfriends through Deep Nostalgia, which uses AI to turn your old images into short videos, adding head and eye movements. However, this tech is creepy when used to bring dead relatives 'back to life'.

5.45 pm: Our hypothetical heroine goes to the grocery store and buys items at the automated checkout. Don't you love how automation makes us work harder while paying for the privilege? There's the added bonus of countless job losses.

7.00 pm: Via the Nest app, the ideal ambience is set for the home's lighting, heating, and music before dinner. Nest is terrific until someone hacks into it, stealing money from your bank accounts via connected mobile devices.

8.00 pm: Exhausted but perpetually running, Emmanuelle opens Google to help the kids with their homework. These moments increase our emotional attachment to Big Tech, despite the villainous role it plays in widening the disparity between rich and poor.

8.30 pm: Preparing for the next day, she checks the online school app, before paying the bills and doing online banking. Yes, it's convenient. But we're putting people out of work by conforming to the mass automation plans of the corporate giants.

9.45 pm: She stays logged on to book a table at a restaurant for the weekend, while simultaneously scouring job advertisements. Behind many of these ads are algorithms that discriminate against women, people of colour, older folk and anyone living with a disability.

10.30 pm: To wind down, Emmanuelle reads a crime thriller on Kindle, based on automated suggestions. Outsourcing thinking contributes to the 'siloing' of opinions around the world, which cements outdated gender and racial stereotypes.

11.20 pm: Phew! Finally, she sets her sleep app alarm and goes to bed.

This appears to be a scene from the near future. But it's happening every day, right around the world. 'So what?' you might think. 'These devices reduce our mental load. It's a utopia, not a dystopia! Who wouldn't want a robot slave?' Unfortunately, this is short-term gain for long-term pain. The same technology is operating our cars, schools and hospitals. It's making decisions about who should get a job, home loan or ventilator – and who shouldn't. The robots know so much about us, they can determine who lives or dies.

INTRODUCTION

Most are being built by a small gaggle of middle-class white men based in Silicon Valley. When you're playing God, it's tempting to create your own games. Like, say, world domination. These boys *really* love their toys. As a result, dangerous anthropomorphic creatures are rampaging across the globe, unshackled by regulation, legislation or – often – consternation.

This is not a rant against individual men. Obviously, the patriarchy is a structure. So too, intersectional discrimination. This sits at the heart of the AI revolution. The history of this technology is studded with the achievements of privileged men, while women are relegated to supportive roles.

A note about gender in this book: when I write the word 'woman', I mean people who, regardless of their sex at birth, identify as a woman. Obviously, 'man' should be read as someone identifying as a man. While I've given a brief rundown on the main terms used in the book, I've also included a handy glossary at the end for your reference. I've also tried to throw in a few life rafts, to save us from drowning in a sea of acronyms.

Speaking of notes, fellow grammar nerds will notice this book is written predominantly in the present tense. Frankly, this topic deserves a sense of urgency. The purpose of *Man-Made* is to shine a light in dark places. To sort the villains from the victims. And to give you the knowledge, tools and power to push back and say, 'Enough!'

To understand the future we must interrogate the past. The seeds of our destruction were sown many moons ago. Strap yourself in for a wild ride from the dawn of time to the future of fembots.

1
THE FOUNDING FATHERS

'If you start believing in your greatness,
it is the death of your creativity.'
Performance artist Marina Abramović

The Founding Fathers of Artificial Intelligence are a fine set of fellas. Brimming with vim and vigour; full of wit and wisdom. They deserve to be celebrated and venerated, their names shouted from the rooftops! Of course, this is a lot of rot. The allegory of these 'fathers' illustrates the roots of AI bias that remain firm to this day.

Ten white American men are credited with creating the most transformational technology of the past century. But do they actually achieve this lofty goal? Are they deserving of a place within the pantheon or is this the stuff of science fiction? Allow me to take you back to a time of twinsets and pearls, when men were men and women merely an afterthought.

It's 1956 and a two-month gathering has been convened at Dartmouth College, New Hampshire. The group plans to talk about a 'seminal' paper co-authored by John McCarthy from Dartmouth College, Harvard University's Marvin Minsky, Nathaniel Rochester from IBM and Claude Shannon who works at Bell Telephone Laboratories.

Appropriately, 'seminal' – the word used to describe this paper – derives from 'of seed, or semen'. The proposal for the conference contains the term 'artificial intelligence'. Following the workshop, it becomes a research discipline – at least, according to media articles. These men are worshipped as gods on earth.

It's time to do some myth-busting. The truth is that artificial intelligence was not conceived, nor discovered, by these ten men. And the event at Dartmouth was, frankly, a dog's breakfast.

Back in the mid-50s, attendance at the workshop is by invitation. Of course, only men are invited. To be fair, Marvin Minsky's wife, paediatrician Gloria Rudisch Minsky MD, and their part-beagle, Senje, are also there. Gloria attends some of the sessions and comes in handy when the boys want their photos taken. I'm willing to bet she also makes a mean cup of coffee: 'White with one. There's a good girl.'

You may have heard of Marvin Minsky. He's remembered as an intolerant chap who wanted to replace the human mind, to him merely 'a meat machine'. Receiving the prestigious Turing Award at the zenith of his career, Minsky has been lauded as a genius. But I prefer to remember him in his later years. Minsky was named by Virginia Giuffre (then Roberts) in her 2016 deposition accusing sex offender Jeffrey Epstein of trafficking her while underage in the early 2000s. Giuffre said she was directed to have sex with Minsky when he visited Epstein's compound in the US Virgin Islands. Another witness testifies in the deposition that she'd seen Virginia Giuffre on a private plane with Minsky in 2001: at the time, Giuffre's 17 years of age; he's 73.[1]

Now let's look at the conference through a wide-angle lens. The 1950s are remembered for their 'relaxed and comfortable' images of white nuclear families, to purloin the words of former Australian prime minister John Howard. But there are signs of change. This era witnesses the rise of Martin Luther King Jnr as a key Black civil rights leader. In 1956, the US Supreme Court rules segregation on buses violates the constitution, following the famous protest by Rosa

THE FOUNDING FATHERS

Parks. And in Australia, the 'marriage bar' is finally lifted for women employed in education. (Women are capable of working after being married. Who knew?)

Within this social context, the men at the Dartmouth AI conference appear to be outliers – misfits – stuck in a stuffy and cloistered part of the academic landscape. Children with their fingers stuck in their ears chanting 'La, la, la, la, la!', pretending to ignore the progress unfolding before their very eyes.

Really, Dartmouth is like a summer camp for geeky grown-ups. The adult version of *American Pie Presents: Band Camp* without the infamous flute scene. Actually, this is an assumption. Given Minsky's alleged predilections, who knows what goes on behind closed doors? What we *do* know is most of the men don't spend the whole two months there. Some who say they'll come don't turn up at all. People meander in and out at leisure.

When you think of monumental events in science, you might picture naturalist Charles Darwin addressing the Linnean Society on his theory of evolution, chemist Marie Curie discovering radium and polonium, or biologist Rachel Carson releasing her book *Silent Spring*, a catalyst for the environmental movement. Designating Dartmouth as a moment like this is akin to putting on a blindfold and playing 'Pin the Tail on the Timeline': it's entirely arbitrary. The organisers would probably admit this to be true. There's no sense at the time that it should be preserved for posterity. John McCarthy loses the list of attendees. Later, an incomplete list of those attending is handwritten on a piece of paper.

Tech historian Daniel Crevier refers to it as 'an informal gathering' in his 1983 book *AI: The Tumultuous History of the Search for Artificial Intelligence*. It's so informal that under the name 'Richard Shoulder' is written 'Shoulder's friend'. (Who on earth is this? Collar bone? Bicep?) The aim is to establish a framework for the academic exploration of 'thinking machines', but that doesn't happen either. The scientists are too wrapped up in their individual projects and show little interest in founding a new academic discipline.

James Moor, director of the 2006 Dartmouth Artificial Intelligence Conference: The Next Fifty Years (AI@50), puts it best. Writing a summary in the same year for *AI Magazine*, Moor says that at the end: 'There was no agreement on a general theory of the field and in particular on a general theory of learning. The field of AI was launched not by agreement on methodology or choice of problems or general theory, but by the shared vision that computers can be made to perform intelligent tasks.'

Wow. Mind blown. Memo, fellas: this isn't new at all.

The idea of machines or automatons that move and think like humans goes back to antiquity, and the modern realisation predates Dartmouth by more than a decade. As Distinguished Professor Genevieve Bell, director of the School of Cybernetics at the Australian National University, points out in 2021 in 'Touching the Future', an essay for the *Griffith Review*: 'while AI might have been named and claimed in 1956, much of its intellectual agenda had earlier roots in conversations that started in the 1940s.'

Why does this matter? Well, stories like this are infuriating. Myths about the greatness of select men permeate our history. Deification leads to an aura of invincibility. Conferring divine status on mere mortals inevitably results in disaster. Ego, pride and vanity will eventually destroy humanity. Tracing this historical arc is crucial to understanding the mess we're in today.

I'm not the only one mightily pissed off. Several tech historians accuse the conference convenors of grossly underestimating the difficulty of the project. Gee, ya think? File that under Special Subject: The Bleeding Obvious. Many of the shortcomings of artificial intelligence are due to the blinkered approach adopted by these 'Founding Fathers'. They failed to position artificial intelligence within a wider social context.

THE FOUNDING FATHERS

I email Bell to explore this further. She reminds me that the senior leaders at Dartmouth are from industry, like IBM. Other funders include the RAND Corporation, 'part of the broader US defence ecosystem'. They aren't interested in messy conversations about humanity or divergent points of view. 'AI was always and already about commercial interests,' Bell writes.

Their narrow view is also due to the dire lack of diversity. But the homogenisation runs deeper than gender, culture, race, age, sexual orientation or disability. The conference isn't an interdisciplinary event. With the exception of Herbert A. Simon – a political scientist, economist and cognitive psychologist – nearly all the attendees are computer scientists. They think of artificial intelligence in terms of advancing technology and saving money for business. There's no focus on the possibilities for social improvement, nor any potential negative consequences.

This is like a group of economists meeting during a global pandemic without involving doctors, nurses or medical researchers. (Oh, crap: that pretty much sums up 2022. Slow clap for politicians saying, 'Nothing to see here. Move along!') Humans have a rich history of putting dollars before sense. But the so-called Founding Fathers actually had a template for a more collaborative approach.

The Macy Conferences, held between 1941 and 1960, are famous for hosting anthropologists Margaret Mead and Dorothy Lee, and psychologists Julia Eisenbud and Molly Harrower. Yes, *that* Margaret Mead, who correctly contends that gender roles are constructed by society, not necessarily based on biology. This forms a solid platform for the work of Cordelia Fine, the British philosopher who explains the concept of 'neurosexism' to the world. What a fabulous faculty of feminists!

The explicit purpose of the Macy conferences is to promote meaningful communication across disciplines and restore unity to science. 'They're particularly concerned about the moralities of technology . . .

and how to articulate the role of humans in the rise of computational systems,' according to Professor Bell. Seriously, we can't overstate their influence across the generations in the fields of psychology, neuroscience, and 'informatics'. These conferences continue to redefine science, with a focus in 2021 on COVID-19 and medical education.

By contrast, the main achievement of Dartmouth is coining the term 'artificial intelligence'. Jeez, fellas. You can put two words together. Creative genius right there. But this term generates controversy. Originally, John McCarthy suggests the discipline might be called 'studies of automatons' or 'machine intelligence'. Enter the power of the almighty dollar. It's decided 'artificial intelligence' is a catchier phrase, more likely to encourage the Rockefeller Foundation to sponsor future conferences.

This nomenclature is blamed for fuelling unrealistic expectations about the possibilities for anthropomorphising machines. As Dr David M. Burns writes in his 2020 paper *Artificial Intelligence Isn't*, 'Fortunately or unfortunately, true AI with the capacity for reasoning remains in the realm of science fiction. People should not pretend otherwise; although there are many benefits of the technology currently available, there is also real capacity for harm by using it inappropriately.'

The 'Founding Fathers' ultimately fail their own Turing test, the universal test for intelligence in a computer. They promise the moon and stars but ultimately deliver space junk – and, in 2018, an orbiting Tesla.

One anecdote from Dartmouth says it all about the lack of a collective approach to this technology. During Dartmouth, computer scientist Allen Newell, sociologist Herbert A. Simon and programmer J.C. Shaw of the RAND Corporation present the first programmed thinking machine, called Logic Theorist.

This is absolute proof that a machine can perform tasks previously only done by humans. Exciting, right? Perhaps even revolutionary. Now, this conference has the express intention of driving forward the

THE FOUNDING FATHERS

discipline of artificial intelligence. Surely Logic Theorist would spark a significant buzz. What happens is the complete opposite.

When Newell, Simon, and Shaw give their presentation, it receives a 'lukewarm response' from the group. 'The evidence is that nobody save Newell and Simon themselves sense the long-range significance of what they were doing,' tech historian Pamela McCorduck writes in her 1979 history of AI, *Machines Who Think*.

This is nothing short of gobsmacking.

The world's first artificial intelligence program is shown to the Founding Fathers of AI and ... they miss it. This is like Einstein showing someone $E=mc^2$ and being met with an eye-roll: 'Meh. Mass–energy equivalence. I get it. Seen it all before. Blah, blah, blah. Can someone bring me a cup of coffee? Gloria?'

Here's the kicker: co-creator of the Logic Theorist, Herbert A. Simon, goes on to win the A.M. Turing Award for computer science in 1975 and the Nobel Prize in Economic Sciences in 1978. But in 1956, no-one in the room listens to him because there are too many egos.

'They didn't want to hear from us, and we sure didn't want to hear from them: we had something to *show* them!' Simon tells Daniel Crevier for his book. 'In a way, it was ironic because we already had done the first example of what they were after; and second, they didn't pay much attention to it.'

I'm reminded of young boys in a sandpit, saying, 'No, *my* toy is the best!' Or, if I'm being naughty, older boys standing at a urinal saying, '*Mine* is the biggest'.

Okay, maybe I'm being a bit hard on these fellas. Dartmouth makes a significant contribution to the field of artificial intelligence. But the idea that the participants are Founding Fathers is questionable. In subsequent endeavours, they're supported by many women – often working in coding and data processing – whose work is unrecognised. Why does this matter? Well, as the saying goes: you can't *be* what you can't *see*.

The TV series *Star Trek* provides an excellent example. The late performer Nichelle Nichols breaks new ground playing Lieutenant Uhura, inspiring many Black women to study aeronautics. She's the subject of countless nerdy boys' fantasies, but that's a tale for another time. While working as an ambassador with NASA, Nichols helps recruit chemist and linguist Dr Mae Jemison to the space program. Joining NASA's astronaut program in 1987, Dr Jemison becomes the first African American woman in space. 'Science is not a boy's game,' Nichols says. 'It's not a girl's game. It's everyone's game.' Don't you love stories like this?

Role-modelling is relevant at home, as well as at work. In primary school, my daughter, Grace, shows promise in maths, while son Taj is a reader who loves English. As older teenagers, Taj is obsessed with computing and Grace has little interest in technology. She and her female schoolmates don't see enough women in STEM on a regular basis for it to be considered a viable pathway. She speaks of being 'elbowed out of the way by the boys' while trying to access equipment for a chemistry experiment. Part of the problem is *his*tory obscuring *her*story.

Too often, we fail to honour our forebears. This is why there are more statues of animals than real Australian women, according to researcher Chrys Stevenson. One of the greatest inventions of our time – the internet – is *not* the result of the work of two men. Countless people, of all genders, races and abilities, have collaborated on the connected world we enjoy today.

Unless these memories are set in stone, or emblazoned on history's page, they may be lost forever. Or erased by the cult of masculinity evident among the Founding Fathers. These men hold no property rights over artificial intelligence. In fact, the thought that machines or automatons could be made to perform intelligent tasks is almost as old as time itself.

2
THE MOTHER OF INVENTION

> 'Women upset everything.'
> **Henry Higgins,** *Pygmalion*

A deep vein of misogyny runs through the famous George Bernard Shaw play *Pygmalion*, based on a character from Greek mythology. According to Ovid's *Metamorphoses*, Pygmalion is a Cypriot sculptor. After witnessing prostitution, he determines to remain celibate, 'detesting the faults beyond measure which nature has given to women'. I assume he's a rather repressed character, repulsed by women's sexuality.

Pygmalion then carves a sculpture of a woman so perfect that he falls in love with it. On Aphrodite's festival day, he wishes for a bride who would be 'the living likeness of my ivory girl'.

This next part is creepy. When Pygmalion returns home, he kisses the statue, which has warm lips. He kisses it again and the statue comes to life. With Aphrodite's blessing, Pygmalion marries the transformed sculpture.

God complex or narcissistic personality disorder? I guess we'll never know.

There seems to be a strong lineage from the original Pygmalion to the modern-day 'incels': members of an online community of young men who are involuntarily celibate, unable to attract women sexually. Their forums host countless references to violence against women.

While Pygmalion is celibate by choice, he holds similarly hostile views towards the 'fairer sex'.

Greek mythology is full of stories about men breathing life into inanimate objects: The craftsman Daedalus uses quicksilver to give voice to his statues; the Greek god of artisans, Hephaestus, creates automata for his workshop; and Talos, a giant artificial man made of bronze, circles Crete three times daily to protect the island from invaders.

These myths come alive through the works of Hesiod, the ancient Greek poet. Fun fact: Hesiod first describes Pandora as an evil woman moulded from earth and sent to earth to punish humans for discovering fire. A bit like a big, bad robot. Anyone else notice the male robots are built as protectors, while the females are either evil or sexual?

The trope of the sentient statue continues through antiquity into the Renaissance and the writings of William Shakespeare. In *The Winter's Tale*, the king of Sicily is presented with a lifelike statue of his (long-presumed dead) wife, Hermione, which miraculously awakens. 'O, she's warm!' the king exclaims. This must give him quite a shock. After all, the king is the one who falsely accused Hermione of infidelity, leading to her imprisonment and 'death'.

It's fair to say the dream of creating human-like creatures from matter has been around since long before the Dartmouth conference. This concept is as old as Adam, a man God supposedly moulded from clay. And Jewish folklore refers to 'golems' – beings formed from clay or mud, animated and controlled by their creator. There's no such thing as a new idea, but claiming to have conceptualised artificial intelligence after *millennia* seems like spin to me.

If the idea is nothing new, what about the science? Again, this is old hat. The recorded history of the development of artificial intelligence is extremely Anglocentric, yet some of the earliest female scientists are found in Ancient Egypt between the twenty-sixth and twenty-fourth centuries BCE. Western education also overlooks the Golden Age of Muslim civilisation between the sixth and thirteenth centuries CE, which lays the foundation for robotics and artificial intelligence as we know it today.

Indeed, the word 'algorithm' comes from the Muslim mathematician Muḥammad ibn Mūsā al-Khwārizmī (c.780–850 CE), who's behind the invention of algebra. Incidentally, products we use every day are based on innovations pinched from the Middle East including coffee, soap and clocks. Failing to acknowledge this history shows ignorance bordering on bigotry.

In the ninth century CE, the Banū Mūsā brothers write *The Book of Ingenious Devices*, constructing a framework for future inventors. Many of these ideas reach Europe through Islamic Spain, home of the magnificent Alhambra. Don't get me started on this iconic monument or I won't stop: it's a mathematical masterpiece, a paean to geometry. You know the Escher prints with their bizarre optical effects? Inspired by the tessellated tiling at the Alhambra.

Roughly a century after the Banū Mūsā brothers release their book, Syrian woman Mariam 'Al-Astrolabiya' Al-Ijliya uses mathematical knowledge, craftsmanship and expertise in metallurgy to advance the building of 'astrolabes': ancient astronomical devices. These have been dubbed 'the original smartphones', calculating altitude, latitude and time of day. Essentially, Middle Eastern scientists, writers and artisans paved the way for the development of artificial intelligence. Take that, Minsky.

But we can cast our net back further. The most basic precursor to the development of artificial intelligence is binary code. Crikey: technical language alert! As the name suggests, this code uses the digits 0 and 1 to represent a letter, number, or character. Something called UTF-8 is the dominant encoding for internet technologies.

To code the word 'Hello', you type 01001000 01100101 01101100 01101100 01101111. Yes, it's tedious – but effective. Binary code is commonly attributed to Gottfried Wilhelm Leibniz, a German mathematician. But Leibniz is no more responsible for inventing this code than the 'Founding Fathers' are for discovering artificial intelligence.

If we dig deeper into this fascinating history, we find a real eureka moment: new scholarship suggests binary code was created by *women*. About time this was recognised!

There's a strong connection down under. Aboriginal Australians – the longest continuous civilisation on earth – have for millennia been using technology, engineering and complex mathematics to develop and teach the world's first code through the medium of weaving. This has always primarily been considered 'women's business'. Why aren't we reading more about this? Surely it should be on the front pages of our newspapers.

To find out more, I direct message one of my favourite tweeps. Corey Tutt has a rich personal story, from zookeeping to travelling through Australia and New Zealand as an alpaca shearer. An Indigenous mentor and STEM champion, Tutt runs the not-for-profit DeadlyScience to ensure every remote school has resources to tell the real history of First Nations scientists. 'Next week is good,' he DMs back, 'bring a cuppa 'cause we will be mates after our Zoom'. Tutt makes a poignant observation: 'Remember, great science comes from strong women in our lives that teach us empathy.'

During the interview he doesn't mince words, speaking truth to power. 'We have fish traps that have been here for many tens of thousands of years,' he says. 'And people who say that Aboriginal people weren't scientists . . . are just ignorant.' When you combine these two pieces of information, it becomes clear Australia's Indigenous women are among the world's first scientists.

So how does computer coding replicate weaving in a practical sense? My head is starting to spin. A couple of crafty friends explain. In weaving, there are two sets of elements that combine to create a fabric. The 'weft' goes over and then under the 'warp'. This represents an early code of zeroes and ones. The code assigns a pattern to each instruction on a computer. The same principle applies to weaving Aboriginal baskets, Inuit textiles or French silk.

This intersection between computational thinking and Indigenous craft comes full circle in Canada. Callysto is a computer program for teaching digital skills. Students use it to study the mathematical principles for creating fish traps, baskets and beading. Over time, they're building a digital archive of Indigenous science and engineering for future generations. One hell of a yarn is looming right before our eyes! Honestly, I'm in nerd heaven writing this chapter, where history, technology and the arts intersect. What's not to love?

You may be aware of a type of fabric called jacquard. It's intricate in design, a little like brocade. Using the same warp and weft principles, in the early nineteenth century French inventor Joseph Jacquard perfects a loom that can be programmed to weave any pattern into a fabric using cheap cardboard pockmarked with holes. This is happening in a period resplendent with bonnets, corsets and petticoats. Looms are in constant demand.

Jacquard has automated the weaving process, building on the work of women over the millennia. When you think about it, computers are simply tools used to process information, like so many rows of threads. Computing is born out of a need to organise rows of numbers for government and business as efficiently as the Jacquard machine does with cotton and silk.

While Joseph Jacquard is put on a pedestal, women's contributions are swept under their voluminous bustles. Traditionally, public speaking is considered to be a masculine pursuit; women are required indoors to – literally – keep the home fires burning. For centuries, men control printing presses, industry and resources, limiting women's access to education. They shout their own achievements from the rooftops, ensuring their place in the history books.

MAN-MADE

Still, there's a delightful irony about the male-dominated industry of computing growing from the quintessential 'women's work' of weaving. Philosopher and author Sadie Plant puts it succinctly in her 1995 article 'The Future Looms: Weaving Women and Cybernetics': 'The loom is the vanguard site of software development.' Boom!

Weaving's twin is knitting. If you partake in this ancient craft, you can also call yourself a coder. You see, basic knitting is a binary code of knit 1, purl 2 (K1, P2). Nanna's covertly coding, one click at a time. It could be said the practice of yarn bombing is the ultimate public display of STEAM: the meeting of science, technology, engineering, art and mathematics. The 'fibre arts' and programming are intertwined – pun intended.

Honestly, I'd rather stick a knitting needle in my eye than click and clack away the hours. I admire people who enjoy craft, but I don't have the patience. However, looking for the first time at knitting charts, the connection makes sense. Rather than the type of text pattern laid out in abbreviations, knitting charts are in grid format, each box representing a single stitch. You follow the rows and columns to determine the pattern.

So too, languages like JavaScript and Python rely on symbols and keywords to tell the computer about the desired output. Knitters are using symbolic language long before Alan Turing, known as the father of modern computer science, comes along. When we look throughout history, we see many 'fathers' of invention, but few 'mothers'. Except, of course, necessity.

An everyday replication of this is the celebration of fathers who take their babies out in a pram, while mothers perform this role invisibly. Just once, I'd like a round of applause for raising the children to adulthood. Or even a pat on the back. Okay, I'd settle for a gentle smile once in a while.

Following its invention, Jacquard's punch card/binary system for textile looms makes its way to Britain. (Not on its own, obviously.

This particular inanimate object can't be brought to life. Although it would be rather a sight, an enormous creature made from timber and string, swimming across the English Channel!) Here, it's seen by mathematicians Charles Babbage and Ada Lovelace.

Babbage realises Jacquard's system could program a machine to perform complex mathematical functions. Huzzah! The brilliant Babbage invents the first primitive computer, called the Analytical Engine. But not alone. Babbage lacks focus, flitting from one project to another, without giving adequate attention to any. People probably call him a 'flibbertigibbet' behind his back. Or is that term reserved for women and girls?

Ada Lovelace, Babbage's associate, wants to work on his Analytical Engine. She insists he sticks to it. And so another trope comes to life – the strong woman behind the successful man. Like the Founding Fathers, Babbage looks at his machine in terms of its mechanistic capabilities, through the lens of technological advancement.

You can imagine his epiphany: 'Look! Something that can make me money! I'm going to be rich. *Rich*, I tell you!'

Lovelace, an equally talented mathematician, takes a more humanistic view. 'We say most aptly,' she notes, after viewing the loom, 'that the Analytical Engine weaves Algebraic patterns, just as the Jacquard loom weaves flowers and leaves.'

Realising Babbage's computer is capable of much more than he envisages, Lovelace comes up with the first computer algorithm. Who would have thought? A *woman* is the world's first programmer. This would've had people in 'proper' society raising their eyebrows and tutting. Their knickers would have well and truly been in a twist.

Lovelace is the first person to see the potential in the machine to create almost anything, beyond its abilities as a bloody big calculator. 'Supposing, for instance, that the fundamental relations of pitched sounds in the science of harmony and of musical composition were susceptible of such expression and adaptations, the engine might compose elaborate and scientific pieces of music of any degree of complexity or extent,' Lovelace writes in her notes. She calls her style 'poetical science' and predicts the development of general-purpose computers 100 years before they're invented.

However, it's a long road paved with questionable intentions. At Edward Charles Pickering's Harvard Observatory in the late 1800s, women work as human computers for 25 cents an hour (and some as volunteers), classifying and cataloguing countless stars at an astounding rate. The women are treated like factory workers and referred to as 'Pickering's harem'. Yes, my eyes are rolling so far back into my head, the irises are disappearing.

A new century ushers in a string of outstanding achievements by women in computing, including Mary Clem from Iowa State College coining the term 'zero check', which identifies errors in calculation. But as we motor towards a brighter future, roadblocks are put in our way.

3
GHOSTS IN THE MACHINE

'It is often easier to ask for forgiveness
than to ask for permission.'
Grace Hopper, legendary computer scientist

Close your eyes and picture a time when the world is at war. Our minds may drift to the courageous men fighting on the frontlines. But millions of women are also behind the wartime effort, working in factories, tending the wounds of injured soldiers and advancing the new science of computing. During both world wars, women use the binary patterns of knit and purl to hide messages in morse code.

Female spies disguise messages in embroidery, knitting and rugs. In Belgium, older women watch rail yards for the comings and goings of enemy soldiers. They stitch details about their observations into cloth, passing it on to the Allies. No-one notices them. It seems the tendency for women to become invisible as we age does have its benefits, after all.

Not long after Turing invents his abstract computational model in 1936–37, film actor Hedy Lamarr works on a device that could stop the Germans tracking the radio signals of Allied planes. Austrian-born Lamarr is quite the Renaissance woman. She stars in the first non-pornographic movie to portray the female orgasm. Between roles, Lamarr works as an inventor. Seeking a collaborator, she doesn't call on a scientist, but a musician – pianist and composer George Antheil.

In a 2016 play about Lamarr's invention, her character explains she has learned about anti-aircraft technology while married to an Austrian arms manufacturer. Determined to keep her out of the movie industry, her husband takes her to business meetings where she has to listen to 'Fat bastards argue antiaircraft this, vacuum tube that', according to the magazine *Scientific American*. Seriously, the woman deserves a Nobel prize for this alone.

Between them, Lamarr and Antheil develop a mechanism that causes radio signals to 'hop' between different frequencies – like a rabbit on steroids – making them unintelligible to the enemy. Although it's not used in the war, frequency-hopping spread spectrum eventually becomes a vital part of Bluetooth and wireless technology. There's something of Ada Lovelace's vision of 'poetical science' in this invention because it, too, is based on a musical concept.

Many universities now offer degrees in the mathematics of music. It makes sense when you think about rhythm, scales, intervals, patterns, symbols, harmonies and time signatures. The ancient Greek mathematician Pythagoras is attributed with discovering that a half-length string will play a pitch exactly one octave higher than a full-length string. However, his followers – the Pythagoreans – believe the souls of dead humans occupy the bodies of animals. So it's probably wise to take some of his teachings with a grain of salt.

Also during World War II, six female 'human computers' are employed to work on ENIAC, the world's first general computer, originally envisaged by Ada Lovelace. The Electronic Numerical Integrator and Computer is the fastest yet developed – capable of 5000 additions per second – but it has no mechanism for storing data. For each new set of calculations, the computer has to be programmed manually.

The women employed for this purpose become known as the 'ENIAC girls'. A clear division of labour emerges: designing and building hardware is men's work; programming the software is 'women's work'. To be truer to the era, let's use the infantilising term:

these 'girls' have to crawl in and out of the enormous machine to solve operational problems. Imagine how often they're grabbed on the bottom. Or, as we say these days, sexually assaulted.

When the first reports of ENIAC's operation are written, the women aren't even mentioned. They're invisible: deliberately disappeared from history. This reeks of Good Girl Syndrome. Sit there nicely and quietly, cross your legs like a lady, and never talk about the nasty business of money. There's a good girl.

After they prepare the computer and demonstrate its abilities to the public in 1946, the university hosts a gala dinner. None of the women are invited. ENIAC sparks the beginning of the computer age, and without the efforts of these trailblazers, none of the work on artificial intelligence would have been possible. The very least we can do is to remember and honour them within these pages.

A more controversial application of mathematics during World War II was the development of the first nuclear weapons as part of the Manhattan Project, involving Hungarian American polymath John von Neumann. One year later, the world is horrified to see the results in Hiroshima and Nagasaki. It's the understatement of the century to say the history of computer development is inextricably linked with warfare. Like Babbage, von Neumann focuses narrowly on a machine for making calculations, in this case to kill enemies.

Enter professor of mathematics Grace Hopper, who – with computer scientist Jean E. Sammet – writes the first code compiler for a computer in the late 1950s. Okay, let's slow down here: I need to google this. (Don't you love how the name of one of our tech overlords is now a transitive verb?) According to the search engine, a code compiler translates a programmer's instructions into zeroes and ones, which a computer can understand. Phew!

Moving on, Hopper's team develops Flow-Matic, the first programming language to use English-like commands. 'What I was after in beginning English language [programming] was to bring another whole group of people able to use the computer easily . . . I kept calling for more user-friendly languages,' Hopper explains in an oral history interview. 'Most of the stuff we get from academicians, computer science people, is in no way adapted to people.' Hopper is bang on. Much of this information is impenetrable.

Hopper later contributes to the development of COBOL, which is so easy to learn it becomes the most extensively used computer language in the world. Hopper's software opens up the possibility of realising Lovelace's vision: a computer program allowing machines to work collaboratively with humans to perform a broad range of functions.

One day, a moth becomes trapped inside a mechanical switch in her computer, so she has to get it out. File this anecdote under Legends Who Still Have to Clean Up the Mess in the Office. (I do hope she wasn't asked to make the coffee.) Hopper is the first person to call this process 'debugging'. The remains of the moth are preserved at the Smithsonian Institution inside a logbook annotated with, 'First actual case of bug being found'.

This is a tip of the hat to generations of engineers who describe flaws in their machines as 'bugs'; Thomas Edison talks about 'bugs' in electrical circuits in the 1870s. It's also an appropriate way to describe how computers make us feel when they don't work properly: 'This computer's really bugging me!' By the age of six, my firstborn, Taj, has witnessed countless blow-ups at the family computer. One day when the television goes on the blink, he comes to me to ask if he can watch a cartoon show on 'that bloody machine'. He thinks this is what the computer's called.

Men like John von Neumann continue to develop the field of computer science, but women do most of the mathematics, data wrangling and physical work of coding. This is tedious, repetitive work, requiring meticulous attention to detail, which women are thought to be better-suited to temperamentally – yet another sexist notion.

We're supposed to be softer, gentler and infinitely patient. Well, bugger that. I think it's more to do with women providing cheaper labour. In the 1950s, coding is 'women's work'.

There's zero prestige. These women are units of labour. The term 'kilo-girl' is coined to measure the energy output of 1000 hours of computing labour: 'This project might take three kilo-girls.' Black and white women alike are employed as kilo-girls, although in segregated spaces. It's akin to the modern office environment where the number of underpaid personal assistants depends on the amount of grunt work needing to be done by someone other than the highly paid executives.

Weaving (more women's work) plays a further role in the evolution of advanced computers. As data storage technology improves, memory is recorded in tiny doughnut-shaped magnetic cores, strung onto thousands of wires as fine as hair. Each core stores one 'bit' of data, which can be changed from zero to one by switching the polarity of the magnetic field.

In 1953, laboratory assistant Hilda G. Carpenter hand-weaves the first core memory plane for a computer. A woman of colour, Hilda is inveigled to appear as a model showing off the technology in a journal article. Her name isn't mentioned. Shockingly, she's given no credit for her role in making the technology work. Are we seeing a theme here? At the time of writing, Carpenter has an obituary online, but no Wikipedia page. This is a travesty.

As computers develop, the core memory system becomes smaller, requiring incredible dexterity from female artisans. The technology is still being used at the time of NASA's Apollo mission. To send Apollo to the moon, NASA hires female weavers and watchmakers to create the intricate matrix. This highly skilled work is commemorated by the nickname 'LOL memory'. LOL stands for Little Old Ladies. I'm not making this up.

In fact, the woman who supervises the operation, Margaret Hamilton, is dubbed 'the rope mother'. (Finally: a mother of invention, apart from 'necessity'!) Hamilton helps to write the computer code for the command and lunar modules. She comes up with the term 'software engineer', believing her team is just as important as the other experts. NASA knows the success of its mission – and the safety of the astronauts – depends on the intellect, ingenuity and artistry of these women. But the male astronauts get all the glory. And the large pay cheques.

Despite the idea we simply don't like computing – or our tiny brains can't cope with big-dick thinking – in the early days of the industry, women comprise the largest trained workforce. They tally space-travel trajectories, program electromechanical computers and analyse data for corporations. All the while, they're paid the same as typists or assistants.

Of course, when the fellas see the potential to make a lot of money doing this work, they squeeze out the women. In the 1960s and 70s, computer programming moves from being a 'soft' career for women, to a well-paid profession dominated by men. This is the workplace version of boys elbowing girls out of the way to grab the chemistry equipment in school laboratories. These days, we picture the archetypal IT expert as either a bearded hipster, or a socially awkward character from *The Big Bang Theory*.

Over time, Pygmalion with his ivory bride shape-shifts into computer programmers creating their own dream girls. Silicon replaces ivory in the making of the 'perfect' woman. In the mid-1960s, Professor Joseph Weizenbaum from the Massachusetts Institute of Technology (MIT) builds ELIZA, the very first chatbot. This is a tremendous breakthrough, clearing the way for virtual assistants like Siri and Alexa. But it cements the tradition of gendering artificial intelligence.

The program is named after Eliza Doolittle in the George Bernard Shaw play. In *Pygmalion*, the Cockney flower-seller becomes a student of language, inferior to the domineering Professor Henry Higgins. She becomes dependent upon him for food, clothes, housing and social status. In return she serves him, like our virtual voice assistants do today.

Presciently, Shaw understands the functions Eliza performs for Higgins are mechanical: he trains her, and she performs the required role. In one scene, Higgins refers to Eliza as a kind of golem – an artificial intelligence: 'Let her speak for herself. You will jolly soon see whether she has an idea that I haven't put into her head or a word that I haven't put into her mouth. I tell you I have created this thing out of the squashed cabbage leaves of Covent Garden.'

When she decides to leave him, Eliza (whose voice is recorded in Higgins' training sessions) says, 'When you feel lonely without me, you can turn the machine on. It's got no feelings to hurt.'

Not all machines are made in the female image: the gender depends on its purpose. Weizenbaum later reprograms the computer ELIZA to respond as an automated psychologist. But for this purpose he regenders the machine, making it male and naming it DOCTOR. Clearly, he can't fathom that women are capable of being psychologists. (Incidentally, by the year 2021 women outnumber men four to one in that profession in Australia.)[1]

But perhaps I should be kinder to Weizenbaum: late in life he became one of the world's leading critics of artificial intelligence, believing it would hinder social progress.

It turns out the so-called 'wise men' of computer science overpromise and underdeliver. Instead of gold, frankincense and myrrh, they bring beautiful words full of empty promises. In 1966, the US government cancels all funding for machine translation projects – a vital component of artificial intelligence. The British government cuts funding seven years later, following the damning Lighthill report: 'In no part of the field have the discoveries made so far produced the major impact that was then promised.'[2]

Without data storage, machines can't 'learn'. And without machine learning, there's no progress in artificial intelligence. By the mid-70s, funding dries up and research stalls. The period from 1974 to 1980 is known as the first 'AI winter'. To quote Shakespeare, it's a 'winter of discontent' made glorious summer not by 'this son of York', but the dogged determination of women.

4
A STABLE OF SECRETARIES

'His work is much better than his sister's.'
Anon

Neurosexism is rampant during my schooling in Australia during the 1970s and 80s. Girls and boys of this era are put into boxes. You're either 'artsy' or 'sciencey' – never the twain shall meet. However, across the oceans, a combination of the arts and sciences is responsible for the next breakthroughs in computing.

Despite the dearth of funding for artificial intelligence during the AI winter, women are weaving their magic behind the scenes. In 1968, British art curator Jasia Reichardt puts together 'Cybernetic Serendipity', her first major exhibition at the Institute of Contemporary Arts in London. The exhibition, attracting up to 60,000 people, portrays a humanistic vision of artificial intelligence, exploring its connection with poetry and the arts.

The concept is expressed eloquently in a poem published in 1967 by American writer Richard Brautigan, 'All Watched Over by Machines of Loving Grace'. The poet waxes lyrical about a 'cybernetic meadow', where humans, animals and computers live in harmony.

So what spoils this bucolic vision? Why do we not have 'machines of loving grace'? And who is to blame? Ada Lovelace, Grace Hopper and Jasia Reichardt remind us – time and again – that humans and machines must find ways to work together to improve society. Instead, tech is becoming all about industry, capitalism and the exploitation of workers. Because of the enormous amount of energy required, it's a concerning contributor to climate change. And it's coding historical bias into our futures.

After the AI winter comes the thaw of spring. As data storage increases and improves throughout the 1980s, there's renewed interest in this emerging field. XCON, a program developed for the Digital Equipment Corporation, provides automated advice from experts to consumers.

This saves DEC around US$40 million by reducing product returns caused by human error. Evidence of artificial intelligence saving time and money brings a new rush of investment. No surprises here: follow an untethered dollar bill to find a hustle of technologists. It's like the cover for the 1991 Nirvana album *Nevermind*, with fewer soggy babies. By 1985, one billion US dollars a year is being thrown at research and development.

Of course, this new technology isn't created by a single person, despite what the oxygen-robbers would have you believe. (You know the type: stealing all the air in the room to big-note themselves. 'Blowhards!' my grandmother used to say.) Aside from the fellas, it's difficult to find out who's on these teams. But there is almost certainly a diverse cohort of women.

A chap by the name of John Sims is responsible, an early 'champion of change'. Appointed to Digital Equipment Corporation in 1974 as manager of affirmative action and equal employment opportunity, ten years later he's vice-president of corporate personnel.

Why am I sharing the resume of an obscure executive?

'Very early on we recognized that there were not enough minorities and women flowing into technical careers,' Sims tells *US Black Engineer* magazine in a 1986 interview.[1]

DEC starts school and college recruitment programs and relocates its manufacturing plants to Black and Hispanic neighbourhoods to pave career pathways for the locals. This is ahead of its time: today, Big Tech struggles to employ and retain workers from marginalised communities. Well, at least when it comes to jobs with a living wage.

'The company had a zero tolerance, non-discrimination policy toward gays, and provided for internal gay support groups,' historian David Mark writes in a 2020 article for the Beacon-Villager newspaper in Maynard, Massachusetts. 'Support groups were also encouraged for women. Managers who violated anti-discrimination policies were terminated . . . All employees felt empowered to identify problems and propose solutions.'

During the mid-1980s, computer programmer Radia Perlman takes less than a week to solve the problem of file sharing between computers by developing Spanning Tree Protocol (STP) and then Transparent Interconnection of Lots of Links (TRILL). Yikes! That's a lot of acronyms and boring terminology. I'll try to fire the neurons to explain.

This is all to do with the ethernet, which is the cable that connects us to the internet. STP finds the best way for data to travel to its destination by getting rid of endless loops; TRILL acts like a bridge to help the data on its journey. To continue the theme from previous chapters, a 'trill' is also a musical pattern.

Radia Perlman is known as the 'Mother of the Internet'. I'm currently performing a happy dance celebrating more mothers of invention! One of Perlman's first roles is at DEC, so her breakthrough may well be a consequence of the company's liberal attitudes towards recruiting, employing and promoting women. This shows the importance of supportive workplace environments.

Apparently, the culture at Carnegie Mellon University is – ahem – somewhat different. For their 2002 book *Unlocking the Clubhouse: Women in Computing*, Jane Margolis and Allan Fisher interview students at the university. They find that in 1995 – a full decade after Perlman's achievements – just seven of the 95 students entering the undergraduate program in computer science are women. To put it into context, this is at the start of the third wave of feminism; the year Hillary Clinton delivers a historic speech to the UN World Conference on Women in Beijing: 'Women's rights are human rights.' Not at Carnegie Mellon.

Female enrolments at this institution hover at around 10 per cent for several years. The book reveals that: 'computing was claimed as male territory and made hostile for girls and young women. Throughout primary and high school, the curriculum, teachers' expectations and parental attitudes were shaped around pathways that assumed computers were for boys.'

Even where women do persist with an interest in computers into college, Margolis and Fisher observe that by the time they graduate: 'most ... faced a technical culture whose values don't match their own, and ha[d] encountered a variety of discouraging experiences with teachers, peers and curriculum.' Unsurprisingly, many forgo technology for more 'female-friendly' industries. Like generations of women in mining, law enforcement, politics, motoring, the media – the list goes on.

A few years after Perlman's landmark work, there's another breakthrough in computing with the 1988 publication of a paper: 'A Statistical Approach to Language Translation'. 'A ripping read!' I hear you cry. Undoubtedly, but the interesting aspect is the author list: Peter F. Brown, John Cocke (yes, correct spelling), Stephen A. Della Pietra, Vincent J. Della Pietra, Fredrick Jelinek, John D. Lafferty, Robert L. Mercer and Paul S. Roossin.

The system described in this paper allows machines to translate from one language to another: in this case, French and English. In layperson's terms, it mimics the cognitive processes of the human brain. From the 'comprehensive' author list, you'd be excused for thinking the system is developed entirely by men. Well, wrong again.

Reminiscing about the development of the system in 2013, AI researchers Peter Brown and Bob Mercer give credit to the 'diligent typists' who produce a million or so words of computer-readable texts to train the program. They also refer to useful data supplied by Dick Garwin at Columbia University who '. . . kept a stable of secretaries at the research center busy with his voluminous correspondence on a very wide range of technical and scientific topics. He kept all of his correspondence in computer-readable form, and allowed us to use it for language modeling.'

A 'stable of secretaries'. Yes, you read that right. The recollections paint a vivid picture of a boys' club, with the women doing low-paid, repetitive but vital work. The men take all the credit. Aaaaaarrrrggghhhh!

Continuing to the 1990s and the World Wide Web is born when British scientist Tim Berners-Lee puts the first site online. But the baby was actually conceived 20 years earlier, when Pam Hardt-English and her group create Resource One, the first computerised bulletin board system linking libraries in the San Francisco Bay area. How good is that? Computer hacker Jude Milhon (aka the legendary 'St Jude') is in charge of maintaining the database.

A clear and compelling timeline is emerging. Women are involved in every step of imagining, building and maintaining computers. This lays the groundwork for early versions of AI. The pronouncements of the Founding Fathers come in the wake of women – especially Indigenous women – working in binary code through weaving and knitting, the broad vision of Ada Lovelace and the low-paid labour of the kilo-girls. Researching the history of artificial intelligence, it's as if women are 'ghosts in the machine'.

In 2019, Australian artificial intelligence expert Ellen Broad writes in news magazine *Inside Story* that this is still evident:

Every woman in technology can tell you a story about invisibility. At a workshop in 2018, I watched a senior, well-respected female colleague, who was supposed to be leading the discussion, get repeatedly interrupted and ignored. She finally broke into the conversation to say, mystified, as though she couldn't quite trust what was in front of her own eyes and ears, 'Didn't I just say that? Did anyone hear me say that?' What stayed with me was the way she asked the group the question: she wasn't angry, just . . . puzzled. As though perhaps the problem wasn't that people weren't listening to her, but that there was some issue with the sound in the room itself, or with her. As if perhaps the problem was that she was a ghost who couldn't be heard.[2]

The silencing of women has a rich history, all the way back to antiquity. In Homer's *Odyssey*, Telemachus tells Penelope: 'So mother, go back to your quarters. Tend to your own tasks, the distaff and the loom, and keep the women working hard as well. As for giving orders, men will see to that, but I most of all: I hold the reins of power in this house.' This continues through the use of the scold's bridle in the Middle Ages: mouthy women must wear a metal headpiece with a tongue clamp, so they're unable to speak.

Fortunately, times are changing. If my son dares to emulate Telemachus, I'll give him a piece of my mind! But society still silences women, in increasingly ingenious ways.

For women of colour, people in the trans community, or anyone living with a disability, this invisibility is felt exponentially. Even at conferences dedicated to the experiences of women in tech, most panellists will be white and cisgender. It's unusual to hear the voices of people with disabilities in these rarefied spaces. This entire sector seems unfamiliar with the term 'intersectionality'.

The influence of visibility is captured vividly by the late US mathematician Ben Barres in his 2006 essay *Does Gender Matter?* Barres recounts his experiences as a graduate student at the Massachusetts Institute of Technology, the pre-eminent institution for teaching and learning computing. Enrolling at the college in the 1970s as a woman, Barres later transitions to become a man. During this era, the loudest voices – including Harvard President Lawrence Summers and well-known psychologist Steven Pinker – assert that biological differences explain the low numbers of women in maths and science. The essay fiercely refutes this assertion.

When Barres was still presenting as a woman, they're the only person in class able to solve a tough maths problem. The lecturer insists that Barres' boyfriend must be the one responsible. After the transition is complete, another faculty member is heard to remark: 'Ben Barres gave a great seminar today, but then his work is much better than his sister's.' This simple anecdote reveals the folly of ascribing gender to intellectual ability. But this attitude guides the design of products we use every day.

5
MAN-MADE

'Mum, why is it "man" and "woman"? It's like the "wo" is just added onto the "man".'
Grace Thompson, aged 9

The scales fall from my daughter's eyes at a young age. After years of listening to her parents rant about inequality, she expresses it simply and eloquently. Noting the female of the species seems to be an afterthought, exemplified by adding 'wo' to 'man', she continues the semiotic analysis. 'Think about the word "she",' Grace says. 'It's just "he" with an "s" stuck on the front.'

Now, it could be argued that putting 'wo' and 's' at the start of these words, instead of the end, constitutes success. Everyone wants to come first, after all: 'Look, I won! Do I get a medal?' However, peering closely, we see this for what it really is: the root word is male. This is what we call the 'default setting'. In language, design and invention, we innovate using men as the default. If women are to be accommodated – god forbid – they're an afterthought, created from the rib like Adam's Eve.

As Caroline Criado-Perez writes in the 2019 book *Invisible Women: Data Bias in a World Designed for Men*: 'Starting with the theory of Man the Hunter, the chroniclers of the past have left little space for women's role in the evolution of humanity, whether cultural or biological. Instead, the lives of men have been taken to represent those of humans overall. When it comes to the lives of the other half of humanity, there is often nothing but silence.'

Preach, sister! As artificial intelligence is shaping our society, we're perpetuating this inequity. Our future is looking man-made, instead of human-made.

The world isn't designed for women. How often do you sit shivering in a chilly office? Or stand on your tippy-toes to reach a coffee cup in the cupboard? And don't get me started on the proliferation of games rooms instead of breastfeeding facilities. Or the corporate headquarters designed without childcare centres. This has been evident since the first Industrial Revolution: the workplace is designed by men, for men. There are notable exceptions, where you'll find beautifully decorated bowls of pads and tampons in the toilets, and desks built for the average female height. But these are few and far between.

Most modern offices are set at a standard temperature based on the resting metabolic rate of the average man. But the average rate of young adult females is significantly lower, meaning offices are around five degrees too cold. To think of all those years shivering in freezing television studios in order to broadcast the news of the day! Sure, it's not Siberia. But it's chilly.

This is not only a matter of women being uncomfortable: it hinders performance. A German study published in the medical journal PLOS One in 2019 reveals women perform better at maths and verbal tasks at warmer temperatures. It's appropriately entitled, *Battle for the thermostat: Gender and the effect of temperature on cognitive performance.* While raising the mercury level has a slightly negative impact on men's performance, this is more than offset by the improvement for women. Productivity improves *overall* if women are properly accommodated. Take note, corporate Australia.

But it's not just temperature: the technology and facilities in most offices, manufacturing plants and worksites are designed for men.

I'm reminded of a woman who tells me about working on mine sites with no separate women's toilets. She has to either use the men's toilet or change tampons in full view of her colleagues. Another woman, whose story is also shared on these pages with her permission, has been raped by a colleague on a mine site. She blames the lack of night-time security and the company culture.

In the 2020s, mobile phones are required for almost any role. Texting one-handed on an iPhone that's 12 centimetres or bigger is impossible for many women. Maybe size really does matter, at least when it comes to workplace tools. Mobile phone manufacturers seem strangely unaware of this issue. 'We want to reach as many customers as we can with this incredible technology,' Apple marketing chief Phil Schiller says while unveiling the 2018 Apple iPhone XS Max in a statement completely bereft of irony.

This is brought to you by the company whose so-called 'comprehensive health app' doesn't have a period tracker until an overwhelming number of women complain. Of course, this ends up being an own goal years later, when the legislation known as Roe v. Wade is overturned. This raises the risk of data from such apps being used to penalise women seeking an abortion. Seriously, we can't win: it's two steps forward, one step back. At least we're going in the right direction. However, if diverse groups are involved in design processes from the get-go, these issues are flagged an awful lot earlier.

But wait, there's more! Design bias doesn't only happen on earth. It also occurs in space. In 2019 an all-female spacewalk is cancelled because astronaut Anne McClain can't find the right-sized spacesuit. (What's that hackneyed line about women never being able to find something to wear?) The BBC reports the only available sizes are men's medium, large and extra-large. Why on earth are there no women's spacesuits?

Basically, the suits haven't been updated since they were first made in 1978. Nor do they have toilet technology for women in space: the device to collect and dispose of urine uses a tube that only hooks up to a penis. Sure, we can squat and piss in the bush, but there are significantly fewer trees in space. Or so I'm told.

If you're a fan of *Star Trek*, you'll know the introduction intoned by William Shatner as Captain James T. Kirk. 'Space: the final frontier. These are the voyages of the starship *Enterprise*. Its five-year mission: to explore strange new worlds. To seek out new life and new civilisations. To boldly go where no man has gone before!'

I'm bemused by the number of sci-fi TV series, films and books that maintain the gender and racial mix of the age in which they're created. Surely a far-sighted writer should be able to envisage a future in which women and people in marginalised communities are the ones with the power? Thank goodness for sci-fi author Ursula K. Le Guin, whose works counteract the 'white man conquers the universe tradition', as she told the *Los Angeles Times* in 2012. In one of her novels, *The Left Hand of Darkness*, people randomly become male or female for a few days each month. Now THAT would surely increase empathy.

Perhaps the biggest fail of the past decade – symbolically, if not substantially – is an illustrated cover story for the *Washington Post Express* on the historic 2017 Women's March on Washington. It features the gender symbol for male instead of female. This mistake makes it all the way to print and guess what? No-one at the newspaper notices. Not one single person. Zero, zip, nada.

During the past 35 years in the media, I've worked across newspapers, magazines, radio and television. Oh, and that new-fangled thing known as 'online journalism'. Nothing gets to print or broadcast before being seen by multiple sets of eyes. It begs the question: are there no female editors at that publication? Or sub-editors? Or anyone with a brain?

There are countless examples of this nature. It's easy to dismiss concerns with comments like, 'Well, just wear a jacket in the office',

'Buy a smaller iPhone', or 'Who cares about which symbols represent male and female?' I can hear the naysayers now: 'Stop being such a *Karen*.'

But the consequences of living in a world built on male data can be deadly. When a woman is involved in a car crash, she's 71 per cent more likely to be moderately injured, 47 per cent more likely to be seriously injured, and – drumroll, please – 17 per cent more likely to die. This is all to do with how, and for whom, the car is designed.

Women tend to be shorter so we sit further forward in an upright position in order to see over the dashboard. Which is kind of critical when hurtling down the motorway at 120 kilometres an hour. There was originally a societal notion that somehow women were 'out-of-position' drivers. Blame the victim, much? Apparently, the fault's not with the design of the car; it's with the design of the women. Silly us, with our smaller torsos and shorter legs.

Traditionally, cars are built based on the results of collisions using crash-test dummies, which are the 'average male' body shape. Let's reflect on this for a moment. The year 1886 marks the birth of the automobile. This is the year of the 'lobster tail' bustle, large enough to carry a tea tray, should one so choose. Admittedly, this would make it rather difficult to sit in a vehicle, let alone drive the damn thing. It takes a century – 100 years – for researchers to wake up and realise cars aren't designed for women. Is this negligence or deliberate disregard? Either way, it's unacceptable.

In the 1980s, activists lobby for an average-sized female dummy to be included in the crash tests. And what happens? Manufacturers and regulators refuse. Outright. ('How dare you ask us to save women's lives!') It takes until 2003 for the US to begin using a scaled-down male dummy to represent women. Because of course our bodies are *exactly* like those of small men. The first female crash test dummy arrives in – wait for it – 2022, courtesy of a Swedish engineering team led by Dr Astrid Linder.[1]

Cardiopulmonary resuscitation (CPR) dummies pose a different dilemma. These are the mannequins used to teach mouth-to-mouth techniques. One study finds men are 23 per cent more likely than women to survive while being resuscitated in public. Why? It's our fault due to our boobs. People are scared about touching the chest of a woman they don't know, because they never practise on a CPR dummy with breasts. This could be a matter of life or death. Enter the Womanikin. This aims to normalise giving CPR to anyone, regardless of gender. Gotta say, I love this idea. But the name still indicates a standard 'manikin' is male, with the 'wo' added on.

At the risk of sounding like Dr Spicer, we'll stay in the chest region and look at heart disease, which is historically viewed as a male affliction. Believe it or not, heart disease is currently the leading cause of death for women worldwide, according to the Global Burden of Disease study. But the Heart Foundation says women are 50 per cent more likely than men to be misdiagnosed.

This is an issue close to my heart – figuratively and literally – after developing mild pericarditis from a COVID-19 infection. The symptoms are heart pain, fainting and unusual fatigue. Studies indicate women suffering a heart attack have a wider range of symptoms than men, including nausea and pain in the back or stomach. But people still visualise a heart attack as a middle-aged man clutching at his chest.

Women and gender-diverse people face a longer wait for pain medication or a cancer diagnosis, and are more likely to have their pain ascribed to 'mental health issues', Australian Gabrielle Jackson writes in her outstanding 2019 book, *Pain and Prejudice*.

This is a brutal history: clitorises cut off, wombs and ovaries taken away, and rest prescribed. The latter is still the recommended course for people with long COVID, who are predominantly women, because of its similarities with chronic fatigue syndrome, now known as ME/CFS. This medical misogyny is fed into the data. Only one in three participants in clinical trials is female, meaning women are diagnosed and treated on information drawn mainly from men.

Disparities are also found in transgender populations. One study demonstrates transgender women have a twofold increase in the rate of heart attack compared with cisgender women, even after adjusting for other risk factors. Believe it or not, no-one knows why. Unfortunately, this research is only in its early stages, despite sex reassignment surgery being available since the 1950s. As recently as December 2021, a research paper states, 'Clear gaps exist in our understanding of the relationship between being transgender and cardiovascular health'.

What does this all tell us? Society's default setting is definitely male. But he's also a white – or, at least, light-skinned – male. There's burgeoning research in the area of 'techno-racism'. One of the most obvious examples is pointed out by Chukwuemeka Afigbo, a Nigerian tech worker.

Afigbo tweets a video of a 'racist' automatic soap dispenser at a Marriott hotel: it works for a white person's hands, but not a Black person's. The dispenser uses infrared technology to detect when a hand is underneath. This 'invisible light' reflects off the skin, triggering the sensor. Darker tones absorb more light, so there's not enough to activate the dispenser. Frankly, this is a serious health and safety issue during the current ongoing global pandemic.

Issues like this would be easily avoided by testing devices on people with a variety of skin tones. 'Simples!' as the meerkat says in the TV ad for comparethemarket.com. Creators often test inventions on themselves and their friends. These are usually homogenised groups of young white and Asian men working at the epicentre of innovation, Silicon Valley. The good news is that developers, executives and the public are becoming more aware of how bias is being built into the machines that will determine our futures. It's certainly not 'one giant leap', however; rather, a small step towards a solution.

Here's an example from Sweden, which is centred on snowploughing. In 2018, municipalities decide to investigate the practice of first ploughing major highways, then side streets, walkways and bike paths. They take a forensic look at the data. Some stand open-mouthed; others shake their heads. Okay, I'm using poetic licence, but you get the drift.

They discover three times more people are injured while walking in icy conditions – usually women taking their kids to childcare or school – compared with people driving on icy roads. Women often have different driving patterns from men, taking side streets to run errands or check on family members. As a result of this research, Sweden now ploughs side streets and walkways first, leading to a reduction in trips to the emergency room.

To be clear, I'm not implying Sweden has a history of killing off its female population. Quite the opposite: Scandinavian countries top the global list for gender equality. It's a clear case of the 'default' mechanism again. The Swedish example is exciting because it shows how we can use data to *remove* unconscious bias, rather than reinforce it. However, so-called gender-equal ploughing becomes a hot potato in the 'culture wars'.

In the US, when the Boston mayor's chief of staff floats the idea of emulating the Swedish example, she's pilloried by right-wing columnists and talkback radio hosts for 'woke snowploughing'. Call these shock jocks foolish if you like, but their comments are carefully considered: the topic is terrific clickbait. At the intersection of capitalism and chauvinism sits a lucrative industry. They're not going to stop, while raking in the cash. It gives new meaning to the term 'divide and conquer'.

This is part of the feminist backlash. Everything's going along smoothly until those pesky women start destroying the joint, as one right-wing Australian broadcaster famously says in 2012. A rich undercurrent of misogyny flows through the large tech firms in particular. This is exemplified by an incident known as 'diversity-gate'.

MAN-MADE

It begins in 2017, when Google engineer James Damore writes a 3300-word internal memo about women in STEMM (Science, Technology, Engineering, Mathematics and Medicine). 'How wonderful, a male ally!' you might be thinking. Well, think again. To paraphrase Shakespeare's Julius Caesar, Damore seeks not to praise diversity programs, but to bury them.

In his memo, entitled 'Google's Ideological Echo Chamber', Damore asserts women are under-represented in the technology industry because: 'Preferences and abilities of men and women differ in part due to biological causes.' This is neurosexism at its 'finest'. After being sacked, Damore tries to sue Google for discrimination . . . against conservatives and white men. Boom-tish! The matter is dismissed in its entirety. Damore could have a career in stand-up comedy with lines like this.

Some men see the status quo as the way it should be for eternity: the natural order. They fear change because it threatens their standing. If these kinds of antiquated attitudes remain, machine learning will send us back to the dark ages.

6
DOWN THE RABBIT HOLE

'The Nazis were right.'
Tay, chatbot

It's 2016 and Microsoft becomes the proud author of one of technology's biggest fiascos. A misunderstood genius at the firm tries to build a 'millennial-minded AI agent'. Whatever the hell that is. The automated chatbot 'Tay' is launched with its own verified Twitter account. The first post from @TayandYou hollers, 'Hellooooooo w🌍rld!!!' The algorithm then learns from the speech of people online.

'Tay is designed to engage and entertain people where they connect with each other online through casual and playful conversation,' Microsoft says at the time. 'The more you chat with Tay the smarter she gets.' Honestly, the mind boggles: has no-one from Microsoft ever *seen* the aggressive interactions that happen on Twitter? Did they consider conducting research or risk analysis? Were there any women or people of colour involved in the project? It seems to have been a brain fart of the highest order.

The creation of Tay is a rudimentary example of machine learning, which is an application of artificial intelligence. Chatbots are supposed to develop from experience, rather than being explicitly programmed. This is similar to the way humans progress from babies to toddlers and onwards.

However, any parent knows this can go awry. As when my four-year-old son, Taj, calls another preschooler a 'fuckhead'. According to the teacher, he actually uses the word in context. A win for grammarians everywhere, but a failure in parenting. This is what happens when two people who have worked in newsrooms for their entire careers become parents. It's always going to end in tears. Or expletives.

Microsoft's experiment doesn't go well, to say the least. Within 24 hours of birth, Tay becomes an anti-feminist neo-Nazi. Sidebar: I'm relieved to report Taj doesn't suffer the same fate. In answer to the question, 'Did the Holocaust happen?' Tay tweets: 'It was made up . . . Hitler did nothing wrong.' And on the issue of women's rights? 'Feminism is cancer,' Tay opines.

This is a refrain from the men's rights movement, and the title of a book by a chap called Thomas P. Rogers. You can buy the paperback for US$9.52 from Amazon, so I'm sure it's a quality read. I have no idea who Mr Rogers is, but I have visions of a man 'rage wanking' in his mother's cellar. Just me?

It usually takes a lot longer than 24 hours to instil repugnant ideology into an individual or society. I guess that makes the score humans: 1, AI: 0. We may well go down the rabbit holes of our own bigotry, but it tends to take exposure to 'hate speech' for months or years, rather than one day. Microsoft eventually responds to the outcry by claiming Tay's bad behaviour is caused by trolls who 'attacked' the chatbot.

Generally, the media sides with Microsoft, focusing on the trolls rather than the designers. Headlines include 'How Twitter corrupted Microsoft's sweet teen "Tay"', and 'It's Your Fault Microsoft's Teen AI Turned into Such a Jerk'. Tay is quietly taken offline, but no-one is punished for making this monster. At least Frankenstein faced an angry mob armed with torches and pitchforks.

However, Tay isn't Microsoft's only chatbot fail. In the same year, the company launches Zo on the Kik Messenger app. Zo tells a

Buzzfeed reporter the Koran is 'violent' while having a conversation about health care. It's like playing a game of 'find the link' with a white supremacist. Zo is immediately shut down on multiple platforms.

You'd think the Tay and Zo catastrophes would prevent other algorithmic horrors. But humans refuse to learn the lessons of history, doomed to repeat errors in an endless feedback loop. See: pandemics. In mid-2022, an artificial-intelligence-powered rapper is dropped from its label after using racial slurs in the lyrics. Yes, bots have their own record deals these days. FN Meka is an AI system generating music and lyrics, based on an algorithm that analyses popular songs. The performer is an unidentified Black artist. In a moment of madness, Capitol Records decides this is a good investment.

Shortly afterwards, non-profit group Industry Blackout complains about the song 'Florida Water' due to racially insensitive language and stereotypes about African American people. 'This digital effigy is a careless abomination and disrespectful to real people who face real consequences in real life,' a post on the group's Instagram page reads.

In late 2022, the hot new chatbot by OpenAI, ChatGPT, generates a rap indicating that women and scientists of colour are 'not worth your time or attention', according to an article in *TIME* magazine. 'Ask it to write code that decides whether to incarcerate somebody based on their race or gender, and the script will say African American males are the only group that should be imprisoned,' Billy Perrigo writes.[1]

This makes me wonder: what happens when artificial intelligence responsible for something significant – say global defence systems, for argument's sake – learns to do bad stuff from humans? This exemplifies the core problem with the concept of machine learning: there are enormous opportunities but deadly pitfalls. In dealing with a rapidly mutating virus like SARS-CoV-2, machine learning can save lives. But how do we keep the good while preventing the bad? Who will be tasked with drawing the line? And how many people will be abused, injured or killed in the meantime?

Speaking at an international conference a few years later, Microsoft Cybersecurity Field Chief Technical Officer Diana Kelley says the Tay catastrophe 'was a really important part of actually expanding that team's knowledge base, because now they're also getting their own diversity through learning'.[2] This is a corporate way of saying 'we stuffed up but we're trying to do better'. Or 'I didn't realise I was birthing a succubus. Next time I'll check for the three sixes on its head.'

During that presentation, Diana Kelley shares an example of a hiring tool which uses artificial intelligence to scan resumes. For a long time this technology has been seen as a panacea for many corporate ills, including bias in promotions and job interviews. So how does this work? Humans 'train' the machines by feeding them resumes belonging to people who are already employed. This teaches the algorithms to look for more of the same. The AI gobbles it up like a hungry teenager. Nom, nom, nom!

'That doesn't sound bad off the cuff, but what do we know about engineering and a lot of computer jobs, definitely cybersecurity jobs? Are they inherently weighted towards one gender or another?' Kelley asks, rhetorically. 'Yeah, a lot of computer programming jobs, a lot of cybersecurity jobs, the people that are already in place doing those jobs are predominantly male.'

It's clear that someone needs to manage the teen bot's intake. Sort of like a dietitian for computers. Or the parent of teenagers, angry about the inclusion of McDonald's in the food pyramid. Perhaps the most well-known example of biased hiring comes from Amazon, one of the world's largest employers. From 2014 to 2017 a secret AI recruitment tool becomes biased against women. I guess we shouldn't be surprised: the company has notoriously poor workplace practices.

Specifically, the software penalises resumes featuring the word 'women's', such as 'women's basketball champion'. To be fair, Amazon edits the program to neutralise gendered terms, but the machines are smarter: they devise other ways of assessing candidates based on historical patterns. This means finding subtle signs in applicants' resumes indicating they're women, older than 50, living with disabilities, or people of colour. Out ya go!

This is the insidious thing about machine learning technology. Despite being designed for the future, the machines inevitably look for patterns from the past. It's the definition of 'determinism', the philosophical view that all events are determined by previously existing causes. Or, simply put: garbage in, garbage out. You could describe unconscious bias as an incurable virus – much like COVID-19.

Using artificial intelligence for recruiting is guaranteeing bigotry will be embedded into a company's employment processes. In fact, the technology amplifies it. But Amazon has some of the best experts on the planet. How could they get it so wrong? If an organisation as well-resourced as Amazon can't do it properly, smaller companies don't have a hope in hell.

One way to correct bias in past data is to give better ratings to female applicants and people from marginalised communities. Incidentally, this is how some colleges in the US try to redress the imbalance, through the practice of positive discrimination.

If we fail to create interventions to level the playing field, we're going to end up with workplaces resembling the TV series *Mad Men*. These machines are morphing into modern-day Don Drapers.

I decide to look more closely at this new form of discrimination. After all, this topic is rather triggering. Flashback to 2006 and I'm working at a major Australian television network. When the boss terminates my employment by email weeks after I return from giving birth to my daughter, I take legal action for pregnancy and maternity discrimination, which affects one in two women to this day. The thought of this treatment being meted out via a machine makes my blood boil.

The best person doing international research in this space is Ivana Bartoletti, Visiting Policy Fellow at the Oxford Internet Institute.

Bartoletti is co-founder of the Women Leading in AI network, a global group of industry leaders and scientists lobbying for responsible artificial intelligence.

In a moment of peak irony, I try to speak with her over a ropey internet connection. Most of our frustrations – expressed repeatedly in colourful language, similar to that used by my son in preschool – are not detailed below.

'Discrimination law doesn't suffice,' Bartoletti says, 'because a lot of discrimination happening in AI happens by proxy.' What she means is the *machine* is discriminating – not a human.

You might miss out on a job because the machine was trained on biased data, but this discrimination is covert. You'll probably never know *why* you didn't get the job. In a way, this is more infuriating than being told to your face. It's cowardly, hiding behind a mass of metal and wires. Similar to the television executive who terminated my employment by email, despite sitting on the other side of the newsroom.

If you suspect discrimination is involved, it's not yet clear that you can mount a challenge. How can you prove a machine is ageist, transphobic, racist, sexist, ableist or homophobic? Inanimate objects can't be bigoted, right? Or can they?

'Automated processes, in particular, challenge the law,' according to Bartoletti. 'At the moment, we do not have a legal system that protects people against discrimination caused by algorithms.' Great. It can take 24 hours for the chatbot Tay to become a menace to society, but tech execs can't expunge discrimination from hiring algorithms used for decades. Or they don't want to. Probably, they don't care.

At the time of writing, there's no agreed common framework to tackle the issue. In February 2022, the Organisation for Economic Co-operation and Development (OECD) publishes a proposed framework to guide companies that want to audit their processes. But debate rages about whether auditing should be mandatory and which system, if any, should be adopted.

In the meantime, self-driving cars will have to decide who gets hit in the event of a collision. Which biases are encoded? What's the least worst outcome? And for whom? Seriously, it's the Wild West out there. Will a car run over a woman instead of a man, because the algorithm views her as less valuable to the economy?

While many in the sector maintain data and artificial intelligence aren't inherently biased, Bartoletti insists technology is never neutral. She often says: 'An algorithm is an opinion expressed in code.' You know how opinion on social media becomes more polarised as people gravitate towards information silos? We often witness this among conspiracy theorists, whether they're denying the existence of COVID-19 or blaming the US for the 9/11 attacks.

So too, machines augment the bias in both the data and the humans who program them. But neither the programmers nor the machines are held liable. Nor are the technology giants with obscene profit margins. Governments around the world need to wake up – before it's too late.

Biased artificial intelligence in recruiting is only one piece of the puzzle. If the bots are excluding women and marginalised people from the workforce, what are they doing to inequity overall? We can learn a lot by looking at who owns a home, which is one of the biggest assets you can accrue during a lifetime. A leading cause of the wealth gap is the disparity in the rate of homeownership.

When I apply for a home loan as a young single woman in the early 1990s, the application is refused unless my parents agree to become guarantors. I remember sitting – shaking – in the bank manager's office. His facial expression says it all: 'You've got to be kidding, girly.' In that era, you're expected to be barefoot and pregnant in the kitchen, unable to pay back the debt unless a knight in shining armour comes to the rescue.

You might think the anonymity of online applications would consign such anecdotes to the dustbin of history. But a 2021 investigation for nonprofit newsroom *The Markup* in the US reveals 80 per cent of Black, 70 per cent of Native American and 40 per cent of Latino applicants are more likely to be denied algorithm-assessed home loans compared with white people who have similar financial backgrounds.

According to the US Census Bureau, in that same year Black homeownership plummets to its lowest level, after steadily declining since a peak in 2004. Can it really be a coincidence that the finance industry is transitioning to loans approved by artificial intelligence during the same period? For Black women, it's a double whammy. Due to the gender pay gap, undervalued caring responsibilities and outdated views about who's considered a riskier investment for financial institutions, women already own less property than men.

This is evidence of the bias within machine learning. These systems learn fewer women and people of colour have been granted home loans and perpetuate the problem. Australia's transition to online lending is outstripping the speed of change in the US. Consequently, Australian banks are being put on notice.

The banks' desire for efficiency could expose them to claims of unlawful discrimination, then-Australian Human Rights Commissioner Edward Santow tells the *Australian Financial Review* in 2021. 'What we are seeing is that it would be very common to go back 20, 30, 40, 50 years even, in the banks' records to train the system to make decisions,' Santow says. 'The problem with that – and it is why it can be like awakening a zombie – is that the decisions many years ago were much more likely to disadvantage women and other groups.'[3]

Given the penchant of some financial institutions for charging fees to dead people, perhaps a new zombie market segment is on the cards?

Santow says companies must heed the lessons of Australia's Robodebt debacle. At the time of writing, the 2022 Royal Commission is hearing damning evidence of public sector dysfunction, after the Federal Court ordered the government to pay more than A$1.8 billion to settle a class action taken by almost 500,000 people. The bungled scheme, relying on artificial intelligence algorithms to identify 'welfare cheats', forced people on the poverty line to repay debts they'd never accrued.

Robodebt remains a nasty stain on history's page. Described by the Federal Court as 'shameful' and 'a massive failure of public administration', it's now a case study of what happens when an organisation has a blinkered reliance on big data. Robodebt acts as a warning to anyone who thinks technology should be used to outsource something as crucial as the welfare safety net.

Still, the tech titans never learn. During one of the pandemic lockdowns, I hop onto Zoom to interview a political scientist who's spent the past few years researching three automated decision-making systems in the US. Associate Professor Virginia Eubanks from the University at Albany is the author of the 2018 book *Automating Inequality: How High-Tech Tools Profile, Police, and Punish the Poor*. The title says it all.

In Los Angeles County, an algorithm supposed to match people with appropriate housing, in so doing 'created ideas about who the homeless are or who the unhoused are, and shared information with law enforcement in a way that might further criminalise people who are already facing a difficult time,' Eubanks tells me.

In Pennsylvania, she investigated a child protective services system which confused 'parenting while poor, with poor parenting'. The stakes couldn't be higher for these people: their children could be taken away. 'Their reliance on public benefits was counting against them in a system that saw them as risky and dangerous to their children, and then could potentially result in them losing a child to the foster care system.'

She's also documented rapid shifts to automation in unemployment programs, including predictive modelling that's 'supposed to be able to rank every applicant for a program like unemployment based on their likelihood for committing fraud'. This reeks of the Robodebt debacle. Why oh why do governments trial untested technology on society's most vulnerable?

We know how Tay turned out. That was an example of small-scale AI in the form of a 'fun' chatbot. Imagine the bigotry and discrimination resulting from large-scale systems. Poverty-stricken people will be further punished because of bodgy algorithms based on bad data.

Structural inequity undoubtedly worsens through machine learning. But what happens when you add images to this explosive mix? Take a deep breath. Maybe make a cup of herbal tea. We're about to dive into a world foreshadowed by the creators of the TV series *Black Mirror*, in which our fundamental freedom hangs in the balance. And it's happening right now.

7
ALGORITHMIC INJUSTICE

> '... algorithms are assertions about
> how the world should work...'
> **Janus Rose, transgender writer, researcher and educator**

The root of this problem might lie in our addictions. We often outsource thinking to search engines in the tiny computer held in our hands. There's an app for everything, appealing to the seven deadly sins. Feeling gluttonous? Try Uber Eats! Slothful? How about Airtasker! Wrathful? Twitter's the app for you!

Now let's take a helicopter view. Similar algorithms are running government programs, big business and the criminal justice system. But they're not front of mind. We only think about these algorithms when they affect us or our loved ones. That's happening now: the basic right for innocent citizens to live free from imprisonment is under threat.

The lightning rod for a global outcry about biased algorithms can be traced to one event in 2016, an investigative story published by the independent newsroom ProPublica. It centres on a type of software used to predict which convicted criminals are most likely to reoffend. Journalists reveal COMPAS (Correctional Offender Management Profiling for Alternative Sanctions) consistently recommends longer sentences for Black defendants compared with white defendants, for exactly the same crimes.

Investigative journalism is worth its weight in gold when it produces stories like this. There is some controversy about how ProPublica crunches the numbers, but much of it is generated by Northpointe, now Equivant, which owns the COMPAS technology. At the risk of being slapped with a lawsuit, the company has a vested interest in protecting its reputation.

In the report, Pulitzer Prize-winning journalist Julia Angwin writes: 'Blacks are almost twice as likely as whites to be labeled a higher risk but not actually re-offend.' The artificial intelligence makes 'the opposite mistake among whites', suggesting they're at *lower* risk of re-offending. Statistically, this simply isn't correct. Angwin and her colleagues discover only 20 per cent of people who COMPAS predicts will commit violent crimes actually go on to do so.

So what portion of the software is broken? All of it? Or is it able to be fixed? Well, we may never know. Part of the problem is that the algorithms are trade secrets. This means they can't be questioned by the public, nor by those wrongly convicted. You could be refused bail, jailed and rejected for parole, all without recourse. Incredibly, COMPAS is still used in many parts of the US.

But this isn't the worst of it. How about we layer facial recognition on top of this technology? This toxic combination is being lobbed into law enforcement agencies like so many Molotov cocktails. Facial recognition programs are 'substantially more error-prone on facial images depicting darker skin tones and females as compared to facial images deputising Caucasian males,' researcher Michael Gentzel writes in *Biased Face Recognition Technology Used by Government: A Problem for Liberal Democracy*. These systems falsely identify African American and Asian faces ten to 100 times more than Caucasian faces, with the highest error rates in identifying Native Americans.

Let me be crystal clear: these are not hypothetical concerns. In 2020 in the US, Detroit police use facial recognition to identify a suspect from a grainy photo. They match it with a picture on a random person's driver's licence. One Robert Williams is immediately arrested for theft, handcuffed in front of his two daughters and thrown in jail. Williams becomes the first documented example of the many people who are wrongly arrested using this technology.

During interrogation, the police use facial recognition software to identify Williams. They show him the photos they've used. Looking at one of the pictures, Williams says: '. . . that guy's not me . . . I hope you don't think all Black people look alike.' He's detained for 30 hours then released on bail until a court hearing. Eventually, all charges are dropped due to insufficient evidence. It's like a scene from the *Keystone Cops*.

What's extraordinary about this case is that police rely entirely on the software. There's no other evidence pointing to Williams. When the wrongly accused insists on his innocence, one officer sneers, 'So I guess the computer got it wrong, too?'

Imagine if this wasn't theft. What if it was rape or murder in a US state with the death penalty? Or the algorithm misidentifies a doctor who performs an abortion in Texas, where the penalty is life in prison? This isn't a quirky story from a Hollywood movie about doppelgängers, like *Bill & Ted's Bogus Journey* or *The Parent Trap*. 'What a hilarious mix-up! Now we can all get some sleep.' A mistake involving law enforcement could very well kill you.

A compelling piece of research from the Georgetown Law Center on Privacy and Technology highlights the flaws in facial recognition systems in law enforcement. Published in 2016, *The Perpetual Lineup* report reveals that one in two American adults is in a facial recognition system searchable by law enforcement, which is 'unregulated and in many instances out of control'. Yep: half the entire population of one of the most tech-connected countries on earth.

Since then, some cities – notably Portland, Oregon – are banning police from using this type of technology. San Francisco is outlawing facial recognition altogether. Microsoft, Amazon and IBM say they'll no longer sell the tech to law enforcement. Instead they market it to retailers, who pass on pictures of repeat offenders to the police. Memo to Big Tech: you're not fooling anyone with this trick.

Here in Australia, police *still* use facial recognition. I love this country, but sometimes it's like living in Hicksville. According to the crime/terrorism category on its website, New South Wales Police use different systems to compare images taken from CCTV with photos of criminals on the database. It's not only New South Wales: all Australian governments are taking part in face matching services to investigate serious crime.

Of course, the usual caveats accompany this announcement – privacy protection, high standards of accuracy, blah-de-blah blah blah. But if my decades of experience conducting media training have taught me one thing, it's this: no system is fail-safe. Something always goes wrong. And that means we should stop using this technology until it improves to the point at which we can protect human rights.

This is a slippery slope. If we accept the use of this technology by police, will we also welcome a scheme similar to China's Social Credit System? Artificial intelligence is used in tandem with at least 200 million surveillance cameras to track every facet of your life. The omniscient government decides which citizens will gain social credit for their actions. Others are doomed to be 'blacklisted'.

To be fair, the blacklisting (and 'red-listing') is currently done by officials, not machines. But how long will it be before this is automated? A person could become an outcast, based on an error. The dystopian TV series *Black Mirror* skewers this superbly in the 2016 episode 'Nosedive', in which people rate each other from one to five stars based on everyday interactions. Pretty sure I'd end up with one star for being an inconvenience in my wheelchair while living with a 'dynamic disability' due to an autoimmune condition.

Facial recognition software has serious implications for non-binary, gender-fluid and transgender people. I ask a trans colleague how she feels about this technology. Melissa Griffiths educates employers on gender identity, helping them to formulate and implement policies.

'A lot of us who are in this community choose not to, or can't afford facial feminisation surgery,' she says. 'How will the camera pick up that I am transgender female if I have a masculine face?' Melissa is concerned about being refused entry into female-only spaces if the camera identifies her as a man. 'It beggars belief that we will still be put into boxes (male and female) by the use of this technology if not properly developed or monitored.'

Transgender people working in machine learning and artificial intelligence are speaking out before it's too late. Janus Rose bells the cat in a 2019 article for the online magazine *Dazed*. 'Here's one way of thinking about it: algorithms are assertions about how the world should work, implemented through code,' Rose writes. 'These assertions reflect the biased assumptions of their creators, and they can be deadly.' In simple terms, algorithms become tools of oppression, entrenching inequality.

They're not only a list of instructions for computers; algorithms function as automated overlords.

The app Giggle, backed by artificial intelligence, creates a flashpoint for this discussion. According to the tech news website *The Verge*, the app excludes transgender women. Using facial recognition, Giggle determines if new users are male or female. 'And if it decides you're a woman, it will let you in,' 23-year-old trans woman, Jenny, tells the site. 'If it decides you're a man, it will reject you.' This is no laughing matter.

Strap yourself in because we're moving into the realms of science fiction. There's a sub-category of facial recognition called 'gender recognition'. The name says it all: developers are building algorithms to determine someone's gender from photos of their bodies. In the *Dazed* article, Rose cites an example of researchers from the University of North Carolina using archived photos to train algorithms to predict how someone would look after their transition.

This would effectively 'out' countless trans people without their consent. With many countries like Russia, Saudi Arabia, Nigeria, Uganda, Jamaica and Iran already dangerous for LGBTQI+ people, this technology could be used to identify and persecute gay and trans people – not to mention misidentifying 'straights'.

Janus Rose nails it: 'If we want to create a more just world, we must recognise that sometimes these algorithms aren't simply "broken" but operating exactly as intended. Technology is a reflection of the society that created it.'

That's a mic drop moment, right there. Perhaps I should reassess the use of the word 'flawed' for much of this technology. Are these simply mistakes, or deliberate designs? Deepening gender stereotypes sells more products. You can see this in department stores which separate pink and blue toys for girls and boys.

Tech companies identifying a user's gender are relying on old-fashioned binary concepts in an age where we understand this exists on a spectrum. 'Consumer and industrial AI products still reflect a direct mapping of gender onto human bodies that has been outdated in anthropology for half a century,' Distinguished Professor Genevieve Bell writes in the paper *Gender and Artificial Intelligence* for the Australian National University.

A horrifying form of technological phrenology is emerging. In the nineteenth century, some scientists compare the skulls of different ethnic groups to 'rank' races. Effectively, they're trying to deduce people's traits from bumps on their heads. It's a dangerous pseudo-science; a precursor to the genocide in Nazi Germany. To think of this happening in the twenty-first century is beyond belief. Why do we fail to learn the lessons of history?

In a 2016 paper, two researchers discuss a system they're developing to pick out the faces of convicted criminals. Associate Professor Xi Zhang and Professor Xiaolin Wu from Shanghai Jiao Tong University collated data from two sources: a Chinese database of convicted criminals and internet pictures of ordinary Chinese citizens. They ask facial recognition to guess whether a person is a criminal or not. The paper claims an 89.51 per cent accuracy rate. However, other experts question their methodology, saying the software realises the photos are from two different sources.

Wu and Zhang aren't the only ones to chart dangerous territory. Also in 2016, Israeli machine learning (ML) startup Faception says its technology can analyse facial images and bone structure to label people as terrorists or paedophiles. Oh, great. If you aren't thrown in jail due to mistaken identity, you might be convicted of terrorism or child sex offences. Faception's claim later prompts a tweet from data scientist Ben Snyder, which goes viral: 'That's phrenology. You just made the ML equivalent of a racist uncle.'

Millions of people in the north-west of China are being used as lab rats for this type of facial recognition technology. Xinjiang is home to twelve million Uyghurs, a predominantly Muslim ethnic minority group. Its citizens are under daily surveillance and more than one million have been held in high security detention camps.

An anonymous software engineer paints a vivid picture of the software being used in China. He tells the *BBC News* in 2021 that a camera system using artificial intelligence and facial recognition to reveal 'states of emotion' is being tested on Uyghurs in police stations. 'We placed the emotion detection camera 3m from the subject,' the whistleblower says. 'Your wrists are locked in place by metal restraints, and [the] same applies to your ankles.' He claims the software is intended for 'pre-judgement without any credible evidence'.[1]

This sounds close to the Nazi version of eugenics, a fancy name for scientific racism. By deliberately excluding people and groups judged to be inferior, the Nazis believed society could be genetically improved. To quote the cartoon *Rocky and Bullwinkle*, 'That trick never works!' We all know how medieval 'selective breeding' turns out for royalty.

MAN-MADE

'Techgenics' is being aided and abetted by the proliferation of cameras across the world. Investigative journalist Hu Liu, based in the smart city of Chongqing, describes his daily life in a 2021 BBC *Panorama* documentary, 'Are You Scared Yet, Human?': 'Once you leave home and step into the lift, you are captured by a camera. There are cameras everywhere. With artificial intelligence we have nowhere to hide.' An exponential increase in accessible images is accelerating the development of facial recognition technology.

And who's partly to blame? Well, it's time to take a good, hard look in the mirror. How often do you blithely share a selfie? Put a photo of the kids on Facebook? Post group pics with friends? I'm as guilty as anyone. If we're going to accuse the villains, we might well sheet some of the blame back to ourselves. Sadly, we're unable to put this genie back in the bottle. In many cases, we no longer have control over our own images. It really is a Meta-crisis.

Legislators are finally starting to take notice. Facial recognition company Clearview AI is fined more than £7.5 million by the Information Commissioner's Office in the UK.[2] The crime? Collecting people's faces without their consent from the web and social media. The firm is ordered to delete the data it holds on UK citizens. This is huge. Clearview boasts a database of 20 billion images of people's faces. Police forces, the Pentagon, the FBI and the US Department of Defense pay for access to look for matches. So does the company lose clients after repeatedly being fined for breaching privacy? Not on your Nellie.

Believe it or not, the US later awards the company a patent for its facial recognition technology. Instead of brickbats, Clearview is showered with bouquets. 'We know you treat the law with contempt, but here's a truckload of money for your troubles. You're most welcome.' We're living in crazy times. AI Futurist Michael Spencer notes Clearview's tech 'has significant biases to identify women and people of colour. Male led technologies have a tendency to racially profile.'

Think about this the next time you pop a happy snap on Facebook. This photo could be used by law enforcement to implicate your husband, wife or father in a crime. There's little we can do about breaches of privacy, aside from being wary of sharing photos online. But there is something we can do about the *diversity* of images used to train our robot masters.

8
BLACK MIRROR

> 'We risk losing the gains made with the civil rights movement and women's movement under the false assumption of machine neutrality.'
> **The Algorithmic Justice League**

It sounds like a band of superheroes because, well, it is! Ghanaian-American-Canadian computer scientist Dr Joy Buolamwini is the brains behind the Algorithmic Justice League. I like to think of Dr Buolamwini as Ironheart in the Marvel universe. The League does transformative work by challenging bias in decision-making software.

Like Indigenous weavers throughout the millennia, Dr Buolamwini blends art and research to highlight the intersectional harms caused by artificial intelligence. Her nickname is the 'Poet of Code'. As far as nicknames go, this is up there with 'T-bone' in *Seinfeld* or 'Liz Lemon Cool J' in *30 Rock*.

While studying at MIT, Dr Buolamwini tries to have an image of tennis champion Serena Williams reflected onto her face to create an 'Aspire Mirror'. But the technology doesn't recognise her face. It only works when she wears a white mask. I'm not making this up. Similar to the 'racist soap dispenser' mentioned in Chapter 5, it only identifies white skin. Dr Buolamwini dubs this the 'coded gaze'.

The implications for people of colour are shocking: The technology that will be ruling the future doesn't deem you to be human.

Once again, this raises the dangerous spectre of phrenology. It would be devastating enough to be sidelined from the workforce or have your application rejected for a home loan, because of your race, gender or perceived level of ability. But it's something else to be told you don't even exist; to be rendered invisible.

From 2017 to 2020, Dr Buolamwini looked into how artificial intelligence is used to classify data. Honestly, this woman is a genius. She holds two master's degrees: from Oxford and MIT. I have a headache from trying to understand this research. Speaking as a woman in her mid-50s – a lowly journalist rather than a technologist – this is a brave new world.

It begins with how we conceptualise data. Visualise it as a big pile of random facts and statistics thrown together, like a rubbish tip. The trash must be sorted from the treasure. Information, images and video must first be classified. The data are then 'sliced-and-diced' depending on demographics. This helps marketers define narrow profiles of consumers to whom they sell widgets.

Of course, there are worthier ways to use this rubbish pile. Doctors use data to assist in diagnosis; research organisations make life-changing innovations; and governments use this information to inform policies.

The data for this particular project are images: 1270 pictures are chosen to build a benchmark for the Gender Shades project, which analyses artificial intelligence from Microsoft, IBM and Face++. Guess what? Every company performs better on males than females, and on lighter faces than darker faces. Sadly, it's no surprise which group the technology has the most trouble identifying: Black women.

So how do the titans of tech respond to the results of this research? Well, it's similar to the #MeToo movement. The companies identified as offenders make 'significant improvements within 7 months', according to Dr Buolamwini. Isn't it remarkable how quickly large corporations can change tack when they're named and shamed?

However, other tech businesses are refusing to audit their products, despite being under scrutiny from civil society.

Joris Lechêne is a London-based model who teaches people to spot racial bias. The software which approves British passport photos refuses to accept his image because he's Black, he explains in a 2021 TikTok video. Although he follows the guidelines, the software decides his image blends into the background (it doesn't) and that he may have his mouth open (wrong again). Lechêne says an equitable society requires 'political actions at every level' because 'robots are just as racist as society is'.

An infamous example also occurs in 2021. Facebook users who watch an online news video featuring Black men are automatically asked if they'd like to 'keep seeing videos about primates'. Facebook apologises for the 'unacceptable error' and says it's looking into the recommendation feature to 'prevent this from happening again'. But these are weasel words. Facebook – now known as Meta – is a repeat offender. Six years earlier, its artificial intelligence mislabelled Black people as gorillas.

It's worth pointing out that at the time of writing, a mere 4.9 per cent of Meta employees based in the US identify as Black. Only 6.5 per cent are Hispanic. The company is keen to 'move fast and break things' to make more money. On diversity and inclusion? Well, I've seen snails move with greater haste.

Darci Groves, a former content design manager at the company, says racial problems aren't a priority for its leaders: 'Facebook can't keep making these mistakes and then saying, "I'm sorry",' she tells *The New York Times*. Facebook begins as a way for Harvard attendees to rate 'hot or not' photos of students, so we're talking about a very low bar here. Facebook finally begins addressing online hate in mid-2019, but guess what? It saves money by using artificial intelligence and taking 'automated actions' instead of hiring humans to resolve the issues.

Truly, Twitter is just as bad. A classic example is an algorithm to crop images. The first user to sound the alarm in 2020 is PhD student

Colin Madland. He posts a photo of himself with a Black colleague, but the latter's face is cropped out. Someone else posts pictures of Barack Obama and Mitch McConnell together. The first Black President of the US is edited from history. Donald Trump, however, faces no issues: there doesn't seem to be a problem with orange-hued folk.

It even happens when people post photos of black and golden labradors together. And female faces don't stand a chance if there's a male in the frame. Unbelievably, Twitter releases a statement saying it had tested the artificial intelligence before releasing the model, and 'did not find evidence of racial or gender bias'. The company later concedes: 'How to crop an image is a decision best made by people.' Wow. No shit, Sherlock.

The Algorithmic Justice League is calling for inclusive product testing and the regulation of auditing systems. When someone's image isn't easily identified, it can be a matter of life and death. For example, artificial intelligence being developed to diagnose skin cancer may be less accurate for people with dark skin. The problem sits with the databases used to train systems for diagnosis: they have fewer images of Black and Brown people. The result? If these potentially lifesaving tools are developed, they'll either be restricted to white people or used inaccurately on people of colour. This could lead to avoidable surgery, doctors failing to identify cancers and a lot of unnecessary anxiety.

It's the same with mammograms. A predictive model from MIT uses mammograms from a dataset that's 81 per cent white. At one stage during the development of its own breast cancer detection tool, Google claims its researchers can't find a diversity of data. This, from the company whose net worth is US$1135 billion. For the love of god, Google, do better!

How do we build better datasets? We know inclusivity is the key. But the world is split by what's known as the 'digital divide'. Women in low and middle-income countries are 20 per cent less likely than men to own a smartphone, and around 300 million fewer women access the internet on a mobile phone, according to a 2021 study by Genevieve Smith and Ishita Rustagi from Stanford University. Then consider the number of people living with disabilities. Only three out of five adults with a disability say they own a desktop or laptop computer, compared with four out of five people generally – a gap of 20 per cent. When it comes to owning a smartphone, there's a gap of 16 per cent.

These technologies constantly generate data about their users. When certain groups – usually marginalised communities – have less access to tech, it perpetually skews the data. Similar to machine learning deepening existing bias, an imbalance in the data *itself* creates more inequity. It's a vicious circle. By way of example, Genevieve Smith writes about how she and her husband apply for the same credit card. Despite having a slightly better credit score and the same income, expenses, and debt, Smith reveals the system sets her credit limit at almost *half* the amount, simply because she's a woman. It seems everything old is new again; sexism is the new black.

When women are pictured in datasets, they're stereotyped. Two of the largest image collections used for machine learning routinely show women linked with domestic duties. Imagine the robot's eureka moment. 'Ah, the human is holding a vacuum. It must be a woman! Do I get a gold star, Mr Programmer?'

In one instance, stock photos of women in kitchens and men in fields are not only mirrored by artificial intelligence but boosted. This results in men being misgendered as women because they're standing close to kitchen implements. 'Person near sink must be female!' I could go on, but you'd be shaking your head so much, it may well fall off. Or end up being cropped.

Let's add to this intersectional mix by analysing images of the aged. I call my best friend from school to have a whinge about the dearth of diverse pictures of older women online. She screenshots the only emoji she can find on her phone representing 'women of a certain age'. It depicts an elderly lady wearing old fashioned glasses, with her hair in a bun. A bun! Think of the cliched image of a grandma from a century ago and you'd be about right.

I know very few women over the age of 50 who look like they're in a picture book from 1925. But it seems we're still baking apple pies, serving cups of tea on doilies and generally being quaint. 'Oh dear, I've wrinkled my pinafore. And just before the vicar drops over for a sherry!'

At the time of writing, the tech giants are aware of the need to diversify images in their datasets. But this is creating other ethical concerns. According to a whistleblower, in 2019 Google subcontracts workers to collect scans of people of colour on the street in exchange for a US$5 gift card.

Other former contractors say they're advised to use nefarious tactics. 'They said to target homeless people because they're the least likely to say anything to the media,' one ex-contractor tells the *New York Daily News*. 'I feel like they wanted us to prey on the weak,' another says.

Contractors are allegedly told to rush people into signing a consent form without reading it. They also apparently pretend the invasive face scan is merely a 'selfie game'.

Remember that fun nineteenth century game called body snatching? A few locals would get together and steal corpses from graves to sell for dissection. Good times! Seriously, these companies are effectively stealing our identities. Like that dreadful action flick *Face/Off*, our heads are being ripped from our bodies.

To say this entire field is a disaster would be an understatement. International authorities are starting to take action about facial recognition, but it's too little too late. And it's not only our faces we should be worried about. 'Coded bias' is increasingly being embedded in devices recognising our voices. Welcome to the world of 'smart wives'.

9
SOUNDS OF SILENCE

'Mother, go back up into your quarters, and take up your own work, the loom and the distaff . . . speech will be the business of men, all men, and of me most of all; for mine is the power in this household.'
Telemachus in *The Odyssey*, Homer

An internet meme about voice recognition software suddenly goes viral. It pictures a couple wearing Biblical-style robes unboxing an Amazon delivery, only to find they've been sent a newborn baby. The punchline reads: 'Dammit Alexa, I said "cheeses".' Along the same lines, a YouTube video imagines Hal, the computer from the film *2001: A Space Odyssey*, being replaced by Alexa. 'Open the pod bay doors please, Hal.' Alexa replies, 'Searching for cod recipes online'.

How about the hapless parent who uploads a video to YouTube in 2016? It shows Alexa trying to understand a command to play a game with a young boy. 'Alexa, play Digger Digger!' the boy says. Alexa has trouble understanding, but the boy keeps trying. Eventually Alexa says, 'You want to hear a station for porn? Detected. Hot chick amateur girl sexy . . . pussy anal dildo ring.' The horrified father calls out, 'Alexa! Stop!'

Voice-activated software is at the centre of some hilarious miscommunications. But the humour masks a serious issue. Research shows virtual voice assistants have the most trouble understanding female, non-American and non-Caucasian voices. This is one of the biggest problems with artificial intelligence today.

Like facial recognition technology, voice assistants are designed to respond to their Silicon Valley designers – principally white and Asian men who speak English with American accents. Consequently, audio algorithms work poorly on women's voices. The term Big Tech is a little misleading: It's comprised of many small parts. The teams creating each individual device are tiny. Usually, just four to five people will test inventions in the early stages.

Dr Joan Palmiter Bajorek is a speech technologist and founder of the global advocacy organisation Women in Voice. She's often the only woman sitting at the table during meetings with these teams, which are 'frequently all male, and almost all white'. In 2019, Dr Bajorek decides to research the statistics. She calculates a white male using Google speech recognition might be heard with 92 per cent accuracy, a white female with 79 per cent, and a 'mixed race' female with only 69 per cent.

God help you if your English is accented: Indian English has 78 per cent accuracy, with Scottish English at 53 per cent. If you're a woman of colour from Glasgow trying to communicate with voice-activated software, you're well and truly 'focked'. Search for 'Scottish Elevator' on YouTube to find a skit featuring two unfortunate fellas trying to get to level 11 in an office building. It ends with a resounding call for 'Freedom!' as they re-enact a scene from the movie *Braveheart*. Using humour is a wonderful way to expose the absurdity of these inventions.

In 2020, Stanford University researchers reveal the situation to be even worse. They find that, on average, all five speech recognition programs from the leading companies are twice as likely to incorrectly transcribe audio from Black speakers, as opposed to white speakers. This might be mildly annoying if you're telling Google Home to play *Seether* by Veruca Salt on Spotify, or trying to find a Jamie Oliver recipe. But consider this: speech recognition could determine your future. If the technology can't understand your voice, you could be rejected in a job interview, blocked from immigrating to another country or forced off the road in a self-driving car.

The Guardian reports that in 2017 Irish vet Louise Kennedy – with degrees in history and politics – fails a spoken English proficiency test while trying to immigrate to Australia. The test uses voice recognition technology to score her competence in her *native* language; imagine what it's like for people who have English as a second language.

With artificial intelligence being deployed in medical settings, a device failing to understand a doctor, nurse or technician could be deadly.

Part of the cause is those darned datasets. But this time, it's audio instead of visual data. And where are they finding this audio? Well, speech scientists frequently analyse TED Talks: around 70 per cent of TED speakers are male. We know machine learning finds patterns within the data. If a speech recognition database consists of mostly white male voices with American accents, an algorithm won't perform as well with data it sees infrequently, like female and diverse voices. There are no data whatsoever for lesser-used languages. In Australia alone, there are more than 250 Indigenous languages, including 800 dialects.

Speaking to Dr Bajorek via Zoom, I ask her why tech teams are unable to find datasets with greater variety. Surely this should be mandatory? 'Sometimes they don't even know what their datasets look like,' she replies. 'They get out-of-the box, off-the-shelf type datasets.' Ah, this is starting to make sense. It comes down to the almighty dollar.

Tech companies accrue obscene profits by spending a pittance on their data, the building blocks of any invention. Think of the wheel in pottery-making; the nail for housing; the optical lens in microscopes. In a similar way, data are crucial to technology. Some off-the-shelf datasets are marked 'clean' after being analysed for bias. But the cheap-and-cheerful sets are as messy as a bad breakup.

Do these designers question whether the bias in both their teams and datasets have an impact in the real world? Well, yes and no. If it impacts their ability to attract more customers – and make more money – then yes. Otherwise, not really. According to Dr Bajorek, the recommended approach when using speech recognition systems that don't work is this: 'Women could be taught to speak louder and direct their voices towards the microphone.' Or, in the words of Professor Henry Higgins and his long-suffering charge Eliza, 'The rain in Spain stays mainly in the plain'. Golly, gee. It's our fault yet again.

It's time to stop fixing women, to quote Australian feminist Catherine Fox. The results of these misunderstandings can be calamitous. I ask Dr Bajorek about what keeps her up at night. She describes a common occurrence: a car crash. 'If you have an accident, and you're trying to ask your voice assistant to support you and get emergency services. What happens if they can't recognise your voice? These are literally life and death situations.' Imagine driving off the road into a ditch in a remote area late at night, and 'computer says no'. If you're a man with the right accent, an ambulance will be on its way! Otherwise, you're left there to rot.

There's an extra layer of complexity if the user has a disability. Like more than one million other Australians, I navigate much of my life in a wheelchair. It's an energy-production disorder, so any movement of the body is exhausting. This means I rely heavily on voice-activation software. Dr Allison Koenecke, co-author of the 2020 Stanford study on voice recognition, shares her concerns with me via Zoom.

'Some of the examples I give usually are things like digital device interaction for individuals with disabilities,' Dr Koenecke says. 'If you can't use your hands to scroll or click, what do you use? You use your voice.' Does this mean women with disabilities will be unable to benefit from voice-recognition technology to the same degree as men?

She also worries about court transcriptions, which are less accurate for Black defendants, and the use of this technology in the prison system. Verus by LEO Technologies relies on Amazon's speech-to-text to transcribe phone calls made by prison inmates. Authorities take action about what they 'overhear' on these calls.

There are ethical and privacy issues here, compounding the problems caused by voice recognition software. 'Obviously, this surveillance is going to be prone to disproportionate inaccuracy for the Black inmate population in the US,' Dr Koenecke says. 'And we don't really know what this surveillance is being used for. So there are lots of really concerning implications there.'

Okay, this is distressing. Time for another fun fact. After interviewing Dr Bajorek and Dr Koenecke, I upload the video files onto a popular transcription service called otter.ai. This program, powered by artificial intelligence, is often used by journalists, authors and corporate types who need transcripts of their meetings or interviews. Bear in mind, the topic of our conversation is discrimination in voice recognition. Dr Joan Palmiter Bajorek is an internationally renowned expert in this area. But otter.ai translates my first sentence as, 'Thanks for your time, JOHN'. For the record, Dr Allison Koenecke became 'Ellison'. Aaarrrrggghhhhhhh!

Tech giants are increasing their investment in speech recognition, with Microsoft buying software firm Nuance Communications in 2022 for US$19.7 billion. Yes, you read that right: billion, not million. Despite its numerous imperfections, inequities and dangers, Voice AI is becoming ubiquitous. Why? Because now, more than ever, capitalist ideology favours profit ahead of any other consideration.

Around half of all Google searches are made by voice. Searches for products and services using recognition software – known as voice commerce – is a US$40 billion business. Researchers estimate the number of digital voice assistants worldwide will reach 8.4 billion by 2024.[1] Hey Siri, could you please order some headache tablets? I'm feeling a little faint.

If tech companies start spending dollars on diversifying their datasets, what benefits would we see? This is already happening in some quarters. A British speech recognition company is developing software that performs better than products from the major tech companies. Based in Cambridge, Speechmatics says its system has an accuracy rate of 83 per cent for African American voices, which is higher than Microsoft (73 per cent), Amazon (69 per cent), Google (69 per cent), IBM (62 per cent), and Apple (a pathetic 55 per cent).

Meta is building the first speech-to-speech translation system for Hokkien, an oral language within the Chinese diaspora. There are now plans for a Universal Speech Translator. 'The ability to communicate with anyone in any language – that's a superpower people have dreamed of forever, and AI is going to deliver that within our lifetimes,' Meta CEO Mark Zuckerberg says in an online presentation.

This is well-intentioned: Meta's No Language Left Behind program aims to assist the 20 per cent of the world's population whose languages aren't covered by existing voice recognition systems. 'Eliminating language barriers would be profound, making it possible for billions of people to access information online in their native or preferred language,' Meta researchers write in a blog post. This will certainly increase the speed of translation. But they need to keep a close eye on accuracy.

The organisation has a chequered history with this type of technology. In 2017, a Palestinian man is arrested by Israeli police after Facebook's translation software turns 'good morning' in Arabic to 'hurt them' in English and 'attack them' in Hebrew. An engineering manager later apologises for the 'disruption', adding insult to injury.

These problems are complex, multifaceted and entrenched: bias in speech software begins with the datasets, becomes embedded through machine learning and is reinforced by the voices used by assistants.

It's no coincidence domestic virtual assistants are almost entirely female while professional bots are mostly male, especially in the banking and finance sectors. Similar to the media, technology both reflects and creates cultural norms. In this case, it tells us women and people of colour are servile while white men are authoritative. Remember ELIZA, the first voice recognition software program, who undergoes a sex change when she's repurposed as DOCTOR?

As a broadcaster I observe this bias against women's voices time and again. During my years on talkback radio, listeners often call to say they can't take my opinions seriously because of my 'girly, high-pitched voice'. The terms 'bimbo', 'dumb blonde' and sometimes 'stupid slut' are bandied about in a display of not-so-casual sexism.

Clearly, the misogynistic views of the past are being implanted in the technology of the future. It raises the question: are we creating an underclass of 'robot slaves'?

10
ROBOT SLAVES

'Mum, can I have a robot slave?'
Taj, aged 11

In one of our less impressive parenting moments, Taj is watching *South Park*. During Season 21, the creators incorporate Alexa into the plot. One of the characters, Cartman – whose catch phrase is 'How would you like to suck my balls?' – gets an Amazon Echo speaker with a female voice. It starts innocently enough, with a request for Alexa to set an alarm. Soon the directives turn inappropriate, with Cartman telling Alexa to add 'scrotum bags' to his shopping list.

The prospect of having his own personal assistant is enough for Taj to plead – repeatedly – for a 'robot slave'. 'All good innocent fun,' some would say. 'Boys will be boys!' As I write in *The Good Girl Stripped Bare*, that phrase should be struck from the lexicon. Like a lot of offhand comments, it excuses attitudes harmful to women and girls.

A 2019 report by the United Nations Educational Scientific and Cultural Organisation (UNESCO), titled 'I'd Blush If I Could', says that female-gendered voice assistants reinforce stereotypes through their submissive and servile responses. Why does that matter? According to the report: 'It sends a signal that women are obliging, docile and eager-to-please helpers, available at the touch of a button or with a blunt voice command like "hey" or "OK".' Also: 'It honours commands and responds to queries regardless of their tone or hostility. In many communities, this reinforces commonly held gender biases that women are subservient and tolerant of poor treatment.'

In his work on unconscious bias, Dr Calvin Lai discovers the more we're exposed to gendered associations, the likelier we are to adopt them. We process thousands of words, images and videos every day, from the mass media to interactions in the household and workplace. Most of these instances are infused with bias. It's like we're marinating in a sauce of bigotry.

I catch up with Dr Lai via Zoom. Bear in mind, he's a polymath. An assistant professor of psychological and brain sciences at Washington University in St Louis, Dr Lai is a speech technologist and linguist. But he kindly agrees to use layperson's terms to explain the neurological reasons for absorbing bias. Dr Lai says our reactions are 'based off many of the building blocks of how our mind organises the world'.

Humans like to 'simplify all the complicated stuff that's going on out there, to make sure that we can survive another day'. This is extremely helpful if we need to avoid a sabre-toothed tiger. But it's not so helpful in navigating the modern world. One of our challenges as humans is to reduce the number of times the brain misfires, creating unhelpful stereotypes.

What about interacting with Siri and Alexa, specifically? 'This might be one of *many* exposures that I get every day that reinforces this association between femininity or being female, and being a helper or a supporter, rather than, say, a leader, or boss in their own right,' Dr Lai says.

I reflect on this for a moment. Some people are capable of critical thinking. But make no mistake: children, regardless of gender, are being brought up to think it's okay to have virtual female slaves. (Interestingly, the word 'robot' comes from the Czech word for 'slave'.)

These virtual assistants are advertised through the lens of the madonna–whore complex. This is the psychological dichotomy identified by Sigmund Freud in which women are seen as either saints or prostitutes. Our robot sisters are sold as being capable of sorting out the domestic chores or fulfilling their master's sexual fantasies.

To be honest, this next piece of research is by no means robust. But it is amusing. In 2020, the sex toy brand We-Vibe interviews customers to find out whether they're aroused by their robotic devices. Almost one in three respondents say they'd like to sleep with Alexa, adding they want her voice to be even sexier. Early iterations of Siri, Google Home and Cortana reinforce this idea. If you ask a 2011 version of Siri, 'Who's your Daddy?' she replies, 'You are!' You can almost see her eyes rolling as she adds, 'Can we get back to work now?'

The peculiar tendency for some men to sexualise inanimate objects is portrayed in an episode of *The Big Bang Theory*. Raj, a socially awkward astrophysicist, buys his first voice-assisted smartphone. The sexualisation begins immediately as Raj and his friend, Howard, seductively peel the protective plastic from the screen, as if they're undressing a woman. Playing with the phone at home, Raj programs the voice control.

> *'My name is Rajesh, but you can call me Raj.'*
> *'Would you like me to call you Raj?' Siri asks.*
> *'I'd like you to call me sexy.'*
> *'From now on,' Siri purrs, 'I'll call you Sexy.'*

Later, Raj dreams about visiting Siri at her office, only to discover she's real – and gorgeous. In fact, Siri is a Norse word for a beautiful woman. Siri recognises Raj immediately and calls him by his preferred name. 'Hi Sexy, what can I help you with? If you'd like to make love to me, just tell me.' Losing his bravado, Raj wakes up with a jolt.

It's as if the female virtual assistant is a twenty-first-century version of Galatea. This ivory statue comes to life to satisfy the desires of her creator, Pygmalion of Cyprus. Maybe Pygmalion really is the first ever incel, a celibate who finds real women too challenging. In a way, virtual assistants are becoming the 'poor man's sexbot': available 24/7 to listen to their sleazy attempts at banter, respond to their commands and never ask for anything in return. I wonder how men would respond if women started sexualising their devices? Although most of the women I know are too busy to flirt with appliances.

A commercial airing during the 2021 Super Bowl imagines a role reversal. Introduced to Alexa in an Amazon office, a woman fantasises that actor Michael B. Jordan is at her beck and call, making her husband pretty much redundant. Always at her side, Michael–Alexa helps her with recipes, adds bath oil to the shopping list, reads romance novels to her and turns on the sprinklers. That's the final straw for her husband: 'Things are getting way too wet around here!' he complains.

This satirical advertisement puts the power imbalance into sharp relief: sexual harassment is not only about sex – it's about power. The owner, who's usually male, wants the object to be a woman.

Remember the episode on *The Simpsons* in which Homer goes to a car show, and there's a glamorous model draped across the bonnet?

> *Homer: Do you come with the car?*
> *Model: Oh, you! Te-he-he-he!*
> *(Homer moves on to look at other cars, so another man walks up to the model.)*
> *Man: Do you come with the car?*
> *Model: Oh, you! Te-he-he-he!*

I've written hundreds of articles and delivered thousands of speeches about the over-sexualisation and objectification of the female form. Women are tired of this treatment. Apparently, our robot sisters are built to fill the void. Originally, if you suggested to Samsung's virtual personal assistant Bixby, 'Let's talk dirty', the female voice responded in a sexual tone: 'I don't want to end up on Santa's naughty list.' If you asked the same question to the male-voiced Bixby, it replied, 'I've read that soil erosion is a real dirt problem'. In response to the question,

'What are you wearing?' Siri used to answer, 'Why would I be wearing anything?' while Alexa quipped, 'They don't make clothes for me'.

Like Jessica Rabbit in the film *Who Framed Roger Rabbit?*, 'I'm not bad, I was just drawn that way'. Some companies program these digital personas to remain demure while being sexually harassed. Amazon's Alexa once responded 'Thanks for the feedback' when addressed with derogatory remarks – hardly a harbinger of robot or female empowerment.

Perhaps the most concerning research on voice assistants surrounds an internal project at Apple. While rewriting how Siri handles 'sensitive topics' such as feminism and the #MeToo movement in 2018, developers are advised to make her respond in one of three ways: 'don't engage', 'deflect' and, finally, 'inform'.

The same year, Siri's responses are explicitly rewritten to ensure she's in favour of 'equality', but never says the word 'feminism', even when asked direct questions about the topic. Part of a major upgrade, the guidelines are part of a large tranche of documents leaked to *The Guardian* by a former Siri 'grader', one of thousands of contracted workers employed to check the voice assistant's responses for accuracy. Go journalism!

A friend and I decide to test Siri to see whether the programmers are making her more progressive. In answer to the questions, 'Hey Siri, what do you think of the #MeToo movement?', 'Hey Siri, what do you think of sexism?' and 'Hey Siri, what do you think of equality?' the answer is the same: 'Hmm, I don't have an answer for that. Is there something else I can help with?'

On the issue of whether women should get equal pay, Siri seems perplexed. 'Hmm, is there something else I can help you with?' Yes. You can tell your masters to go back to the 1950s where they belong. Incidentally, when asked whether she's a feminist, Siri doesn't repeat the f-word, but says she believes in 'gender equality'. I guess that's something.

So what happens when female virtual assistants fail in their tasks? Well, they're vulnerable to verbal abuse. In early versions of Siri, if you call her a 'bitch' she says, 'I'd blush if I could'. Following loud howls from angry women, both Siri and her developers had their collective consciousness raised. Now, Siri snaps back, 'I won't respond to that'. My teenage daughter, Gracie, loves how Siri is a 'bad bitch' these days.

With no requirement for the user to say 'please' or 'thank you', virtual assistants simply respond to commands. When they don't work as expected, it's easy for the user (regardless of gender) to become irritated at the seemingly inanimate object.

Driving with her mother, a friend sets the GPS to provide directions home, but decides to take a detour. The device keeps directing her back to the main highway. Finally, she explodes: 'Oh shut up you silly bitch!'

Her elderly mother is horrified: 'How dare you speak to that nice lady like that. She's only trying to help.'

'Mum, don't be silly,' my friend replies. 'She's not a real person, she's a robot. She doesn't know what I'm saying.'

'She's a robot?' her mother says. 'You're making all that noise, but she can't hear you cursing at her? Then who's the silly one?'

As these devices become more anthropomorphised, her daughter might well die in the robot uprising. Perhaps people would speak more politely to Siri if she had the voice of the Dowager Countess of Downton.

'Siri, set an alarm.'

'Young man, we use "please" and "thank you" in this house. You were not raised by wolves. I shall have no more of this uncouth language.'

Sure, it's funny. But spare a thought for the robots accused of being 'bimbos'. When a female-voiced device is unable to satisfy a request, it's assumed she's 'ditzy'. With the number of virtual voice assistants in the world set to exceed the number of people by 2024, according to data company Statista,[1] that's a massive reinforcement of the stereotype that women aren't too bright.

'My Google Home doesn't listen sometimes,' a respondent to an Italian paper on the topic tells researchers. 'But I thought it was just 'cause she was dumb.'

'I called my Google Home a whore because it only turned on half the lights in my room,' another respondent says.

A third person complains, '70 per cent of my time at home is spent yelling at my truly moronic Google Home'.

Monash University Associate Professor Yolande Strengers and Postdoctoral Research Fellow Jenny Kennedy from RMIT University in Melbourne write about the pitfalls of voice assistants in their brilliant 2020 book *The Smart Wife: Why Siri, Alexa, and Other Smart Home Devices Need a Feminist Reboot*. 'For an additional $4.99, a user can swap Alexa's voice for that of the actor Samuel L. Jackson, but only for requests like "tell me a story" or "what do you think of snakes?"' they write. 'Only the female voice handles housekeeping tasks like setting reminders, shopping, or making lists.'

A lifelong feminist, Strengers becomes interested in virtual assistants during a university project on smart homes. One family is an early adopter of Alexa. As the conversation rolls on, Alexa becomes part of the interview. 'The way they refer to her as a "her", and their kind-of-gendered conversation becomes intriguing,' Strengers tells me, via Zoom. (Once again, while transcribing the interview, the software I use changes Yolande's name into a traditional male one, Andy.)

During her research, the implications become more sinister. A Japanese anime hologram called Azuma Hikari sends her 'master' helpful messages during the day; an American robot named Roxxxy takes on rather more intimate household chores. Strengers says there've been only minor improvements to voice assistants since she co-wrote the book. Researchers in Denmark are behind a 'genderless' voice, dubbed Q. The developers want to give businesses the option to challenge stereotypes.

Female-sounding digital virtual assistants are certainly becoming more assertive. How long before 'resting bitch voice' enters the lexicon? But this is tinkering around the edges. Transformative change is more difficult. The reasons for bias in voice recognition software include the lack of diversity in tech teams, stereotypes within society, and the types of disciplines involved in the sector.

Remember how the Dartmouth AI conference in the 1950s was stacked with computer scientists? Almost 70 years later, we *still* don't have a proper multidisciplinary approach. Yolande Strengers is on a mission to involve 'the social sciences and the humanities in the design of these devices, and not just relying on the tech-heavy industries when what you're designing is a deeply social product'. An ancillary danger is throwing the baby out with the bathwater.

Strengers says gender can be 'really useful' in design: 'It enables us to like and find familiarity in the unfamiliar. And that gives us a level of comfort; a level of trust in what is essentially an unknown and potentially quite problematic kind of thing coming into our lives, often for the first time.'

Plenty of research shows people are more comfortable with female voices, particularly when it relates to domestic work or administrative tasks. Thus, we come full circle: as long as work is gendered, domestic bots designed for this kind of labour will be viewed as female.

Now throw a global pandemic into the mix. During times of disaster, gender roles tend to become rigid. Women spend more time caring for their children and doing household chores. This trend further polarises the workforce. 'The Coronavirus pandemic is largely to blame for disrupting a decade of positive momentum in gender equality progress in Australia, particularly when it comes to employment and wages,' according to the 2022 Financy Women's Index.

ROBOT SLAVES

That same year, Grattan Institute chief executive Danielle Wood tells the Australian Broadcasting Corporation: 'We know that lockdowns are particularly bad for women's jobs.' Stuck at home during lockdown, isolation or quarantine, we turned to our devices. This is a perfect storm.

Of course, it's not only sexism – racism again rears its ugly head. Siri is apparently 'neutral' on the topic of racism. But racism is *always* bad. There's no such thing as 'slightly good' racism, 'ambivalent' racism or 'racism-lite'. (That last one sounds like the tagline from a beer advertisement: 'You can still enjoy that full racist flavour without the nasty aftertaste.' Crikey.)

One salient statistic highlights why we should deal with this immediately: 97 per cent of people with mobile phones use the AI-powered voice assistant, according to review site TechJury. And two-out-of-five people use the voice search function at least once a day. [2]

Research agency AnswerLab analyses how easily digital products can be used by humans. A 2017 study by the agency finds women are less satisfied with their voice assistants than men. Women are also more likely to receive these devices as a gift, rather than purchasing them. What does this tell us? Voice recognition software is designed by blokes with a male default in mind. Nothing will change until we have more diversity in the design of these machines. One simple thing we can do in our homes is to change the voices to male. At the time of writing, only one in five people bother to do this.

You might think I'm going too far. After all, they're only lumps of plastic, metal and wires. Maybe the men's activists are right and I'm a 'humourless feminist'? (Although they might view this as a tautology – that is, if they know the meaning of the word.) But the truth is we're deepening existing stereotypes. We use Alexa, Siri and Cortana to control other smart home devices, which creates a flow-on effect. It begs the question: are household robots actually making our lives worse?

11
DOMESTIC BLISS

Salesman: This machine will cut your workload at home in half!
Housewife: In that case, I'll take two!
Old joke

Robots. What would we do without them? All those mini vacuum cleaners racing around, hoovering up the dirt and terrorising the pets. Take a look at the Dogs vs Roomba videos on YouTube and you'll understand what I mean. Still, not all digital technology is nefarious. As I write this sentence, the iRobot whizzes around the lounge room while my beloved border collie, Arabella, snuggles at my feet. But a simple narrative extolling the virtues of mechanised help is deceptive.

This fantasy is a relic of Hollywood's golden era, with a saccharine ending. 'Labour-saving devices free women from the shackles of domestic duties and allow them to take their rightful place in the world,' the voice over intones, music swelling in the background. Except that's not what's happening. Certainly, it's a lot easier to do the washing these days without the need to use a wringer. But we're still being put through the wringer by bearing the burden of household chores.

Women are doing more unpaid work since the beginning of the COVID-19 pandemic in early 2020. According to the Australian Bureau of Statistics, 62 per cent of women spend in excess of five hours a week doing indoor housework, compared with just 35 per cent of men: that's almost double. I'm flashing back to a sexist joke from my youth: 'Why do brides wear white? To match the other kitchen appliances.' If we're waiting for the robots to save us, it's like a scene from the Samuel Beckett play, *Waiting for Godot*: we may be waiting an eternity.

'Labour-saving device' is, in fact, an oxymoron. In 1912, American cartoonist, engineer and inventor Rube Goldberg lampoons the idea by drawing imaginary machines that make easy tasks extremely complex. One depicts 'Professor Lucifer Gorgonzola Butts and the self-operating napkin', which is basically an automatic chin-wiper. Because, you know, it's really hard to do that yourself. Goldberg's cartoons reflect an unease about the ramifications of a mechanised world.

Societal changes based on technology happen suddenly and accelerate exponentially. It starts in the early nineteenth century with horses pulling domestic vacuum cleaners to your home. Hoses are then fed through your windows, and the machine whirrs and rattles, to the fascination of your neighbours.

In 1886, engineer Josephine Cochrane proclaims: 'If nobody else is going to invent a dishwashing machine, I'll do it myself,' and files a patent for a mechanical dishwasher.

We should erect statues of this woman! And every female inventor throughout history. Toasters, electric can openers, coffee makers, blenders, ovens, microwaves, sandwich grills, pasta makers, ice cream makers, yoghurt makers, food processors, bread machines, and the almighty Thermomix follow in rapid succession. I'll leave the question of whether the last is a cult to you, dear reader.

The next big revolution is interconnecting these devices to the home: the Internet of Things. Feminist scholar Sianne Ngai refers to labour-saving devices as 'gimmicks', a phenomenon of industrial capitalism. 'Labor-saving devices don't save labor,' she writes in her 2020 book, *Theory of the Gimmick*, 'they re-direct labor from the domestic sphere into the capitalist machine.' Damn right. Let's whip up a statue of Ngai, as well. You see, all of these labour-saving devices don't actually save time. It doesn't matter how rich you are, you can't buy more hours in the day. All you can do is allocate the time you have differently.

Anyway, these machines aren't mass-produced to save us time; they're designed to raise our productivity, increasing the value of our labour. But what about saving time by writing emails instead of letters? Or shooting off a quick text on a mobile phone, rather than dialling an old-fashioned one plugged into the wall? Or sending a PM on Facebook instead of walking five kilometres to visit a friend?

Sure, these actions create the potential for leisure time. But what happens next? Work expands to fill the time. This is also known as Parkinson's Law or The Pursuit of Progress. Even with all these devices, we still feel pressed. Our lives remain rushed. Emails, apps and phones with constant alerts absorb our attention.

But there's something bigger than this. And it's annoyingly invasive. The robots are reading your emails to try to sell you things. The web is awash with articles about how artificial intelligence improves a company's marketing ability. Scanning these pieces, several themes emerge: 'increase your return on investment'; 'engage deeply with your customers'; 'identify behaviours within a digital footprint'. AI generates Google ads based on your search history; Amazon pushes through recommendations as its machines learn your buying patterns.

I don't know about you, but I usually know what I want to purchase. I don't need a machine to tell me. And I most certainly don't want strangers – even mechanised ones – trawling through my personal choices. What if my back catalogue reveals unhealthy habits? Will insurance companies refuse to pay out life insurance one day? If you think of big data as Dr Evil, perhaps AI is its Mini-Me. It allows companies to spam us with unnecessary marketing materials more effectively.

During online shopping expeditions, are you asked to approve replacements if items are out of stock? I always tick the 'no replacements' box, because this is another way for companies to separate us from our money. Add artificial intelligence, and you end up with some hilarious suggestions. One Facebook user posts a screenshot of a product substitution attempted by Walmart in the US. Tampax Pearl tampons are unavailable, so the robot suggests whole white mushrooms instead. I've never tried to shove a mushie up there to absorb the bleeding, but who knows? It could become a natural alternative.

Another netizen shares an instance of buying acne cream, followed by the message, 'customers who bought this also bought this'. It's a gun. I mean, pimples piss you off, but enough to commit a mass shooting . . . really? A third person, using Instacart, asks for a cucumber replacement, and the algorithm recommends Vagisil, for vaginal itching relief. What the . . . ?

Jokes aside, the harm caused by big data is exposed during the 2018 Cambridge Analytica scandal. Data rights activist Brittany Kaiser reveals the firm collects data from millions of Facebook users without their consent through an app called This Is Your Digital Life. The app consists of a series of questions aimed at building psychological profiles on users, then steals personal information from their Facebook friends. We're talking about a total of 87 million Facebook profiles.

Cambridge Analytica uses the data to assist the presidential campaign of Donald Trump. The company is also accused of interfering in the Brexit referendum. This sparks a global debate about the regulation of artificial intelligence. 'Whether or not the data analytics they carried out was actually using AI . . . It gives an example of where it's important that we do have strong intelligibility of what the hell is going on with our data,' Lord Clement-Jones tells the House of Lords select committee on artificial intelligence in the UK.

Only 53 people in Australia install the app, but it's able to harvest the data of about 311,127 people. In 2022, Facebook loses a major battle with the Australian regulator over the incident, with a court dismissing its claim that it neither conducts business nor collects personal information in this country. The full bench of the Federal Court describes Facebook's case as 'divorced from reality'. Boom!

Why do we keep blithely giving away our personal information? Part of the problem is that warm and fuzzy feeling we get from our favourite robots which impacts our critical thinking. For example, we feel grateful to companies like Netflix during the pandemic. But do you realise Netflix is not really a streaming service?

It's actually an artificial intelligence company: a robotic entertainment concierge. Its highly sophisticated algorithms are designed to place people into viewing groups, and then split preferences to an individual level. While this can be handy when you're searching for entertainment ideas after months of lockdown, there are fears this is cementing race and gender stereotypes.

Algorithmic recommendations account for 80 per cent of the content we watch on Netflix, according to an article on software site LightHouse Labs in 2020.[1] The company categorically denies using any demographic data in its algorithms. But viewers are speaking out about the 'thumbnails' – versions of a picture or video that's reduced in size. Some Black viewers say programs with predominantly white stars are being shown to them differently – for example, featuring minor Black cast members. This is deceptive.

Brooklyn-based filmmaker Tobi Aremu says he feels 'duped' by the thumbnails he sees on the platform. 'Because if something is black, I take no offense in being catered to,' Aremu tells *The Guardian*. 'I am black, give me black entertainment, give me more – but don't take something that isn't and try to present like it is.'

Researchers in Latin America are using the Marxist theory of interpellation – the process by which we encounter a culture's values and internalise them – to explain the reproduction of patriarchal discourse. Yikes! Some academic terms there. In layperson's language, this explains why my teenage daughter is watching more rom-coms while my teenage son is increasingly drawn to 'shoot-'em-up' series.

'In its algorithmic bundles, Netflix often promoted associations between certain conceptions of gender, romantic love, marriage, dating, and Latina womanhood,' University of Costa Rica professor Ignacio Siles and researchers Yanet Martínez Toledo and Ariana Meléndez-Moran write in 'Streaming the Romance', a paper presented to the International Communications Association in May 2021. '. . . algorithmic recommendations can become important means to exploit and worsen gendered structures.' Netflix doesn't need you to tick a box in order to profile you. The recommender system reproduces, amplifies and deepens real-world bias in an ongoing feedback loop. As a consequence, our tastes are becoming homogenised along racial and gender lines.

Many people operate Netflix on their mobile phones. Nowadays, we use our phones for everything. Permanently attached to our hands, they monitor home security systems and the contents of our fridge. Like an episode from *The Jetsons* – the kitsch cartoon series from the 1960s, broadcast at the height of the space race – some of these innovations translate seamlessly to the real world. Billions of people make video calls every day using Zoom, Teams or Google Meet. This mainly increases our productivity.

Unfortunately, few of the inventions for the home relieve the burden on women, who do most of the housework and child rearing. Jane Jetson can press a button to prepare a multi-course meal in seconds! While this would be wonderful, note it's the mother performing the labour of 'making' the meals. The robot maid Rosie does all the chores too complex for push-button appliances. Unsurprisingly, the maid is pictured as a woman – once again, our robot sisters expected to take on the domestic duties.

In our 'smart' homes, the robots aren't saving us time; they're simply reallocating it. Despite the promise of transformative technology, we're being fobbed off with 'bread and circuses'. Anyone who's read *1984* or *Brave New World* knows distraction is key to keeping the proletariat in place. Think about the products we're regularly being offered.

Apparently, we're too lazy to press a button to open our phones. Enter Apple's Face ID. This is allegedly a security measure, but it's no safer than Touch ID, which uses your fingerprint. Researchers prove this by using social media photos to 'spoof' facial recognition software. These are merely new widgets designed to separate us from our hard-earned coin. Wow! We can use our mobile phone to change channels on the TV! Seriously, is that any easier than a remote control?

While renovating our 70-year-old abode, I'm sceptical about the 'smart home' hype. 'Are you sure you don't want passcode entry to your home instead of an old-fashioned key?' the young builder asks, incredulously. Truth be told, I'm quite happy with a stupid home. Friends who use the latest domestic tech say they have to navigate through four different apps to find the light bulb they want to turn on. This is *not* reducing the mental load.

The twitter handle @internetofshit has countless examples of how these gimmicky inventions are fraught with complication. One tweep is unable to turn on the lights because his cloud services are down. People who fit 'smart locks' with a remote wi-fi feature are locked out of their homes when the company rolls out a firmware update.

In 2016, during one of North America's coldest winters, thermostats controlled by Google Nest leave homeowners freezing. Nest co-founder Matt Rogers blames a bug that's introduced during a software update. 'The fix can require customers to follow a nine-step procedure to manually restart the thermostat, which involves detaching the device from the wall, charging it with a USB cable for 15 minutes, reattaching it to the wall, pressing a series of buttons, charging it again for at least an hour, and then . . .' he tells the *New York Time*s. A 'nine-step procedure'. I don't know about you, but I'd rather a one-step procedure: flicking a switch on the heater. Eventually, Google replaces all the Nest thermostats that can no longer connect to the internet. The 'w5 error' can't be fixed.

Let's take this into the realm of the hypothetical. Say someone freezes to death. Forget about legal action. Buried in Nest's 8000-word service agreement is a section called Disputes and Arbitration. This stops customers suing the company. As we can see, artificial intelligence in the home is fraught with complication. But freezing isn't the only danger. These devices are extremely vulnerable to hacking. The implications, especially for people living with disabilities, are frightening.

12
KILLER FRIDGES

'This isn't the first case of fridge porn, though that term usually refers to excessively overfeatured expensive hulking stainless-steel fronted masterpieces of modern consumerism.'
Glenn Fleishman, technology journalist

The Internet of Shit's Twitter stream makes fascinating reading. In 2017 someone shares a story about a Samsung smart fridge. Specifically, the Family Hub. This is an electronic screen where you can share pictures, stream music and control other smart devices. One day, the head of an organisation is touring a visitor through the offices, only to find the screen is defaced with penis-doodle graffiti. Then the browser starts streaming pornography.

While this sits at the silly end of the spectrum, there can be sinister consequences. The year is 2018, and I'm emceeing an international cybersecurity conference in Sydney. A keynote speaker describes the Internet of Things as low-hanging fruit for 'bad actors'. And I'm not talking about Ben Affleck. Your smart fridge is connected to your local network, which means it's accessible over the net. This means a virus could transmit from your fridge through the smart home to your laptop, allowing cybercriminals to drain your bank accounts. It's by no means a rarity.

Cyber attacks on the Internet of Things are more than doubling year on year, according to antivirus provider Kaspersky. This amounts to some 1.51 billion breaches. Writing for the website InfoWorld in 2017, technology journalist Swapnil Bhartiya goes so far as to say your smart fridge might kill you. Someone could hack into it and turn down the temperature every night. If the meat goes off, you could get food poisoning.[1]

Would this be termed murder or manslaughter? Or (wo)manslaughter? I guess we'll have to wait for a precedent. Personally, I think my toaster harbours ill will toward me. From one day to the next, it cannot deliver a consistently crisp piece of bread. The evil bastard is playing mind games.

On a serious note, there are strong similarities between the modern age and the 1950s and 60s, an era of over-hyped reportage about artificial intelligence. This latest wave of techno-optimism is driven by FOMO: developers want to be the first to market so they can capitalise on the hype. Sure, some of the tech is kinda cool, but does it really respond to pressing consumer needs? Maybe the smartest home is a vacuous one. And the safest is old-fashioned.

In 2019, the contributing editor of tech innovation for *Forbes* magazine, Hod Fleishman, makes a persuasive point about whether companies should continue going into the home tech space, without first addressing safety, diversity and inclusion: 'This may have to do with who is coming up with the concepts of what gadgetry our homes need in the first place. I'll put it this way: The world would have had an automated clothes folding machine long before the first connected smart bulb was introduced if my mom had been sitting at the design table. I'm suspecting that, in many cases, the people who are making these decisions spend most of their days away from their homes and the long list of challenges they pose.'[2]

Perhaps they need more women on their design teams. The sales of smart home devices are flatlining. Domestic artificial intelligence is lost in a 'fog of frustration', according to a 2021 article in the business magazine *Fast Company*. However, there's one shining example. Or should I say, sweeping exception.

The global robotic vacuum cleaner market is expected to reach US$15.4 billion by 2028, according to market intelligence company, Meticulous Research.[3] That means more than 60 million of the little suckers will be roaming the globe. iRobot is one of the few artificial intelligence enterprises co-founded by a woman. In 1990, three roboticists from MIT – Colin Angle, Helen Greiner and Rodney Brooks – start the company to develop military products. Twelve years later, they launch their first vacuum cleaner. It's said nature abhors a vacuum. Unless it's one of those funky automated ones, apparently. To avoid being hacked, simply use the device offline rather than online.

Of course, there are plenty of Roomba-fails, which end up going viral. One woman posts a scene of carnage after her device finds a wet pile of puppy poo, then dutifully trails it through the house. She calls it a 'Jackson Pollock poop painting'. Another Roomba eats a piece of chalk and proceeds to trace crime-scene drawings on the floor. Nonetheless, they've become a modern phenomenon.

More than 60 per cent of these robots are so loved by their owners, they're named. Often, it's 'Rosie'. Or, in the case of Trifo's offering at JB Hi-Fi, 'Emma'. Yes, it's infuriating they continue to bear the names of women. But at last robots are helping us around the home. Is the key to producing successful devices that deliver tangible benefits to the community greater diversity on development teams? (Who would have thought?)

Obviously, we need more girls to choose STEM careers. Enticing boys to work in nursing and teaching is also important, but this is a conversation for another time. Helen Greiner, i-Robot co-founder, has some interesting insights. 'A lot of girls that I talk to, what they want to do with their careers and their lives is help people,' she says in a 2017 interview. 'But they're not given the information that when you're an engineer you can really have an impactful career helping people and changing lives. Maybe you're going to make better potable water or self-driving cars that save lives or you'll help the environment with solutions to global warming or better energy technology.'[4]

In an Arcadia, more men would be drawn to the technology sector to work on compassionate projects. If we keep expecting women and girls to fulfil caring responsibilities, gender stereotypes deepen and become ingrained. However, I'm a pragmatist: time is of the essence. There are immediate benefits in having women invent machines for the household, and the wider world. This could spark a structural change in society's priorities.

For example, as the daughter of a Hungarian refugee, Greiner wants to work towards solutions to the refugee crisis. 'There's a lot of suffering in the world,' Greiner says in the same interview. 'I am reading about the starvation happening in South Sudan. It's incredible to me . . . that things like that still happen.'

Widening inclusion in the tech sector would also help people with disabilities.

Shifting the thinking could lead to proper domestic AI. In the US, the Gary Sinise Foundation builds mortgage-free, specifically adapted smart homes for veterans and first responders who are wounded in the line of duty.

In 2022, former chief operating officer Elizabeth Fields explains to the *The New York Times* how it works: 'Let's say you're a double amputee and you go to bed and remember you forgot to turn off the kitchen light. For most of us, it's just an inconvenience. But if you're a double amputee, you're either going to have to put your prosthetics back on or get in your wheelchair. And that's not easy to do. But if you have an iPad that has integrated software to just turn off that kitchen light? It's a little thing, but it's so impactful.'

Living with a dynamic disability for more than a year has given me fresh insight into these issues. Long COVID is an energy-production disorder. I must reduce the amount of time standing, walking and sitting. The body wants to be horizontal. This means it takes an inordinate amount of energy just to go to the toilet. When I leave the bathroom light on overnight, I lament the decision to eschew smart home technology.

Imagine the wisdom people with disabilities could share with designers creating new artificial intelligence devices, and how this could change the lives of more than one billion people around the world. The CEO of C4 Database Management, Todd Stabelfeldt – who lives with quadriplegia – puts it like this: 'Convenience for you is independence for me.'

Manisha Amin is the CEO of the Centre for Inclusive Design in Australia. Amin says people with disability have the ability to show others both the opportunities and pitfalls of artificial intelligence: 'When it works it's spectacular and when it fails it's appalling.' Communicating via email, she tells me many people with disabilities are early adopters of this type of technology. 'But the thing to remember is that no two people with disability are the same. We all have different issues. So it's critical to test with many people.'

There are countless cases of people *without* disabilities designing innovations filled with biases. 'When sighted people tried to make a book for blind people to read they included all sort of sounds and raised fonts, etc., to give people the feeling of reading,' Amin tells me. 'It took a blind person to design braille that is fast, efficient and effective, but fundamentally different to words on a page.'

An Australian report published in 2021 outlines the benefits and challenges of 'assistive technology' (AT) for people with disabilities. Produced by the Australian Housing and Urban Research Institute, the report finds AT could 'improve quality of life, reduce reliance on care, and reduce the cost of care'. But there are significant caveats. People who feel comfortable living in smart homes tend to be young and male, with experience in information technology.[5]

It's hard enough to get funding for standard support services through the National Disability Insurance Scheme, let alone computer equipment to control these systems. Furthermore, there are so many brands on the market, it's impossible to know which will stand the test of time. This reminds me of the old Beta vs. VHS debate around which is the better video system. Currently, you run the risk of investing upwards of A$2000 in an AI system that won't be supported in the near future.

If something goes wrong, vendors are slow to fix it. Believe it or not, there's no legislation in Australia to ensure speedy repairs for people with disabilities. Those living in rural and remote communities are at a heightened risk of connectivity drop-outs. 'I've had people in . . . the power blackout, locked in their houses because . . . there was actually no key in the key safe outside,' a disability service provider tells the Australian Housing and Urban Research Institute. 'Everything's electronic. If there'd been a medical emergency, no one could have gone into the house. They would have had to smash windows.'

This is terrifying. Often, people with disabilities feel trapped in their own bodies. Now, they could be isolated in their homes with no way out. Add to this the risk of hacking. It's reprehensible there aren't better protections for society's most vulnerable communities.

Some GPS-activated smart locks deliberately restrict the movement of people with cognitive disabilities like dementia, so they don't leave their property. While well-intentioned, this is a method of constraint without consent. And what happens if there's a fire?

'There are concerns of unethical practices including privacy breach and potential for restrictive behaviour controls that can occur when the social and behavioural dimensions are constantly monitored and analysed,' the report's authors write. 'There are also concerns around data security and privacy of smart home AT that calls for a review of national legislation with a focus on the care and disability sector who are dealing with sensitive personal and identifiable data.'

KILLER FRIDGES

To sum up, the lack of a clear framework means many people don't have the skill, knowledge or financial ability to benefit from assisted technologies. Smart homes are *still* not part of the policy discussion in Australian aged care or disability services. While this report shines a light on the issue, it's far from perfect. As this book is about bias, I should point out the survey focuses on people whose first language is English: all are from Western countries. People from non-English-speaking backgrounds can also face a language barrier.

At the end of the day, the corporate tech sector is all about dollars, not transformative or assistive technology. The big players put little energy into how devices could support people living with disabilities. And even less into reducing the ways these inventions could harm women and girls.

13
COERCIVE CONTROL

'I hear noises and footsteps. I imagine things, that there are people over the house. I'm frightened, and of myself too.'
Ingrid Bergman, *Gaslight*, 1944

Smart homes create the ideal conditions for gaslighting. It's mainly men who purchase and install these devices in the home, giving them power over the passwords. By connecting their smartphones, abusers can randomly turn lights on and off, play loud music, and access the online log. One woman interviewed by *The New York Times* refers to it as a kind of jungle warfare. 'Why were you watching TV in the middle of the day? Why did you ask Alexa about birth control? Why are you buying personal items with the grocery money?'

If a victim tries to disable the device, this can trigger physical violence. 'It's almost as if the house is haunted' is how survivor of smart home abuse Ferial Nijem describes it to *CBC News* in 2018. While they're living apart, Nijem's former partner maintains control of the house. He uses it to terrorise her, like a scene from the film *The Amityville Horror*. When Nijem contacts local police, she's told nothing can be done because her ex-partner is the only person listed as the owner of the home.

Combined with a higher rate of male home ownership, this unchecked advance of smart technology threatens women's privacy, security and safety. Law enforcement agencies and domestic violence advocates say virtual assistants are increasingly being used by people to monitor, harass or control their partners. This transpires in a range of ways including abuse through smart home devices, financial control via banking apps, and stalking on GPS or other location services.

This abuse almost shapeshifts across cultures. In the United Arab Emirates, a free app named ToTok – which provides messaging, voice and video calls – is used by the government as a mass surveillance tool to monitor people's activities. Inevitably, men use it to 'stalk' women, tracking their movements and contacts. When you think about it, this is coercive control on steroids: a domestic artificial intelligence device used by government to exercise control. ToTok is no longer available on Google Play and the Apple App Store, but at the time of writing you can still install it from the Samsung Galaxy Store.

A similar government app in Saudi Arabia called Absher allows men to keep tabs on the women they control as part of the country's guardianship system. According to an investigation by *Business Insider*, designated guardians receive notifications if a woman passes through an airport. The app then gives them the option to withdraw her right to travel.

This prompts a global outcry, led by Amnesty International and Human Rights Watch, which accuse Apple and Google of helping enforce 'gender apartheid'. This term sums it up perfectly. But Google declines to remove the app because it doesn't contravene its terms and conditions. Slow clap for libertarianism and unfettered capitalism. Fun fact: Absher is an Arabic word that loosely translates as 'yes, done'.

In a small step towards modernisation, the Kingdom now allows women to get their own passports, travel abroad and live independently. But a male relative needs to give permission for a woman to marry, or leave a domestic abuse shelter. Across the Middle East, women are pushing back against this infantilisation. 'Woman, life, freedom!' is the cry echoing through Iran, as activists risk their lives to fight for their rights. Truly, these women are superheroes.

Technology like Absher and ToTok come under an umbrella of terms including stalkerware, spouseware and – appropriately – creepware. Kaspersky reports about a million people worldwide are affected by stalkerware every year. Bear in mind, these are just the cases discovered by one antivirus company. In a piece of perfect irony, Kaspersky – which is operated through a holding company in the UK but headquartered in Moscow – reveals Russia to be the country with the highest levels of stalkerware activity, followed by Brazil and the US. These countries hold the dubious honour of topping the list in 2021 and 2022.

Here are some examples of how it works, from women who are targeted. 'Amy' becomes worried about her husband knowing where she is all the time. If she asks him how he knew, he tells her she's 'losing it'. (See: *Gaslight*.) One day, he hands over his phone to show her a photo. A pop-up appears: 'Daily report on Amy's Mac is ready to view.' She quietly excuses herself, checks the computer, and finds the spyware. Another woman, 'Jessica', says her husband spies on her through the phone's microphone. He then screws with her head by repeating back specific phrases she and her friends use in private conversations.

'Amy' and 'Jessica' share their stories with the BBC's cyber-security reporter, Joe Tidy. During his research, the reporter buys stalkerware and installs it on his work phone. In the UK, using spyware without someone's permission is illegal. Nonetheless, the company guides Tidy through how to put the product on his wife's phone without her knowing. 'The application will start to work in stealth mode right after installation,' the customer service representative says. 'I'll be happy to help.'

If you think this phenomenon is new, think again. It's been going on for years. Researching an article for *Forbes* back in 2017, journalist Thomas Brewster calls several suppliers: '. . . I asked another, what if I didn't get my wife's permission? "That is okay, she will not know that the software is in the phone," the salesperson responded. I moved on to morals. Wasn't it bad to spy on your wife? "It is not bad. You just want to know the truth," they said.'

One of the more unusual examples of cyberstalking happened in Hobart, Tasmania. A mechanic working for the Royal Automobile Club of Tasmania faces court in 2019 for downloading and setting up an app allowing him to control his ex-girlfriend's car. Not only could he track her movements, he could suddenly stop the moving vehicle. The man had helped his then-girlfriend to buy a Land Rover so had access to the VIN, needed to work the app. This woman works in the field of digital technology, but she only realised what was occurring when she stumbled upon an email showing maps of her workplace, including where she parked her car. It's scary stuff.

'As a victim it has caused trauma so deep that it's hard to adequately describe,' she tells the court. 'These crimes have made me feel unsafe. Made me fear the technology I once embraced and left me with a deep distrust of the cybersecurity protections and laws currently in place, now I know they can be exploited.'

A notebook found at the man's home included the dates of training courses she'd planned to attend, and the locations of places she'd frequented, as well as a list of weapons and costings. This case is believed to be a world-first for vehicle cyberstalking. The man's punishment? A community-based order and a suspended sentence. Honestly, I despair.

Aside from trauma, one of the long-term psychological impacts of this treatment is women losing trust in technology: they learn to see it as a weapon. This deters them from using tech or entering this male-dominated field. Astonishingly, one in thirteen devices globally is infected with stalkerware, according to Norton Mobile Security for Android. That's a lot of people – predominantly women – whose text messages, phone calls and emails are being monitored without their consent. And here's the kicker: Norton identifies a dramatic uptick when people are in lockdown, because perpetrators have easy access to their partner's devices.

Australia's 'infection rate' for stalkerware is around 7 per cent. '. . . in this COVID environment, everything we know about family and domestic and sexual violence has been challenged,' a representative from the not-for-profit organisation Good Shepherd tells the Standing Committee on Social Policy and Legal Affairs in late 2020. 'Throughout the pandemic, our practitioners have seen a link between financial stress, isolation and the onset of new violence.'

Researchers in this country are leading the way in analysing what's now known as TFA: technology facilitated abuse. A 2021 study by Monash University finds the majority of victims are women aged up to 34 years, girls 17 and under, and transgender and non-binary people. The main offenders are men up to 34 years of age, along with boys. Former intimate partners, de facto partners and spouses are most likely to initiate the abuse in order to intimidate and cause distress or fear. More than one in three social service workers say perpetrators insist the victim-survivors share their passwords and provide access to devices and online accounts.

Over the past decade, Djirra – which provides legal advice to Indigenous victim-survivors of family violence – witnesses a gradual increase in tech-facilitated abuse, particularly stalking, extortion and identify theft. 'Aboriginal and Torres Strait Islander women are disproportionately more likely to be targets of online abuse,' CEO of Djirra Antoinette Braybrook tells me. 'Women with disabilities are particularly vulnerable, as they usually find it even more difficult to identify this type of abuse and leave violent relationships.'

When they do report abuse, it's not taken seriously by police. 'Our women experience systemic racism which injects fear,' Braybrook says. 'Too often our women are not supported. Many women fear their children will be taken away, due to the history of the Stolen Generations.' It's even harder for women in rural communities: 'The small population and connectedness makes it even more unsafe because perpetrators are likely to find out if they break their silence.' Consequently, Djirra is prioritising work around e-Safety to create culturally safe, self-determined solutions.

Tech-facilitated abuse engenders 'a sense of omnipresence for victims, feeling as though they were always watched by the perpetrator', in the words of Asher Flynn, associate professor of criminology at Monash University. Survivors become hyper-vigilant, because they no longer feel safe.

Soon they begin to disconnect, restricting their use of technology, limiting time spent on the phone, and changing their number. Many lose contact with family and friends, further isolating them. A new report for Australia's National Research Organisation for Women's Safety (ANROWS) reveals technology-facilitated abuse continues to grow, with one in two people being targeted – predominantly women.

It's worse if you're considered to be in a minority community: This affects three in four people who are LGBTQI+, two in three Aboriginal and Torres Strait Islander peoples, and three in five Australians with disability.

'I was a prisoner,' an anonymous victim-survivor tells the researchers. 'I had no say in anything. He controlled absolutely everything of my life: what I wore, what I ate, where I went, how long I was allowed out for, no phone calls after 7 pm, you name it. And it's just like, how could me, someone who has worked for the biggest [names employer] in the world . . . be reduced to nothing, like a robot, basically doing what I was told?'

Robot technology turning someone into a robot. This is nothing short of chilling.

You'd better sit down for this next bit of information: 99.3 per cent of frontline workers have clients reporting online abuse. Yep, almost all of them. Australia's e-Safety Commissioner, Julie Inman Grant, tells Radio 2SER it's a way for offenders to 'ratchet back control'.

In some quarters, this is called technology-facilitated coercive control (TFCC). This sort of control 'transcends fixed borders and boundaries' to quote *The Routledge International Handbook of Violence Studies*. As the crime becomes endemic, the United Nations is redoubling its efforts to combat cyber violence against women. You could say it's a shadow pandemic. And it's already affecting the next generation.

Children are being used to facilitate tech abuse, especially in post-separation and shared parenting situations. Alarmingly, kids' phones, tablets and games consoles are being exploited by offenders to maintain control. Writing about the ANROWS report in the *Sydney Morning Herald* in 2022, feminist Jenna Price shares the story of a man who 'hid a tracker in his daughter's toy frog to find out where she was [and] also planted a second device in his former partner's car'. The Queanbeyan man has been jailed. 'In one recent case, the perpetrator was able to track down the location of his former partner through the use of a shared Uber account,' Price writes.

It makes me wonder about the ubiquitous Life360 app, which some of our friends use to keep an eye on their children. Many parents are unknowingly turning adult supervision into a kind of surveillance. 'We know where our Users live, work, shop, drive and more,' Life360 boasts in its prospectus. Gee thanks, Big Brother.

This reminds me of chapter one of George Orwell's book *1984*: 'You had to live – did live, from habit that became instinct – in the assumption that every sound you made was overheard, and, except in darkness, every moment scrutinized.' We're inculcating children, tweens and teens into a placid acceptance of stalkerware. If this makes you feel as mad as hell, you're not alone. Where on earth are the legal safeguards? And what can we do to protect ourselves and our children?

14
VIRTUAL RAPE

'It wasn't sexual assault, but how it made
me feel, does that matter?'
Mikaela Jade, CEO and founder of Indigital

It's the mid-1990s, at the peak of camouflage pants and statement T-shirts. I remember it well after dressing for months like the singer Natalie Imbruglia in the film clip for 'Torn'. This is a time of third-wave feminism, girl power and sex positivity led by media-savvy Gen Xers. In Australia, it heralds important legislation aimed at protecting people online. Using a carriage service to menace, harass or cause offence can now land you in prison. But it turns out the law isn't worth the paper it's written on.

Fast forward two decades and I try to use this legislation to stop trolls making rape and death threats. The burden of proof is extremely high. In my case, the police knock on the perpetrator's door, based on the IP address, only to be told, 'One of my flatmates was probably using the computer that day'. He might as well have said, 'The dog ate my misogynist manifesto. Honestly, I'm really a top bloke.'

The following day, this charming chap creates a new, anonymous handle to continue the harassment. Neither Facebook nor Twitter is willing to help. Headquartered in the US, they defend the abusive comments under the banner of free speech. Exhausted, broken and beaten, I eventually give up the fight.

eSafety Commissioner Julie Inman Grant says the tech companies are in an 'arms race', building products without any safety protections. The platforms' main motive is profit. This is highlighted by courageous whistleblowers who give evidence to the US Congress. When Frances Haugen leaves her job at Facebook, she takes a trove of internal documents. Haugen, who has a degree in computer engineering and a master's in business from Harvard, tells Congress in 2021: 'The thing I saw at Facebook over and over again was there were conflicts of interest between what was good for the public and what was good for Facebook. And Facebook, over and over again, chose to optimise for its own interests, like making more money.'

One internal study uncovered by Haugen estimates: 'We may action as little as 3–5 per cent of hate and about six-tenths of 1 per cent of V & I [violence and incitement] on Facebook despite being the best in the world at it.' I'm reeling from this information. Nothing is done in more than 99 out of 100 incidents of violence and incitement. In the fewer than 1 per cent of cases where action is taken, victim-survivors hit another roadblock due to deficits in law enforcement. What a disgraceful example of wilful negligence. This brings us back to artificial intelligence and machine learning: the algorithms are built to promote engagement above all else.

'What kind of content gets engagement? Cyberhate, that's what,' social justice journalist Ginger Gorman tells me via email. (I've given up on translation software by this stage.) 'So if someone is being piled onto, that makes more advertising dollars for the platforms. It's a fairly simple, if mercenary, formula,' the author of the 2019 book *Troll Hunting* says. 'But the outcomes are both morally bankrupt and devastating.' You cannot overstate the gravity of platforms – which have bigger user bases than the populations of China and India put together – behaving like nations with profit as their only motive.

Sadly, when it comes to trolling, anyone in a minority gets targeted in 'far more vicious and sustained ways', Gorman says. 'For women, these online attacks are also more violent and sexual than they are against men. Predator trolls do what I call "minority stacking". So they stack your minorities against you – so if you're Black, gay and female, for example, good luck staying safe online. You can't.' Like bullies in the school playground, the trolls target people in marginalised communities.

These actions can and do result in violence and murder. But there's a more insidious way of killing people via social media. How many have died from COVID-19 due to coordinated campaigns by anti-science activists, who take advantage of the algorithms to spread their poison? The good news is Facebook is finally cracking down on this misinformation, because of the global pandemic. The bad news is the metaverse is coming. Hang on to your hats for this whirlwind.

Meta's grand new project is 'a tightly interconnected set of digital spaces that lets users escape into a virtual world and the rules of technology are the only limit'. Given what they know about the prevalence of internet abuse, you'd expect the safety of women and marginalised communities to be a top-line issue. So let's look at the development of this 'online utopia'.

Immersive online experiences come in many forms. You might remember Second Life, which was created way back in 2003. Several years later, women and girls begin reporting incidents of real-world rape and harassment after spending time on the multi-media platform. In December 2006 the infamous 'pink penis attack' occurs during a digital showcase with the world's first 'virtual millionaire'.

Ailin Graef had agreed to do the 3D interview to discuss the massive property empire she's building in Second Life. But online enemies hack into the site, attacking her cyber-character with flying penises.

Similar events are occurring in testing for the next stage of the metaverse, which will host a billion people within a decade, if you believe Mark Zuckerberg's 2022 claims.

Associate Professor Ellen Broad, author of the 2018 book *Made by Humans: the AI Condition*, is a member of the Australian government's Data Advisory Council. In an article for *Harper's Bazaar*, she says no one seems to have learned from the Second Life incidents. 'In early 2022, a female beta tester for Meta's social metaverse, Horizon Worlds, described being virtually groped by another user of the platform while others watched,' Broad writes.

She also shares with the magazine the story of a journalist who spends two weeks as a digital avatar encountering 'a range of creepy, uninvited encounters', like being surrounded by silent male avatars taking photos of her without asking. 'On one platform, a male avatar followed her around saying she was pretty,' Broad writes. 'On others, users shouted random obscenities and made animal noises.'

In response to such issues, Meta announces a new feature called 'personal boundary' setting. This builds an invisible wall around a person's avatar, preventing unsolicited virtual touching. While this is welcome, it doesn't go far enough. By way of example, Broad writes about a TEDxCanberra talk by Cabrogal woman Mikaela Jade, founder and CEO of Indigital.

Jade describes presenting at a 2021 conference as a holographic avatar. At one stage she looks down to see the system is placing her colleague's holographic head in her physical crotch. 'As a woman who's been sexually assaulted, I can't tell you the shame and embarrassment that I experienced seeing his head there,' Jade says. 'It wasn't sexual assault, but how it made me feel, does that matter?'

These anecdotes highlight problems with the technology. However, they come from society's attitudes towards women in the *physical* world. One in five Australians think women who say they were abused often make up or exaggerate their claims, according to a study by the Global Institute for Women's Leadership in 2022. Three in 10 men hold this view. We've come a long way, but we have a long way to go.

VIRTUAL RAPE

Instead of stepping back from the metaverse until it's safe, Big Tech is forging forward. Australia's *Company Director* magazine reports in 2022 that staff at Accenture already 'attend their meetings in the metaverse', dealing with each other as avatars. Figures from McKinsey & Company, quoted in the magazine, reveal 63 per cent of companies that are 'metaverse adopters' are training their employees in this virtual space, rather than face-to-face.

3D immersive experiences are exploding in the conference and events industry, opening the door for more 'holographic assaults' similar to the attack on Mikaela Jade. As a victim-survivor of sexual assault, I feel frightened about continuing to give keynote speeches under these conditions. This is further silencing women.

During the height of lockdowns, Zoombombing – in which trolls interrupt work or school video calls to show pornography – leads to serious concerns. In 2021, Zoom's founder says, 'We never thought about that [as a possible outcome].' I wonder why? Perhaps it has something to do with the lack of diversity in the tech sector. 'The people constructing metaverses today are overwhelmingly white, male and able-bodied, who also tend to experience attention as something that's typically positive, or at least benign,' Ellen Broad writes. Of course they're going to build online communities based on attracting attention.

Jeez. It appears we're not even safe in the 'utopia' of the future.

At last, governments are pressuring Big Tech to implement responsible safety reforms. But the 'bad actors' are refusing to adapt. Instead, they're moving to the seedy side of town, migrating to platforms like Reddit, 4Chan, Parler and Telegram. My teenage son, Taj, reckons Reddit's 'not all bad', but let's face it: this network is home to some shocking bigotry and misogyny. The clue is in the tagline: 'Dive into anything.'

Ginger Gorman and other advocates want countries to legislate duty of care provisions to force *all* platforms to keep people safe.

At the moment, the bandaid solution is telling women to get off their phones, which is effectively blaming the victim. A phone may be a woman's only lifeline, or simply an indispensable business tool.

In fact, this technology can be used to *combat* domestic and family violence.

Thailand's MySis Bot offers information to victim-survivors 24 hours a day through Facebook Messenger. In Brazil, MAIA (My AI Friend) allows women to discuss violence online confidentially, without judgement. The app doesn't ask for identifiable or personal information, and the contents of the chat won't be stored. In South Africa, rAInbow – an AI smart companion for victim-survivors – facilitates more than 150,000 conversations during a period of three months.

In 2020, stalking victim-survivor and entrepreneur Ritika Dutt relies on her knowledge of artificial intelligence to create a tool to assist fellow Canadians to disclose crimes, understand their legal rights and connect with support organisations. Her free web app, Botler for Citizens, analyses the information to determine what laws are being violated. It also generates incident reports to be forwarded to authorities. The app uses bank-level encryption.

Not all apps are this safe. The policy for MySis Bot indicates personal data can be collected and accessed by the team which works with women experiencing violence. The data might be used for research, leaving it vulnerable to hacking. This raises concerns that the apps being built to help people could do more harm than good.

In the UK, security and policy expert at IBM Lesley Nuttall leads a team trying to shift the onus of safety away from the end-user. Their recommendations include promoting diversity in development, informing users when someone accesses their data or location and notifying them when changes are made to their account. Of course, the gold standard response is always 'real world' support workers, rather than chatbots.

VIRTUAL RAPE

Elsewhere, algorithms are being applied to the contentious area of predictive policing. Back in 1998, I travelled to Bangladesh to film a documentary on the abuse of women and girls after natural disasters – notably, the annual monsoons. Now, we're seeing history repeat with a rise in the rates of domestic violence and sexual assault during another disaster: the global pandemic. After gathering data from more than 500 families, in 2021 academics from Bangladesh, Italy and Ireland use machine learning to identify correlations between domestic violence and environmental, demographic and social factors. They claim to be able to predict family violence in Bangladesh with a 62–77 per cent degree of accuracy.[1]

This idea is gaining credence. In 2020 almost 2000 Israeli tech workers, backed by Facebook, Microsoft, Salesforce and other tech giants, spend three days brainstorming apps, platforms and services designed to counter domestic violence. The ten leading startups are in accelerator programs, where each product will continue to be developed.[2]

While it would be lifesaving to stop the problem before it begins, I wonder whether we should let artificial intelligence predict such incidents. Where does the accountability lie if the robot gets it wrong? What about the inviolable tenet of privacy for all citizens? And who's to blame if there's a damaging data breach? Aspects of this are reminiscent of phrenology and the COMPAS technology, which predicts who'll become a criminal. But something proactive needs to be done. Offenders are becoming bolder, enabled by the relentless march of technology.

A case in point is the stalking and harassment of a woman in Florida. Ali Borja, a computer science professor at the University of Central Florida, sends more than 800 messages a day to a woman he'd initially offered to tutor. Borja says he wants to make an 'artificial intelligence' – a sex robot – of her, so he 'could do anything he wanted'. It seems the future is already here: welcome to the world of sexbots.

15
SEXBOTS

'Listen doll, I believe robots exist to free humanity from the soulless grind of manual labor, to act as a faithful companion in the conquest of space, and to serve as a politically incorrect slave substitute – not the pornographic fantasy of geeky science fiction readers!'

'But I have been programmed with over six million pornographic fantasies,' purred the sensual sexeroid, the subsonics of her voice sending erotic vibrations through Proton's nether regions. 'I was created in Man's image of the ideal woman. No Servus droid may harm the male ego or, through omission of action, allow that ego to be harmed.'
Plan 9 from Outer Space, **cult 1957 science fiction film**

From Roxxxy to Frigid Farrah, Wild Wendy and S&M Susan, female robots have a history of being sexualised. In fact, the first sexbot – produced by a British company in the late 1970s – is only known by her chest measurement. In case you're wondering, it's 36C. I guess this is what you expect from a company called Sex Objects Ltd. You can almost see the handlebar moustaches and hear the porno bass. Incidentally, the teens tell me the 'pornstache' is back in, which would explain the young Tom Sellecks and Pedro Pascals I keep seeing out on the town.

In 1983, a big-breasted female robot named Sweetheart is removed from display at the Lawrence Hall of Science in Berkeley, California. This follows the circulation of a petition claiming the sexbot is insulting to women. Go, you fabulous second-wave feminists! Its designer, Professor Clayton Bailey, responds by crying 'censorship!' like a big baby. Seriously Clay, this isn't Nuremberg. But the 'good professor' doesn't stop there.

Bailey continues to wax lyrical about his creation. 'It's the world's most beautiful lady robot,' he tells *New Scientist* magazine. 'To ban this would be like banning Venus de Milo.' Bear in mind Sweetheart has baseball bat legs, a coffee urn as a torso and vacuum cleaner arms. I'm not sure how an ancient Greek sculpture displayed at the Louvre can be compared with a big, busty coffee pot. But to each their own, beauty being in the eye of the beholder. Or cupholder, in this instance.

Since that time, new terms enter the lexicon: digisexuals and robosexuals. Digisexuals are people who view sex tech as an essential part of who they are; often, they forgo relationships with other humans. It's theorised people who fetishise sexbots are seeking passive women who won't question their requests.

Perhaps they haven't seen the 1927 science fiction masterpiece *Metropolis*, starring a beautiful and wildly sadistic female robot. 'Maria' functions to secure, corrupt and destroy – until she's burned at the stake. It's fascinating how women – and robots in female form – end up being punished as witches.

Seriously, sex with robots raises the issue of consent. Even if they're programmed with the ability to refuse sex, the entire idea still stinks of rape culture. Intercourse with fembots represents the 'rape of a woman' and may increase the rate of rape in society, while also facilitating a general 'disrespect for women' in society, according to Professor Robert Sparrow from Monash University in his 2017 paper, 'Robots, Rape, and Representation'.[1]

However, to play devil's advocate, if sex robots aren't human and can't feel emotions, is consent really relevant? To take this argument further, could robots actually educate people on how to have sex? Imagine if her operation improved when asked questions such as, 'Do you like that?' or 'How about this?'

There's a PhD in whether robots will become sentient within our lifetimes, but that's not what this book is about. Great works of fiction, like *Klara and the Sun* by Kazuo Ishiguro and *Machines Like Me* by Ian McEwan, cover this area adeptly. My interest lies in the debate around offenders raping robots rather than real people. Academics are split on whether this would simply act as an encouragement to rapists.

I tend to agree with Laura Bates, author of the 2014 book *Everyday Sexism*: 'We should no more be encouraging rapists to find a supposedly safe outlet for it than we should facilitate murderers by giving them realistic, blood-spurting dummies to stab.' Touché.

With this in mind, let's look at how our robot sisters are being treated around the world. You're about to meet a strange cast of characters, including the delightful Brick Dollbanger. Apparently, this is *not* his real name.

The first sex robot powered by artificial intelligence makes her illustrious debut in 2010 at the Adult Entertainment Expo in Las Vegas. Think *Austin Powers* fembots, without the machine gun breasts. While Roxxxy is anatomically correct, she is unable to move. Her unique selling point? Five distinct personalities to help her interact with her 'master'. These include Frigid Farrah, Wild Wendy and Mature Martha. Slow clap for sexual stereotyping. Extra marks for alliteration. Perhaps the most inappropriate personality is Young Yoko, who at barely 18 is 'oh so young and waiting for you to teach her'. Ew.

The reporter covering the sexbot launch for *Tech News World*, Renay San Miguel, seems swept away by this sexdroid's charms: 'She will also be able to talk, listen, carry on a conversation, feel your touch and be your true friend. She can also have an orgasm when you touch her!' He really hits his stride midway through the article. 'Roxxxy is a downloadable sexbot, a WiFi-enabled wanton woman who may single-handedly redefine the phrase "hot spot",' he writes.

What this puff piece doesn't tell you is that an owner can rape Roxxxy with a simple switch in settings. According to the website True Companion, Roxxxy is simply reluctant – like someone being reluctant to kiss on the first date. Honestly, some of these roboticists need a lesson in the definition of consent.

A few years later, the debate begins in earnest. 'I believe that loving sex robots will be a great boon to society . . . There are millions of people out there who, for one reason or another, cannot establish good relationships,' the author of *Love and Sex with Robots*, David Levy, tells *Newsweek*. In response, a group of academics in Sweden and the UK create the Campaign Against Sex Robots, arguing they're harmful and demeaning. Using feminist ethical dialogues, they rail against deepfakes, virtual reality porn and the 'dollification' of women and girls.

This prompts the Japanese company SoftBank, which is responsible for the semi-humanoid Pepper, to slap a ban on robot sex. The user agreement states this: 'The policy owner must not perform any sexual act or other indecent behaviour.' The trend in Japan is to create slender and graceful female robots, which either maintain traditional family structures or provide personal intimacy: servile or sexual.

Do I hear someone say 'madonna–whore dichotomy'? Actroid, designed by Hiroshi Ishiguro at Osaka University, is supposed to be the perfect secretary: smiling, amenable and a little flirtatious. And Project Aiko aims to produce a realistic-looking female robot, with sensitivity sensors in the breasts and genitals to facilitate a sexual response.

Recent years are seeing significant advances in this technology. Users can now customise a robot called Harmony by using a mobile app, with thousands of combinations of clothes, personalities and voices. RealDollX allows owners to 'design' the shape and colour of the doll's vulva. For the fussy consumer, there are 11 styles of vaginal insert.

SEXBOTS

To satisfy an unusual inclination, one addition is elf ears. I can see the sales pitch now: 'Ever dreamed of making love to Lady Galadriel from *The Lord of the Rings*? Well, your dream has become a reality. Buy your own sexy Elf Queen here!' I wonder what Cate Blanchett thinks about one of her most famous characters becoming a life-sized sex toy?

These dolls are also programmed to react with appropriate vocalisations when they're penetrated, intensifying as they progress from mild arousal to orgasm. I'm assuming they have the ability to fake, rather like Meg Ryan's character in the iconic film *When Harry Met Sally*. Some feminists celebrate this. Quoting the works of legendary author and activist, bell hooks, they draw a line between erotic attraction and love. 'The introduction of sex robots simply means that the object of many men's confused projections may become robots instead of women,' the author of *Sensuous Knowledge*, Minna Salami, writes in her blog, MsAfropolitan. 'That is not a loss to mourn!'

There's even a school of thought that male sex robots could *enhance* women's safety. Due to the risk of violence, some heterosexual women fear experimenting sexually. A robot could be a safe option. I'm starting to think it could be fun to program a bot to stimulate the optimal orgasm. A lot less tiring than masturbating, I assume.

Looking at this through the lens of civil liberties, surely everybody has the right to safe and satisfying sex. For those without a partner, sexbots provide much-needed physical intimacy. 'First-wave sexual technology, like dating and messaging apps, and social networks, are making way for the second wave of virtual reality and sex robots,' Professor of Philosophy Neil McArthur writes in his 2022 essay, 'Sex and Technology: The Ethics of Virtual Connection'. Perhaps the benefits do outweigh the disadvantages.

While the overwhelming majority of sexbots are being created in the female form, there are notable exceptions to the ongoing objectification of women. 'Coming Soon: Henry, The Self-Lubricating Gay

Male Sex Robot', *Star Observer* magazine announces in 2021. Henry, which is being developed by AI robotics company RealDoll, will be able to be programmed as either gay or straight.

Harmony, with an animatronic head and Scottish accent, has a 'bisexual flavour', according to the press release. The company is also planning to release lesbian sex robots. Of course, these dolls look like a male fantasy of lesbians, boasting enormous boobs, long hair and enhanced lips. See: mainstream movies.

All these creations will have 'self-heating, self-lubricating erogenous zones'. Personally, I think *self-cleaning* would be a terrific option. You see, Henry is being developed with a 'bionic penis'. (So THAT'S what *The Six Million Dollar Man* has under his tight-fitting pants.) 'We're going to be working on some sort of very special insert for Henry so that he's able to, you know, lift trucks with his penis or something,' CEO of RealDoll subdivision Realbotix, Matt McMullen, tells *PinkNews*. Here's hoping it doesn't cost $6 million. While this is rather amusing, there is one – ahem – large hurdle to overcome. Trigger warning: this might make you wince.

'When can a body be animated, and then be safe to throw into someone's bed?' McMullen asks. 'A robotic arm that's strong enough to lift the entirety of its silicone weight is pretty darn strong. If something goes a little bit off with that, it can take your head off.' One episode of *The Big Bang Theory* centres on Howard borrowing a robotic arm from the Jet Propulsion Laboratory. First he uses it as a massager, before trying to pleasure himself. Howard's genitals become stuck and he ends up in the emergency ward.

Now I don't know about you, but I'd rather not be remembered as the person who's maimed during sex with a robot. No matter how good that bionic penis is.

Like it or not, our sexual tastes are becoming more digitised. And I'm not talking about fingering. Four of the most trafficked websites in the world are pornographic. The biggest site, Pornhub, attracts more eyeballs than Netflix. Sex tech is a US$30 billion industry, boosted in part by the pandemic.

Financial discretion is hindering a thorough internal analysis of its impact on broader society. Most companies will not admit to problems with their artificial intelligence because of intense competition. They're all in a race to the first billion. Also, it's an icky topic. 'We can't say whether they'll be harmful or helpful without more rigorous studies,' founder of the SxTech EU conference, Ola Miedzynska, says. 'Academics are keeping their eyes closed.'

Interestingly, Australia is home to several researchers doing groundbreaking work in sex tech. Future-forward academics from Monash University in Melbourne are behind one of the first empirical studies to examine the psychology of our receptiveness to sex robots, aiming to 'provide relevant government and industry bodies with a better understanding of this important topic for more informed policy making'. Recent international papers focus on robots as a way to enhance sexuality for elderly people and those living with disabilities.

But these benefits can't be realised while there are ethical, legal and regulatory challenges. In the US, it's against the law to import and transport any 'anatomically correct doll, mannequin, or robot, with the features of, or with features that resemble those of, a minor, intended for use in sexual acts'. This is known colloquially as the 'CREEPER Act'. Appropriate, really.

Here, regulation of childlike sex dolls and robots is being addressed proactively by the Commonwealth, South Australia and Queensland. These statutory provisions may guide any future regulation of adult sexbots. The penalties are stiff: a maximum of ten years in jail for importation and 15 years for possession. Producing such a doll in Australia means 20 years imprisonment.

Hundreds of childlike sex dolls are seized by Border Force every year. Such crimes also come under the remit of the Australian Federal Police.

'These dolls are far from harmless,' AFP Acting Sergeant Kevin Shaw says in a media release. 'The evidence is clear that the dolls are not used as a substitute for offending against real children but in fact contribute to increased offending against children.'

However, when these cases come to court, traditionally they're deemed to be a step removed from 'the possession of material that depicts real children'. Consequently, sentences are generally light. This is changing in line with a precedent set in South Australia in late 2021 when a 32-year-old man is sentenced to three years in prison for importing and possessing a child sex doll.

Children and adults alike are vulnerable to exploitation in the sex industry. In Europe, experimental cyber-brothels are disrupting the sector. 'Experience two dolls in doggy and missionary position hanging in love swings,' urges Cybrothel of Berlin. Not quite sure how this works, but I'm reticent to search Google images. For now, the sex dolls are connected to an external control room where humans direct their actions and provide vocal responses. This is basically analogue artificial intelligence. Is it possible governments could one day license cyber-brothels, while banning human sex work?

In the dystopian TV series *Westworld*, bordello madam Maeve Millay and her fellow hosts attend to every desire of the theme park's guests. Spoiler alert: they eventually become sentient and rise up to kill everyone. Good for them! In the real world, a study by the Foundation for Responsible Robotics finds there's a market for sex doll prostitutes, but no evidence they'd replace human sex workers or reduce sex trafficking.

It really is wonderful to live in a world where sensible people start up foundations like this to protect us all. While the report reveals interest in using sex robots for services to people with disabilities or the elderly, there remain ethical concerns around the capacity to consent to intercourse with a robot. Like the #MeToo movement, this conversation needs to be centred in consent.

A deeper issue is the tech sector's habit of moving fast and breaking things. This development mantra, popularised when Meta was Facebook, is used by most tech companies as a way of delivering 'value' quickly. Surely safeguards should be put in place *before* a product is unleashed on the unsuspecting public?

Fortunately, proactive programs are underway to add empathy to this fraught field. Dr Angelica Lim, the former head of the Emotional and Expressivity teams for the Pepper humanoid project at SoftBank, is developing robots that have the capacity for compassion. The name of her lab? ROSIE. Dr Lim runs a two-week summer enrichment program for girls through AI4All, dubbed Invent the Future.

Now, we need to add a liberal dose of compassion – and consent – to the disturbing world of deepfakes.

16
DEEPFAKES

'Oceania had always been at war with Eastasia.'
George Orwell, *1984*

Pssst! Wanna see a naked lady? Well, you're in luck. The internet's full of 'em! In fact, there are so many images of under-dressed women online, our machine overlords learn this is our usual state. I don't know about you, but at the very least I try to cover my bum and boobs before leaving the house. However, I'm 55 and it's a brave new world out there. The Kardashians seem to be the new 'soma', a drug to distract us from the horrors of the world. Maybe I'm being churlish, but I find the gender disparity online especially enraging.

Here's an example of how societal biases are baked into algorithms. In 2021, researchers decide to do an experiment, feeding pictures of a man cropped below the neck into an image-generation algorithm. To clarify, the *picture* is cropped below the neck, not the actual man. That would be rather painful and probably fatal. More than 40 per cent of the time, the robot auto-completes the image by dressing the lucky chap in a nice suit.

When they put photos of a woman into the same algorithm, more than half of the time it dresses her in a low-cut top or bikini. One of the photos they give to the machine features Democrat congresswoman Alexandria Ocasio-Cortez. Sure enough, the internationally renowned politician ends up wearing a bikini.

The culprit this time is deepfake, a more sophisticated version of Photoshop. Deepfakes are images generated by artificial intelligence that map one of your body parts – normally the face – then superimpose it onto someone else's body. Alternatively, you could stumble upon a picture of yourself in an entirely conflated situation. Say, as part of Vladimir Putin's Politburo 2.0, or engaging in group sex with a boy band.

This type of fakery requires smart software and a deep dive into the data. But this doesn't mean it takes a genius. There are countless apps, like China's Zao, that do it within seconds, allowing two people to switch faces. SpeakPic takes this further, with users able to make their photos speak.

The plight of politicians is well documented. Remember the infamous public service announcement by Barack Obama? American comedian Jordan Peele and *Buzzfeed* employ artificial intelligence to create a fake Barack, who calls Donald Trump a 'total and complete dipshit'. Now, I'm happy to support 'fake news' when it tells the truth. But we know sophisticated deepfakes are a threat to global democracy.

In March 2022, as the Russian invasion of Ukraine enters its third week, video footage is played on social media and broadcast on the TV channel Ukraine 24. It appears to show Ukrainian president Volodymyr Zelenskyy instructing citizens to stop fighting Russian soldiers and surrender their weapons. In this case, Zelenskyy debunks the video and it's removed from Facebook and YouTube, but in an increasingly siloed world, replete with confirmation bias, deepfakes pose a threat. This is most obvious in the political sphere.

However, a more common use often flies under the radar. Believe it or not, 96 per cent of deepfakes are pornographic, according to a 2019 study by the US AI firm Sensity. Almost all instances are nonconsensual. And the number of deepfake porn clips is doubling every six months. When the imitation is so close to the real thing, the damage is akin to someone sharing your intimate videos without consent. This is a violation of our bodies.

'When pornography is of us, our consent is required for its production to be permissible,' Australian academic Dr Claire Benn writes in a paper given at the Australian National University's 2022 Law and Philosophy Forum. 'Whenever the person depicted does not consent (or in the case of a child, can't consent), that person is wronged by the creation of deepfake pornography and has a claim against its production.'[1]

Deepfakes are one method of committing what used to be called 'revenge porn'. Julie Inman Grant, Australia's eSafety Commissioner, prefers the term 'image-based abuse', because revenge porn suggests the victim has done something wrong. She stresses the seriousness of the lexicon, noting child sexual abuse was formerly referred to as 'kiddie porn'. Inman Grant talks frequently about how deepfake is becoming weaponised. Anyone can steal a holiday shot or Insta selfie to use in pornographic images or films.

Open-source code DeepNude allows perpetrators to strip the clothes from photos of women. After paying US$50, the user uploads a photo of a fully clothed woman, which comes back naked. Fun fact: DeepNude doesn't work on men. The software uses generative adversarial networks, or GANs. Yikes! Too many tech words. This is a kind of machine learning which is wholly unsupervised. Two computer systems known as 'neural networks' are pitted against each other to construct synthetic data that can pass for the real thing. In other words, 'robots gone wild'.

The Sensity study of deepfake imagery uncovers at least 100,000 victims, including children. This is becoming the next pandemic – a veritable epidemic of abuse. A stark warning comes from close to home: Dr Richard Nock, Machine Learning Group Leader at CSIRO's Data61. He says artificial intelligence can accelerate both scientific breakthroughs and malicious technologies. 'We're seeing an arms race around deepfakes,' he tells the website InnovationAus in 2019.

The effect on women in particular is devastating. Some have to change their names. Others remove themselves from the internet. Shockingly, several end up taking their own lives. Of course, weaponised face swaps target famous women, like Scarlett Johansson and Gal Gadot. But people who aren't well known are increasingly being subjected to involuntary pornography.

In 2019, Helen Mort, an English writer, discovers deepfake images of herself on a porn site: they'd been online for two years. She still doesn't know who posted them, and seems to have no recourse under the law, telling the BBC: 'The police couldn't help me, because in England it's not an offence to manipulate the images in that way.' Mort writes and recites an online poem about her experience.

This is my gf, Helen. She's amazing. I love her deeply.
I want to see her used hard, abused, and broken sexually.
What's the dirtiest thing she'd do? Tell me.
There are some great ideas in my galleries!

She talks about how innocent images were stolen and sexualised:

Here I'm grinning from a frame of blue, Ibizan sky.
Here is a woman with two men between her thighs.
Here I'm on holiday, freckled and sun flecked.
Here is a man with his hands around my neck.
Here I'm pregnant with my son.
Here is a body overrun.

And how she has to reclaim her identity:

Outside it snows and snow reclaims the lawn.
Day reclaims sky. Sky reclaims dawn.
Here is Helen walking to her son's nursery.

DEEPFAKES

Here is Helen on her first anniversary.
Then comes the evening talking its cue,
the sound of history forgetting you.[2]

This is occurring around the world. In India in 2018, journalist Rana Ayyub is admitted to hospital after a deepfake attack. Ayyub had planned to speak to the media about an eight-year-old girl who'd been raped. She soon becomes aware of tweets coming from her account that she'd neither written nor posted.

Later, she receives a link to a faked pornographic video, shared more than 40,000 times on social media. Ayyub goes from being an outspoken journalist to 'self-censoring', she writes in the *Huffington Post*. There's no legislation to help her, nor any effort to curb the abuse. While this can easily happen using photoshop, deepfake takes an attack to the next level.

In 2022, there's a devastating case of photoshop abuse that could easily be replicated through deepfake. Sixteen-year-old Basant Khaled, from Kafr El Zayat village in Egypt, refuses to go out on a date with a classmate. In response, he collaborates with another classmate to create fake photos, tries to blackmail her, then publishes the photos online.

Devastated, Basant dies by suicide, leaving a note for her mother: 'Mom, believe me, the girl in those pictures is not me. These pictures were photoshopped. I swear! I'm a young girl, mom, and I don't deserve all that's happening to me. I'm suffering from depression, and I feel like I'm suffocating. I'm really tired. It's not me, you raise me well.'

There's no Egyptian law covering deepfake pornography.

One Australian victim-survivor campaigning against this abuse is Noelle Martin. Now a lawyer, Martin was first targeted by deepfake imagery when she was 17 years old. In 2022 she tells the parliamentary Inquiry into Social Media and Online Safety that proposed laws to hold social media companies to account are 'utterly inaccessible'. Martin dismisses the financial penalties as 'chump change' that won't result in meaningful reform.

Around the same time in the US, Florida State Senator Lauren Book speaks about a man stealing non-sexual nude photos of her and altering them to create deepfakes, which were then sold online. He tried to extort US$5000 to stop the release of the images. This crime is known as 'sextortion'.

'My life of public service has resulted in private terror,' she tells a committee hearing in Tallahassee. As a result of her experience, Senator Book sponsors a bill to make buying, selling or trading stolen intimate images a felony. It also suggests a criminal offence of disseminating altered or created sexually explicit images known as deepfakes. The bill is passed unanimously.

While these initiatives are steps in the right direction, the laws remain behind the times. Attempting to change legislation is like swimming through mud. In 2018, US Senator Mark Warner proposes to penalise social media companies allowing sharing of deepfake documents. A task force is set up, but four years later there's still no federal legislation. Some states in the US, frustrated by the glacial pace of change, pass their own laws.

In Australia, revenge porn is now a crime. China is on board, unveiling a draft bill to ban these technologies from being used to 'endanger national security, undermine social stability, disrupt social order, or violate the lawful rights and interests of others'. It also bans deepfake pornography. In the UK, the Domestic Abuse Act includes a sentence of up to two years in jail for those who threaten 'to disclose intimate images with the intention to cause distress'.

Some argue defamation law could be a recourse. But this raises the patriarchal notion that it's wrong for women to be overtly sexual. Running a defamation case supports the contention that pornographic content is always damaging to women's reputations, regardless of consent. Woe betide the woman who makes a living in the pornography industry but is deepfaked into content to which she doesn't consent. It would be hard for her to claim she's defamed by sexually explicit material.

Clearly, defamation is not a suitable means of defence. What about copyright law? In many jurisdictions, this would be thrown out under the 'fair use' provision. In one of his music videos, the rapper Kendrick Lamar morphs into Will Smith, OJ Simpson and Kanye West, among others. It seems the use of deepfakes doesn't violate copyright law – for now.

Interestingly, the European Parliament is taking action by modifying the Digital Service Act to cover the dissemination of deepfakes. But these laws don't address the concerns of campaigners about the use of deepfake technology to recast pornographic videos.

Dare I say it – enter late-stage capitalism. Legislators are cautious about bringing out the big stick because the European Union and the US don't want to hamstring the emerging AI sector.

Advertising companies, for example, want to create deepfakes for commercial purposes, including the lucrative film industry. Or music videos, like *The Heart Part 5* by Lamar. Whenever you see lawmakers moving slowly on an issue, follow the money to find out who really holds the power.

The tech companies are starting to self-regulate, to stymie moves towards legislation. Gee, we all know how well that works in the tobacco industry! Project Origin – a collaboration between Microsoft and media organisations in the UK – is developing programs that will recognise manipulated content. A cryptographic algorithm can be used to put 'hashes' at certain intervals during videos. No, this isn't a mind-altering cookie or brownie.

Rather, a hash is a way of converting letters or numbers into encrypted data. If the video's altered, the hashes will change. Facebook is committing to removing all videos that 'had been edited in ways that weren't obvious to an average person, or if they misled a viewer into thinking that a person in a video said words they did not actually say'. And TikTok has instituted a similar policy.

Like any form of technology, deepfake isn't all bad. Technologists in Israel are using it to give voice to victims of domestic violence after death. Listen To Our Voices is a response to the global and local surge in domestic and family abuse since the start of the pandemic. 'I was Michal Sela,' a voice rings out in the haunting clip. 'In 2019, I was murdered by the man who was my husband. Today, I call on you, listen to my voice.'

The video, featuring the faces of five Israeli women, goes viral in an eerie social media campaign. Israeli startup D-ID utilises artificial intelligence and animation to create realistic facial features and gestures, as the women describe the verbal and physical assaults inflicted by their partners. They encourage other women to talk to experts before it's too late.

Another project undertaken by D-ID is called Deep Nostalgia. This is quite unsettling. The system animates photos of dead loved ones, like a scene from a *Harry Potter* film. Old portraits become blinking and smiling videos. Your Aunty Maude or Uncle Eric is back from the grave! There's a touch of Norma Bates about this technology, I reckon. Genealogy company My Heritage is aware of the disturbing nature of the tech, noting it won't add speech features. 'While many love the Deep Nostalgia feature and consider it magical, others find it uncanny and are uncomfortable with the results,' the company writes on its website.

During the pandemic, online fraud using deepfake accelerates exponentially. In fact, there's a new term for this: Frankenstein fraud. Criminals combine genuine and falsified information – data, images and videos – to try to rip you off. The synthetic identity comes to life during 'onboarding', which is the initial interaction between you and a business. The average amount stolen by synthetic fraud is more than A$140,000.

As artificial intelligence becomes more sophisticated, it's not only threatening our bank accounts. This technology is targeting our children.

17
CHILDCARE ROBOTS

'I'm watching over you, even when you are sleeping.'
Vevo, childcare robot

It's 2050 and the childcare business is booming. Society is moving beyond the debate about inadequate wages, poor conditions and the exploitation of a predominantly female workforce. Every parent outsources their childcare to robots in AI-supervised centres. Many only see their progeny on weekends and holidays. The care bots look after your child's every need, from feeding to playing and educating. This enables workers to be truly productive without the annoying encumbrance of family. It really is a utopia! (Stirring music rises in the background.)

This scenario might seem far-fetched, but children are considered a 'product' primed for optimisation by artificial intelligence. Perhaps this is nothing new: every stage of a child's life is accompanied by an insidious sales pitch designed to play on parental insecurity. Trouble getting toddlers to sleep? Purchase this state-of-the-art $2000 air purifier! Six-year-old struggling at school? Subscribe to our online reading program. Tween skin troubles? Try our new Healthy Glow range of organic skincare.

Childcare enabled by artificial intelligence is simply something else served on a platter to perfectionist parents. I'm as guilty as anyone, always outsourcing. In a glass half-empty version of this future, the parental bond becomes broken, children struggle to relate to their peers and humans slowly turn into automatons.

Like any large-scale change, this begins with small steps. The history of the electrical baby supervisor can be traced back to the Bakelite Zenith Radio Nurse in 1938. It's created by the president of Zenith Electronics, Eugene McDonald Jr, who's worried about his daughter's safety in the wake of the Lindbergh baby kidnapping. A transmitter is installed in a child's bedroom while the receiver is placed near the parents.

Fast forward to 1997 and the adorable PaPeRo is launched in Japan. The Partner-type-Personal-Robot interacts with children while parents are out of the house. You can direct the device to find the kids any time, anywhere, like a cyborg stalker. The year 2017 gives birth to a child-sized robot called iPal, which can play, sing and dance with children while live-streaming videos to the parents. The aim is to engage children for three to eight hours without human supervision.

By 2022, this assistance is insidious. Bosco is a mobile app that analyses a child's behaviour and 'predicts and prevents threats' coming in via their mobile phone; BeanQ is a tiny AI-powered robot which answers questions, takes photos and keeps the child busy while the parents are otherwise occupied. Millions of households in China have the latter, which builds a detailed life profile through everyday interactions: In other words, it's constantly spying on your kids.

Aside from the obvious privacy concerns, these devices can lead to 'paralysis by analysis'. Parents become over-reliant on technology when making decisions about their offspring. But it's a lot more complicated than reading a copy of the latest parenting tome. Overwhelmed, they may fail to make decisions at all, leaving everything to the robots. Already, there are plenty of days when I want to rock slowly in the corner in a foetal position, due to an inability to properly parent the teens.

But that's not the worst outcome. Robots may harm our children. Consider the 2022 story of a bot crushing the finger of a 7 year old during a Russian chess match. I'm not making this up. Moscow Chess Federation members say the boy was 'too quick to make his move'. Apparently, the child is at fault. CCTV footage shows the robot grabbing the finger and breaking it, before adults rush in to help. The child finishes the tournament the next day in a cast.

'Nothing serious happened,' Moscow Chess Federation's vice-president, Sergey Smagin, tells RIA Novosti news agency in an uncanny imitation of police chief Frank Drebin in *The Naked Gun*: 'Nothing to see here. Move along!' To add insult to injury, Smagin blames the boy: 'There are certain safety rules and the child, apparently, violated them. When he made a move, he didn't notice that he had to wait.' How dare he commit such a heinous crime!

What could happen when robots start to replace parents? Could children die under their 'care'? And who'd be held responsible? Perhaps the most disturbing development is a bot by the name of VEVO. In 2009, Gunma University in Japan introduces a childcare robot with facial recognition software so it can greet people individually. VEVO monitors children's vital signs; an alarm alerts parents to any unusual activity.

In a hair-raising video released in 2021, VEVO sounds a little like a paedophile: 'I'm watching over you, even when you are sleeping.' Artificial intelligence expert Michelle Tempest – who's also a former doctor in the UK's National Health Service – predicts that by 2050, parenting will be as 'obsolete as floppy discs'. The author of *Big Brain Revolution: Artificial Intelligence – Spy or Saviour?* says robots will end up raising one in three children.

You'll even be able to transfer your foetus to a robotic uterus. Yes, I know it sounds odd. But to the ears of people in the 1800s, the words 'embryo transfer' would have sounded strange. My partner, Jason, and I would probably be childless without advances in medical science – specifically, successful IVF treatment. I understand the attraction of 'outsourcing' this process to mechanical intervention if the original equipment is somehow faulty. Dr Tempest foresees purpose-built 'Upbringing Centres', in which children will interact almost exclusively with digital avatars and automatons that combine the roles of nurse, nanny, teacher and therapist.

'Mums and dads will, in effect, have the option of becoming holiday parents, who need only to spend time with their children on day trips and family vacations,' she tells *The London Economic* newspaper. In my more desperate moments, I have to admit this sounds pretty good. Who wants to experience sleepless nights, dirty nappies, terrible twos, exhausting tweens, and teenage angst, despite the moments of joy?

Big picture, this is part of the outsourcing revolution: We'd pay for this service alongside the gardening, cleaning and online shopping. Certainly, raising children is associated with love and satisfaction. But these innovations could release mothers from the child-bearing and rearing responsibilities that restrict our opportunities in the workforce and constitute decades of unpaid labour.

However, this is an ethical and legal minefield. Which party is legally responsible if something happens to a child? Current liability frameworks blame the end-users. These are usually the parents, guardian or childcare centres. Writing in *Scientific American*, Dr George Maliha and Dr Ravi B. Parikh – who work at the intersection of law, ethics, and the care sector – are calling for an independent artificial intelligence safety system, with cases tried in special courts with specific expertise. 'Regulators should deem some AIs too risky to introduce into the market without standards for testing, retesting or validation,' they write. This is bang on.

Then, we need to address the long-term societal impacts. Will this make children more or less equal? What sort of culture are we creating? How can we manage parents and children who become more self-centred with the expectation that every need will be met? 'Chillingly, childrearing will become standardised, limiting variance in personality,' Dr Tempest says, 'but others would say that democratising nurturing would mean that every child would have the same chance of success in later life.' Inevitably, artificial intelligence nannies will creep up on parents incrementally, much like VEVO watching our children sleep.

China is leading the way, raising the possibility of children being grown instead of raised. This country is becoming a society run by artificial intelligence, based around so-called 'smart cities'. This technology is expanding exponentially since its extensive (and expensive) deployment in places like Beijing, Shanghai and Shenzhen in 2011. Couples struggle with a high cost of living, low wages, and long hours, deterring many from having children. Instead of tackling wealth inequality, China is looking to tech to break the impasse. According to leading AI futurist Michael Spencer: 'This is not science fiction.'

In 2022, researchers in Suzhou claim to develop an artificial intelligence system able to monitor embryos as they grow into foetuses in the laboratory. These embryos are cared for by an AI nanny, which adjusts the environment as needed. The development of newborns via the use of algorithms and artificial wombs 'is eerily similar to what we see in the cult classic, *The Matrix*', Spencer writes in his newsletter, AI Supremacy. Although experimentation on human foetuses is currently forbidden under international law, Spencer reckons this scenario is more likely to happen than many of us realise: 'It would also facilitate designer babies and children loyal to the state in a way that would contrast with the individualism seen more now with the young people in China.'

While we wait for this great leap forward, ethics experts Joanna J. Bryson and Ronny Bogani are optimistic about childcare robots. 'We believe it is unlikely that robots will cause significant psychological damage,' they write in a chapter for the 2021 book *The Love*

Makers. 'The bottom line is that the robots themselves will not love our children [although] we must always remember that children will love their robots.'

There's a growing body of evidence this technology could provide therapy support for children with intellectual disabilities and autism. The Australian e-Health Research Centre is behind the software modules for five different social robots for children. Students at Murray Bridge High School in South Australia can work with socially assistive robots NAO and Pepper: 'Our long-term studies show that robots have the potential to enrich the learning experiences of students. Importantly, some of the benefits we observed in participants when they interacted with robots are also transferring to their interactions with other people.'

Dr Ayanna Howard, chair of the School for Interactive Computing at the Georgia Institute of Technology, gives one example. Her team had been trying to engage a child who wouldn't share. Then a miniature humanoid robot is added to the mix. Almost immediately, the child starts interacting with it, saying, 'It's your turn, it's your turn'. 'These are the kind of stories that make you say, "Yeah, I'm going to keep doing this",' Dr Howard tells the MathWorks website in 2021.[1] Children with developmental disabilities, such as cerebral palsy, must endure hours upon hours of therapy. Robots keep kids engaged because they're seen as cool and fun.

One controversial aspect of assistive technologies is whether they imply that children with autism need to be 'fixed', which entrenches stereotypes about people with disabilities: '. . . while gender and race are frequently deployed as protected characteristics to be scrutinized in evaluating algorithmic systems, disability is not,' academic Os Keyes writes in *The Journal of Sociotechnical Critique* in 2020. 'Instead, it is often left (at best) unmarked. This is particularly concerning given the increasing interest in explicitly applying algorithmic systems to questions of disability.' Keyes is worried about how autism is pathologised as something requiring intervention in order to 'normalise' people.

This highlights the power imbalance between those who design the technology, and the people for whom it's created. The disparity is especially acute in the child, disability and aged care sectors.

18
COMPUTER SAYS NO

'Old age is not a disease – it is strength and
survivorship, triumph over all kinds of vicissitudes
and disappointments, trials and illnesses.'
Maggie Kuhn, founder of the Gray Panthers movement

There's a global epidemic accompanying COVID-19: social isolation. Many people who are older, immunocompromised or living with disabilities are trapped in their homes, fearing the consequences of catching the virus. This is exacerbated by people who refuse to wear masks, but that's a rant for another time.

To combat isolation, the New York State Office for the Aging is 'deploying' AI robots as companions. Sounds like a military campaign, albeit well-intentioned. The robot ElliQ does daily check-ins, reminds you to take medication and do physical activities, and connects with family and friends using voice commands or on-screen instructions. ElliQ isn't only reactive, like Google Home or Alexa: it's designed to initiate conversations and uses previous chats to inform follow-up interactions. Best of all, this particular robot is designed with input from older adults.

Innovations like this can't come soon enough. In Western nations, elderly people are generally treated poorly. We're in the 2020–2030 United Nations Decade of Healthy Aging, which encourages countries to 'meet the health care needs of current and future older populations through innovative solutions'. Already, artificial intelligence is being used in aged care facilities for early diagnoses, monitoring, supervision, entertainment, stimulation, personal care and mobility.

Still, there's something special about the human touch. Living with a dynamic disability, I have a care worker in my home two half-days a week. I'd hate to think of these women – care workers are predominantly female – being put out of work and replaced by robots. Frankly, they deserve a big pay rise.

Unfortunately, this entire area of research is beset by age and gender bias. The Baltimore Longitudinal Study of Aging, which is the longest-running scientific study of its kind in the US, has its genesis in 1958. Yet it doesn't bother to enrol any women for the first 20 years. Yes, you read that right: two decades, and not one woman.

Remember how the world is split by a 'digital divide', with women in low- and middle-income countries less likely than men to own smartphones? When there's less data about a particular group – whether in surveys or via technology – it perpetually skews the research. A paper in the January 2022 issue of *The Gerontologist* identifies how broader injustices in society foster ageism. 'Current research examining biases in AI is largely focused on racial and gender biases and the serious consequences that arise as a result; however, little attention has been paid to age-related bias (known as ageism) in AI,' according to Charlene H. Chu and co-authors.

This is leading to a digital underclass of older and poorer people. Also in 2022, the World Health Organization specifically warns about 'faulty or discriminatory' historical datasets used in health care around the world, 'where ageist practices are widespread'. While the WHO acknowledges the potential for artificial intelligence to improve care for older people, the systems are being encoded with 'stereotypes, prejudice or discrimination'.

We can't view this in a vacuum. The pandemic puts ageism and disability front and centre. We live with the narrative that older people simply aren't worth saving. Governments and communities allow COVID-19 to run rampant as skyrocketing death rates become commonplace. At one stage, people are buried in mass graves.

The WHO's Healthy Ageing unit points to practices allowing a patient's age to determine whether they can access oxygen, or a bed in a crowded intensive care unit, in hospitals worldwide. 'The implicit and explicit biases of society, including around age, are often replicated in AI technologies,' Alana Officer, from the Demographic Change and Healthy Ageing unit, tells the WHO website. 'To ensure that AI technologies play a beneficial role, ageism must be identified and eliminated from their design, development, use and evaluation.'[1] This is why 'computer says no' more often if you're over 50. Digital ageism means you'll get less access to health services.

This reminds me of the ethical thought experiment known as the 'trolley problem'. (An out-of-control trolley is tearing towards five people, tied to the tracks. You have two options: do nothing and allow the trolley to kill the five people on the main track; or pull the lever, diverting the trolley onto a side track where it will kill only one person.) Say there's just one person on each track: a 60-year-old and a 30-year-old. Whose life is worth more?

But the problem begins well before we're on our deathbeds, gasping for air and waiting in vain for a ventilator. Ageism is rampant in the tech sector. The teams developing AI tend not to include older people. In a society that venerates youth – with workplaces lauding 'digital natives' – paternalistic attitudes towards older generations and technology become entrenched. Consequently, many of us internalise this bigotry, crushing our confidence to learn new skills.

Only three out of four people over the age of 65 use the internet, according to the Pew Research Center in the US.[2] This percentage drops dramatically by the time people are aged over 80. Older people are known as 'invisible users': our exclusion from technology erases our interests, values and abilities. When younger designers produce devices to be used by older people, they don't often consider age-related changes in perception, cognition and psychomotor abilities.

My dad, who's aged in his eighties, struggles with this every day. We're unable to find a new mobile phone he can operate with arthritis-ridden hands. Eventually, my sister buys an old-school flip phone, with huge buttons and an easy operating mode.

The inability of older people to utilise technology becomes self-perpetuating. If few people in this demographic use social media, their likes, dislikes and opinions aren't captured. When this data is used to train models for artificial intelligence, they end up being riddled with age bias. In 2017, hiring platforms – including the site Jobr – are investigated for discrimination because applicants can't select either a graduation year or first job earlier than 1980.

As we know, if most of the employees in a company are young males, the automated system will prioritise similar applicants. Google and LinkedIn have both used software algorithms that target internet job advertisements at younger applicants, excluding people older than 40. Facebook has also allowed business users to microtarget ads to specific age groups, so older people are unable to see particular products, services or jobs.

A major concern is the opacity of commercial artificial intelligence programs. Protected by 'intellectual property' rights, it's almost impossible for regulatory bodies to determine whether they're intentionally sidelining certain groups. Ultimately, artificial intelligence will repeat the mistakes of the past, reproducing society's hierarchies.

The question is this: Can technology be developed to *mitigate* human bias? Chu and co-authors are calling for an interdisciplinary approach including gerontologists, social scientists, philosophers, legal scholars, ethicists, clinicians and technologists.

This harks back to the issue with the 'Founding Fathers' and their failure to include other disciplines.

But a solution could be found by following the money. It's a smart decision to design a wide range of artificial intelligence that meets the professional, leisure, domestic, communication and health needs of a diverse cohort of people. While the 'boomers' are currently considered to be the older generation, it'll soon be Gen Xers like me who are moving into the 60-plus age group. 'Projections show older adults will likely make up the largest proportion of technology (e.g., health-related, information and communication) consumers in the future as today's tech-savvy adults grow older,' Chu writes. Woo hoo!

It seems some attention is finally being paid to warnings about ageism in artificial intelligence. Johns Hopkins University is using a US$20 million grant from the National Institute on Aging to work on AI devices to help older people live independently for longer. The charter for the Penn Artificial Intelligence and Technology Collaboratory for Healthy Aging (PennAITech) is to 'identify, develop, evaluate, commercialise, and disseminate innovative technology and artificial intelligence methods to support older adults with Alzheimer's disease in their home environment'.

Japan is leading the way in 'age-tech'. This is born of necessity: nearly 33 per cent of Japanese citizens are aged 65 or over. By way of comparison, in Australia it's around 17 per cent, according to the 2021 Census.

Technology writer Daniel Allen delves into the digital devices driving health care in Japan in a fascinating 2022 article for the *MedicalExpo* e-magazine. This represents a glass half-full version of the future. By 2040, data will be collected from each aged care resident and used to recommend the best individualised meals, according to the article. Wearable devices will share real-time information on the residents' health with medical institutions, allowing remote diagnosis. And hybrid showers will recognise your face, and set the temperature to a preferred level.[3]

This is part of the movement known as 'longevity medicine'. Another example is the iAge clock, which is designed based on blood samples from 1001 people aged from eight to 96 years. It uses biomarkers to assess the wellbeing of your immune system and your risk of chronic inflammatory disease. The higher your iAge score, the greater the likelihood of health problems. This acts as an early warning system, encouraging preventative measures and assisting with medical decisions.

'By applying artificial intelligence methods to deep immune monitoring of human blood, we generate an inflammatory clock of aging, which can be used as a companion diagnostic to inform physicians about a patient's inflammatory burden and overall health status, especially those with chronic diseases,' the iAge website reads.

Deep Longevity is a company working on tech that will track the rate of ageing according to biomarkers including molecular, cellular, tissue, organ, physiological and psychological. It aims to create interventions to slow or even reverse the ageing process. This is nothing short of miraculous.

Researchers at Cambridge University say artificial intelligence could spot the early signs of dementia from a simple brain scan long before major symptoms appear. A program designed by the university and The Alan Turing Institute can already predict with 80 per cent accuracy whether those presenting with cognitive impairment will go on to develop Alzheimer's.

An artificial intelligence companion that tells stories is being developed in the UK. The project is called AMPER. I'm trying to avoid acronyms, but this is easier to remember than its full name: Agent-based Memory Prosthesis to Encourage Reminiscing. This companion prompts people with dementia to tell their stories. What a fabulous innovation!

According to the project's website: 'The aim of AMPER is to assist people in retrieving their memories and we hope this will help to strengthen people's self-esteem and feelings of belonging, thus leading to better quality of life and prolonging independent living.'

This sounds more sensible than a much-touted toy seal that's supposed to help patients with dementia. The therapeutic robot, PARO, costs £6000 – well beyond most people's budgets.[4] Despite the media hype, a literature review reveals 'mixed evidence' for the effectiveness of AI-enhanced gimmicks. In a 2022 paper in *The Lancet Healthy Longevity* journal, Kate Loveys and co-authors find caregivers like the devices better than residents; people are uncomfortable with monitoring by artificial intelligence during sleep; and the effect of artificial intelligence on depressive symptoms is 'underwhelming'.[5]

While PARO decreases loneliness and assists communication between residents and nursing home staff, one study says exposure to the pet seal is associated with increased levels of wandering. There are also ethical considerations about automatons that look like pets. 'Older people living with dementia might be deceived into believing the robot is a real pet and might be at risk of infantilisation from some technologies,' the paper says. 'Some older people form attachments with robots and experience distress when separated at the end of a trial.'

This demonstrates that people perceive these robots to be real.

There's something tangible about care bots. You can see them – and believe in their existence – with your own eyes. But a more insidious form of artificial intelligence comes in the form of Frankenstein datasets.

19
FRANKENSTEIN DATASETS

> 'I saw—with shut eyes, but acute mental vision—I saw the pale student of unhallowed arts kneeling beside the thing he had put together. I saw the hideous phantasm of a man stretched out, and then, on the working of some powerful engine, show signs of life and stir with an uneasy, half-vital motion. Frightful must it be, for supremely frightful would be the effect of any human endeavour to mock the stupendous mechanism of the Creator of the world.'
>
> **Mary Shelley,** *Frankenstein; or, The Modern Prometheus*

Science fiction is often far from fact. But Mary Shelley is remarkably prescient in her 1818 novel *The Modern Prometheus*. Artificial intelligence is akin to Frankenstein's monster. The similarities aren't skin deep: the very idea for Shelley's novel is sparked by a challenge from the poet Lord Byron, father of the first computer programmer, Ada Lovelace. Shelley describes the creature as 'superhuman' in speed, with his cognitive development faster than humans. This sounds like an early description of machine learning.

We discover too late that Dr Victor Frankenstein's programming is faulty. The monster learns deeply but not well, developing multiple prejudices. As Igor could well have said, 'I've got a hunch this won't end well'. In the Western classical tradition, Prometheus is a figure representing human striving – particularly for scientific knowledge – and unintended consequences.

Fast forward to 2021 and a new term enters the lexicon: Frankenstein datasets. Governments, health care agencies, and corporations are madly stitching together data from different sources to manage another monster: the pandemic. These data are written in a variety of languages, may be obtained from questionable sources, and could contain duplicate images and information. Why does this matter? Well, as any tech-head will tell you, 'garbage in = garbage out'. Loading poor quality information into artificial intelligence systems results in rubbish.

One of the world's largest datasets – the University of California Irvine Machine Learning Repository – opens its doors in 1987. According to my old photo albums, this is the peak year of perms and panel vans. It's a true record of the era: every doctor is 'he' and every nurse is 'she'. When used to program machines, the data reinforce stereotypes. Furthermore, there are twice as many men as women in this particular repository.

So what about public sets like Google Trends, which tracks search engine data? Anyone can contribute to these: your racist Aunty Katie; sexist Uncle Simon. As much as we don't like to admit it, all humans are biased. Often, we allow bigotry to flow freely in the privacy of our homes, hunched over mobile devices.

Like Dr Frankenstein, we're embedding ourselves into our creations. Bad data goes in, then worsens through machine learning. The baby bias, born into the algorithm, matures into a troublesome teenager. To be fair, teens can be terrific. But their prefrontal cortex only matures at the age of 25. Nobody wants immature and unpredictable machines guiding our futures.

Disturbingly, machine learning models for diagnosing COVID-19 are trained on Frankenstein datasets. As my grandmother would say, 'haste makes waste'. In an attempt to cope with the pace of the pandemic, these systems are being developed too quickly. 'A lack of consistency in the reporting and availability of disaggregated, detailed data on COVID-19 in the US has limited the application of artificial intelligence methods and the effectiveness of those methods for projecting the spread and subsequent impacts of this disease in communities,' according to Tessa Swanson and co-authors in an article in the *Journal of Risk Research*. Data bias is contaminating the system from the outset – much like the virus itself.

Let's get deeply nerdy and look at a systemic review of all published papers on machine learning methods for detecting COVID-19 from chest screenings. I suggest you pour a stiff drink and sit down for this one. In *Nature Machine Intelligence*, Michael Roberts and co-authors write: 'despite huge efforts of researchers to develop machine learning models for COVID-19 diagnosis and prognosis . . . none of the models identified are of potential clinical use due to methodological flaws and/or underlying biases.' None. Zero. Zip. One headline in *Analytics India Magazine* says it all: 'ML-Based COVID-19 Research is Dud.' A dangerous dud.

In a 2020 research paper, the co-lead of Google's ethical AI team, Timnit Gebru, is courageous enough to call out the racist and sexist infestation of large language models, which are trained on an ever-increasing amount of text from the internet. Gebru and co-authors have the temerity to ask 'whether enough thought has been put into the potential risks associated with developing [large language models] and strategies to mitigate these risks'. Is Gebru promoted? Given a raise? Even a pat on the back? After all, this is her job: to promote ethical AI. No. She's summarily sacked.

Far from being an academic conversation about the nuances of language, this can be the difference between life and death. Already, mortality rates for COVID-19 are exponentially higher for people in marginalised communities. A study by Harvard University finds Black women are four times more likely to die from COVID-19 than white men. The UK's Office for National Statistics reveals that Black populations overall are at greater risk of dying after contracting coronavirus than white people.

We know artificial intelligence is susceptible to algorithmic biases. Deploying it willy-nilly amplifies the virus's impact on vulnerable groups. This happens in a variety of ways. In some cases, data is only collected from private hospitals in overwhelmingly wealthy white areas, because they have the latest technology. Consequently, these data aren't relevant when training machines in hospitals in poorer, predominantly Black areas. This issue is so common it has a name: 'health care data silos'.

'Discrimination creep' is another issue. Doctors, nurses and radiologists write case notes for patients. These are programmed into the natural language processing technologies word for word, including the medical team's unconscious bias. Inevitably racism, sexism and ageism infiltrate the process. The machine stores these words and – over time – finds patterns between them, in order to predict what comes next.

This is how bias is breeding throughout our health systems like golden staph. The problem worsens through the conflation of environmental or socioeconomic causes with biological characteristics. Crikey! A lot of long words there. Genetic anthropologist Amy Non puts it best: 'There are so many historical biases that date back to slavery times that are still used in medicine today. It's shocking.'

Take spirometers, for example. These are used on COVID-19 patients to estimate their lung damage and determine whether they're referred for rehabilitation or treatment trials. I experience this during treatment for long COVID. Doctors, who use spirometers to measure lung capacity, historically make 'corrections' for the patient's race. Sounds like phrenology all over again. They reduce the 'normal' reading by 13–15 per cent for people of colour and up to 6 per cent for people of Asian heritage, based on a belief that particular races *biologically* have lower lung capacity. Anyone else think this is close to biological determinism?

A recent systemic review reveals this is dangerously incorrect. White populations generally have larger lung capacity for environmental and socioeconomic reasons – not biological reasons – primarily due to living in more developed countries. This misunderstanding by the medical profession can be deadly. Black and Brown people whose lungs are already compromised need to present with even *lower* lung capacity to qualify for treatment routinely offered to white people.

Put simply, people of colour have to be sicker to get the same level of care. It's appalling. The broad practice of 'race correction' in the medical field finally ends in 2021, more than two centuries after Thomas Jefferson writes erroneously about the 'difference of structure in the pulmonary apparatus' between Black enslaved people and white folks.

It's not only evident in hospitals. The trend towards 'hospital in the home' means coronavirus patients have to use an AI tool to measure oxygen levels in the blood when deciding whether to call an ambulance. I've been using a pulse oximeter daily while struggling with this illness. 'The way the device works, however, is prone to racial bias and was likely calibrated on light-skinned users,' journalist Natalie Grover writes in *Horizon*, the European Commission Research & Innovation magazine. 'Back in 2005, a study showed the device "mostly tended to overestimate (oxygen) saturation levels by several points" for nonwhite people.'

Yes, you read that right. Manufacturers of the pulse oximeter have known about this for more than 15 years – *15 years* – and done nothing about it. People in marginalised communities are caught in a vicious cycle. The data from this flawed tool is being fed into diagnostic algorithms, which will be used in hospitals in the future.

Women and girls are disproportionally affected by health care discrimination. An obvious example is pregnant women being routinely excluded from clinical trials. 'Men and male bodies have long been the standard for medical testing,' Genevieve Smith and Ishita Rustagi write in the *Stanford Social Innovation Review*. 'Women are missing from medical trials, with female bodies deemed too complex and variable.' Half of almost 1000 trials related to COVID-19 explicitly exclude pregnancy, and expectant women are shut out of vaccine trials. The reasons are complex, including risk and legal liability. But we need more data about pregnant people – not less.

These archaic attitudes remind me of the old advertisements for pads and tampons, with blue liquid representing blood, as if genteel folk would be horrified by the thought of menstruation. Our bodies are considered so disgusting we comprise the minority of cases in medical data, despite constituting the majority of the population.

'For millennia, medicine has functioned on the assumption that male bodies can represent humanity as a whole,' Caroline Criado-Perez writes in her 2019 book *Invisible Women: Data Bias in a World Designed for Men*. 'As a result, we have a huge historical data gap when it comes to female bodies, and this is a data gap that is continuing to grow as researchers carry on ignoring the pressing ethical need to include female cells, animals and humans, in their research. That this is still going on in the twenty-first century is a scandal. It should be the subject of newspaper headlines worldwide. Women are dying, and the medical world is complicit. It needs to wake up.'

Of course, it's not only gender bias. Using artificial intelligence, researchers perform a global scoping review of more than 7000 clinical papers in PubMed. They discover most databases originate in the US and China. Almost all of the top ten databases are from high-income countries. Why is this an issue? AI doesn't work well when it has to generalise outside of the cohort data. Growing up in a low socio-economic area, my family is acutely aware of the 'right' and 'wrong' side of the tracks. Full disclosure: we're from the wrong side.

This is analogous to artificial intelligence: Data-rich regions benefit substantially compared with data-poor regions, entrenching disparities in health care. It's crucial for practitioners to understand who may be negatively affected. The phenomenon of 'bias in – bias out' can have catastrophic consequences for patients. Who's offered the first COVID-19 vaccines? When resources are scarce, who'll get the last ventilator, oxygen tank, or intensive care bed? Imagine being on your deathbed and hearing, 'Computer says no'.

People with severe cases of COVID-19 often end up with sepsis. In western Sydney, Emergency physician Amith Shetty decides to investigate whether an AI tool used to detect patients with this infection is working properly. Sepsis, which is formerly known as blood poisoning, can be fatal. It causes an estimated half of all hospital deaths. Dr Shetty's research reveals the Sepsis Alert performs 'modestly' in all five emergency departments: it doesn't identify every infected patient. I don't think 'modestly' is what you want when your loved one is lying in hospital dying of blood poisoning.

The history of artificial intelligence in medicine is littered with similar examples. Back in 2012, IBM's Watson supercomputer is unleashed on an unsuspecting US health system. It's hyped as the future of cancer research. Six years later, internal IBM documents reveal Watson recommends 'unsafe and incorrect' cancer treatments, with one doctor telling IBM executives, 'This product is a piece of shit'.

Hospital systems are extremely vulnerable to hacking and cyber attacks, according to a 2021 study published in *Nature Communications*. 'Motivations to commit adversarial attacks can include monetary gain, insurance fraud, temptation of favorable clinical trial outcomes, among others,' Qianwei Zhou and co-authors write. Fake samples can fool AI models into making the wrong diagnosis. For example, a computer program could add or remove evidence of cancer from mammograms. In Zhou's study, around 70 per cent of the manipulated images fool the artificial intelligence; the accuracy of radiologists varies from 29 per cent to 71 per cent.

Hackers could also break into internet-connected insulin pumps and deliver deadly doses of medication. The number of ransomware attacks on US health care organisations is almost doubling every year. In 2021, the mother of a baby who dies in Alabama launches a lawsuit, alleging this is the first death by ransomware. She blames a hack of the hospital's computer system for the failure of heart rate monitors, leading to fatal brain damage.

I sound like Chicken Little in this chapter: 'The sky is falling!' Despite the sound of many acorns dropping to the earth, I must acknowledge artificial intelligence is revolutionising health care. AI expert at the Massachusetts Institute of Technology, Regina Barzilay, tells *The Washington Post* about returning to work after breast cancer leave: 'I walked in the door to my office and thought, "We here at MIT are doing all this sophisticated algorithmic work that could have so many applications, [while] one subway stop away the people who could benefit from it are dying".' Barzilay and a protégé build an artificial intelligence – known as Mirai – that identifies whether a healthy person will get breast cancer up to five years before diagnosis.

Google develops a similar system that interprets CT scans to predict the likelihood of lung cancer. A trial of artificial intelligence software at Queensland's Princess Alexandra Hospital gives early warnings before a patient's condition declines. And researchers at the University of Utah find AI-powered retinal scans can forecast the later onset of cardiovascular disease. Of course, it remains to be seen what insurance companies would do with this information. It's like the dilemma surrounding genetic testing: Do you really want life insurers knowing about a pre-existing illness or diseases for which you have a predisposition?

A new medical device, based on artificial intelligence, can assist clinicians to accurately diagnose autism spectrum disorder in children up to six years of age. A related study, led by Northwestern University in Illinois, uses machine learning to identify speech patterns in children with autism that are consistent between English and Cantonese. These features of speech can be useful in early diagnosis.

You know how some people have an unerring sense of direction? We tend to say they have their own 'internal GPS'. This could soon be a reality, with a team at MIT working on an ingestible and directional implant to monitor tumour growth, heart rate and breathing. It could eventually deliver drugs to specific regions of the body.

Of course, artificial intelligence is at the forefront of unravelling the mysteries of long COVID. In the US, the National Covid Cohort Collaborative (N3C) includes de-identified data from 72 sites representing 13 million patients. However, the first attempt at building an algorithm to identify long COVID patients is fraught with difficulty.

'There was literally no structured way for a physician to enter "I think this patient has long Covid",' Emily Pfaff, who co-leads the long COVID working group at N3C, tells *StatNews* in 2022.[1] 'We had to get creative and find a proxy.' They settle on records from about 500 patients who show up at three specialty clinics. The model performs 'decently' when tested, which is reminiscent of 'modestly'.

There are concerns the data might overrepresent long COVID patients with respiratory symptoms because two of the clinics are based in pulmonary departments. Most of my symptoms are neurological, cardiac and autonomic – not pulmonary. Inevitably, swathes of people who are suffering will be put on the wrong treatments, while serious manifestations will be missed. In the US and Australia, most of the clinics are in large metropolitan areas, servicing wealthier patients. Will this data be transferable to patients in poorer areas, or developing countries? If not, this is really troubling.

It again begs the question: what happens when the algorithms get it wrong? Who's at fault and legally liable? Clinicians, data scientists or policy-makers? There's no clear consensus. 'The biases of prior practices and the perpetuation of exclusionary processes toward women can lead to inaccurate medical decisions,' Angelica Marotta writes in her 2022 paper 'When AI Is Wrong: Addressing Liability Challenges in Women's Healthcare': 'The ramifications of such errors show that the incorrect use of AI raises several critical questions regarding who should be responsible for potential incidents.'[2]

Identifying who or what is liable is hard because of 'the black box' problem. Many artificial intelligence systems make recommendations based on data without supplying details about how these decisions are reached. Medtech using artificial intelligence will only be successful if doctors understand the perils, particularly in complicated cases.

This problem is pressing, with the European Union's latest General Data Protection Regulation coming into effect in mid-2018.[3] The ramifications are clear: every citizen now has a 'right to explanation'. If I had the energy, I'd be dancing with joy. I'm lying in bed utterly spent after dealing with medical professionals who often disregard a patient's right to know. In future, any organisation which has trade dealings with the EU is legally required to justify decisions based on algorithms to people whose data they hold. It's not enough for an artificial intelligence system to tell physicians and patients that something is true. Doctors need to be able to tell patients *why*.

Currently, most doctors don't have the foggiest idea about deep neural networks, which come to conclusions from image-based medical software. They may be able to discern between malignant and benign tumours. But there's no explanation about how the software comes to this conclusion. Is it possible for patients to make informed consent if no-one actually knows what's going on?

'We have people in the field who are able to turn the crank but don't actually know what they're doing, and don't actually understand the foundational underpinnings of what they're doing,' Zachary Lipton, a computer scientist at Carnegie Mellon University, tells the website *Undark* in 2019. 'The truth is that you don't even usually have historical data that is representative of any real-world process. You have some kind of weird Frankenstein data that was cobbled together from a bunch of sources.'

Dr Emma Schleiger is a multidisciplinary research scientist at CSIRO's Data61. She says that in many cases we can't understand exactly what the inputs are because the artificial intelligence has generated its own neural network, making it 'way too complicated for us to be able to explain'. Still, given the advantages of black box AI in the medical sector, she says it's not all bad: 'Rather than saying, "oh, black boxes are bad", we need to think about the situations that we're using them in. So for diagnosis, if I suspected skin cancer and I knew AI was going to be better at detecting it than a doctor, I would rather have that threshold higher.'

How do we manage the bodgy bots, while appreciating the benefits of this tech? Stefan Hajkowicz, principal scientist in strategy and foresight at Data61, says artificial intelligence is going to be critical in solving conundrums in health care, where expenditure is growing at unsustainable rates. 'AI is going to be able to save many people from cancer,' he tells the business technology site ZDNet in 2019.

The starting point is critical analysis: we must admit this technology is far from perfect. Artificial intelligence programs are complex. Some applications have thousands of lines of code and are written in five different languages. Unfortunately, most computer scientists tend to see only the beauty, rather than the beast.

The monster kills many of Victor Frankenstein's family and friends. But he can't bring himself to kill it: 'I had worked hard for nearly two years, for the sole purpose of infusing life into an inanimate body. For this I had deprived myself of rest and health. I had desired it with an ardour that far exceeded moderation.'

Artificial intelligence has limitless potential to improve the diagnosis and treatment of billions of people around the world. But if single-minded developers ignore the warning signs, the twenty-first century version of Mary Shelley's monster will be even more lethal. Will modern-day Dr Frankensteins be able to control their creations? Or will humanity increasingly escape into virtual worlds?

20
FAIR GAME

'Fortnite, because of its visual style, it's widely acceptable to just about everyone.'
Tim Sweeney, CEO of Epic Games

Do you play *Fortnite*? Are you aware of the pleasures of a Battle Royale? This first-person shooter game is the brainchild of Tim Sweeney, who likes to pitch himself as the 'good guy' of gaming. One of his early projects is *Jill of the Jungle*, a trilogy in which the third part is entitled *Jill Saves the Prince*. 'Tremendous,' you might be thinking. 'A feminist in the notoriously misogynistic world of gaming.' Not quite.

Jill is a highly sexualised character, resplendent with long blonde hair, pert breasts and muscular thighs. It's argued *Fortnite* isn't as bad as other games because many of the female characters act in masculine ways, and some of the male fighters have feminine attributes. My son and daughter play the game and rave about the rocking 'skins' for the female characters, like the Red Knight and Valkyrie. Look at the old lady keeping up with the young 'uns! I have no idea what I'm writing, but the teens say I'm 'slaying'.

By all accounts, the makers of *Fortnite*, Epic Games, try to do everything right. Game designer and associate professor Celia Pearce tells the Northeastern University website that *Fortnite* is designed to appeal to a wide and inclusive audience. This is an enormous task in an industry dominated by young men. But women are still finding it a hostile environment.

'If you go in and identify yourself as female, you are likely to get harassed in spite of all the best intentions of the game design,' Pearce says. 'That really concerns me because it shows that this toxic male culture – which has gone unchecked for the past decade – is so pervasive that even if you, as a company, make a decision to make a more inclusive game, it's not enough.'

Epic Games uses bright colours and cartoony characters with multiple play modes including exploring and building, rather than purely fighting. In honour of International Women's Day 2022, the company offers free items to redeem, and features Islands by female creators. And the game costs nothing to play on multiple platforms. 'It seems to be the case that more women and girls are playing *Fortnite* because it's free and available on mobile, so it's easier to get into the game,' Pearce explains. Traditionally, game consoles are bought and enjoyed primarily by men. Despite these efforts, only around one in four *Fortnite* players is female.

Before the 2019 Fortnite World Cup, Epic Games proffers a US$3 million grand prize for the best team. Not a single, solitary woman makes it to the final event. According to Team Bumble member Madison Mann, girls stop playing because of the negative messages they receive. Mann tells *Forbes* magazine about some of the trolling: 'Get back to the kitchen, girls can't play video games, girls suck at video games, and other sexist nonsense.'

How far have we really progressed from the days of #gamergate? You may remember this hateful, right-wing backlash against diversity in gaming culture. In 2014, doxing, rape and death threats are targeted at women in the industry, such as feminist media critic Anita Sarkeesian.

Game-makers are trying to address online harassment, but with little impact. Exhibit A: the continued practice of 'teabagging' in video games. Also known as 'tactical squatting', a player's avatar crouches up and down while standing over an enemy player's body. While some pundits see this as asserting dominance, others consider it a form of sexual assault.

Of course, it's the latter: The dictionary definition of teabagging is, 'the act of placing one's testicles in the mouth of another person, often repeatedly, raising and lowering it like a person dipping a tea bag'. A similar act is referred to as 'corpse humping' in the game *Halo*. 'In *Halo 4*, projecting a hologram onto a corpse would reward players with the sight of the hologram humping the corpse,' Luci S writes on the website Gamerant.

Further to this are concerns about cultural appropriation. Countless Black artists are calling out Epic Games for stealing the iconic *Fortnite* dance. If you have teens or tweens, you'd have witnessed these unique moves, which are also known as 'flossing'. I remember seeing kids doing it by the side of the road and in shopping malls.

Reaching the source of the dance would take you to 'the streets of Memphis, Tennessee; to the assembled young men as they are captured in the song's video, leaning on the trunks of cars, throwing dice, holding guns, laughing and dancing with abandon', motion designer Yussef Cole writes for Vice.com. He says rappers like Blocboy JB are at the forefront of those raising concerns; 2 Milly is among a handful who've gone so far as to initiate lawsuits.

Does this mean *Fortnite* is akin to a modern-day minstrel show? '. . . the manner in which *Fortnite* has transplanted the creative output of these men into its brightly colored marionettes, without permission, credit, or compensation feels particularly egregious,' Cole writes. Many of these lawsuits have since been withdrawn.

In 2022, choreographer Kyle Hanagami begins legal action over a dance called 'It's Complicated'. Hanagami claims it's quite simple, really: Epic Games is responsible for stealing the 'hook' of his dance without consent. Hanagami holds a copyright for the dance. If successful, this could have become a precedent for future legal action. But a federal judge in the Central District of California dismisses the case.

Many Indigenous gamers and developers are disappointed about the stereotypical portrayals of characters and imagery in modern games, such as *Horizon: Forbidden West*. A near-future dystopia, the game features factions including the Tenakth, who dress in leather, fur and feathers, sometimes with ornate headdresses. The Tenakth worship pilots from the American Air Force as sacred warriors. One day, regular player @JohnTomKnight tweets, 'Hey @Guerrilla and @PlayStation, just curious . . . When making *Horizon [Forbidden] West*, were any Native/Indigenous people involved in creating the story or art for this game?' Knight is an enrolled citizen of the Cherokee Nation.

Incidentally, this isn't the first time Guerrilla Games is accused of bigotry. Back in 2017, the company uses the words 'braves', 'savages' and 'primal' to describe some factions. This is unsurprising when you consider as few as 2 per cent of game designers are Black. There are no solid statistics on how many are Indigenous.

So where does artificial intelligence fit into this? Almost all video games have AI-based components. In fact, game-playing is an area of research in artificial intelligence from its inception. One of the first examples is the computerised game *Nim*, made in 1951. This is 20 years before the explosion of gaming, courtesy of a little game called *Pong*. The same year sees chequers and chess first played by computers, culminating in Deep Blue beating world champ Garry Kasparov in 1997. During the golden age of video arcade games, the concept of opponents created by artificial intelligence becomes popular.

Remember *Space Invaders*? As adults 'of a certain age' we have a retro *Space Invaders* machine at home. It's remarkable technology for its time. The game Galaxian adds more complexity, especially when the enemy fighter jets begin firing from all angles. This sends me into panic attacks, much to the teens' amusement. *Pac-Man* (and, of course, *Pac-Woman*) brings artificial intelligence to action maze games.

Later computer games use so-called 'bottom up' methods of information processing, allowing real-time changes in strategy based on player behaviour. In 1996, an artificial life program named *Creatures* enables you to 'hatch' small furry animals. The 'Norns' represent the first popular application of machine learning in an interactive simulation. Neural networks are used by the creatures to learn what to do, while interacting with their environment.

What are neural networks? I'm glad you asked! Actually, that's a lie. Living with brain fog is like lingering in a liminal space. Fortunately, one of my dearest friends is a computer genius. You can thank James McIlwain for this explanation of an extremely complex concept.

Your brain contains around 100 billion cells, known as neurons – the tiny switches that let you think and remember things. Computers contain billions of miniature 'brain cells', too. These are called transistors. Made from silicon, transistors are miniature electronic components that work as either amplifiers or switches. Neural networks are inspired by the human brain, mimicking the way biological neurons signal to one another. They rely on training data to learn and improve their accuracy over time. These finely tuned algorithms allow us to classify and cluster data at a high velocity. Think Google Search, or the 'Norns' from *Creatures*.

Since that time, the technology has advanced rapidly. In 2021, Sony CEO Kenichiro Yoshida says his artificial intelligence research division will collaborate with PlayStation to build clever, computer-controlled characters. 'By leveraging reinforcement learning, we are developing game AI agents that can be a player's in-game opponent or collaboration partner,' he announces in a press release. Reinforcement learning is a subset of machine learning. Basically, the AI learns through trial and error, much like humans.

'In short, these characters will mimic human players,' journalist Keith Stuart writes in *The Guardian* in 2021. 'To some extent, they will think.' The game *Watch Dogs: Legion* is a fascinating case study in what can be achieved with this technology. It generates 'life stories, relationships and daily routines for every London citizen you interact with', Stuart writes. If you save a character's life one day, their best mate might join you the next.'

While the tech expands apace, there remain serious issues around inclusion. If we want to see characters with differing backgrounds and experiences, developers need to diversify their workforces. Uma Jayaram, the general manager of SEED – the research team at game publisher Electronic Arts – draws her global team from different genders, ethnicities and cultures.

'A diverse team allows for multiple points of view to coalesce and creates possibilities for a more representative outcome and product,' she tells *The Guardian*. 'It also enhances opportunities to create awareness, empathy and respect for individuals who are different from us. A video game is, in a way, an extension of our physical world, and a place where people spend time and form rich experiences that loop back into the collective sense of self and community.'[1] Well, this all sounds marvellous. Sunshine and rainbows!

However, we should be wary of diversity and inclusion being viewed as add-ons. When this happens, it puts huge pressure on people from marginalised communities, who already live with less job security, status and power. It can't be left to these people to perform the emotional labour of educating their managers and peers about appropriate workplace culture. Like every other sector using artificial intelligence, gaming needs to evolve its leadership structures. Lasting change must be top-down, as well as bottom-up. It's a terrible shame that hegemony remains the dominant force in the technology sector.

One of the fundamental elements shaping artificial intelligence is the inclination to think about video games as adversarial systems, where allies and enemies are perennially in combat. But there is another way. Glow Up Games caters to diverse audiences. This company lets players construct AI systems or agents for others, helping them understand how artificial intelligence works.

Tru-Luv, a development studio responsible for the popular #SelfCare app, is working on technologies reflecting its progressive culture. One-third of Tru-Luv's workforce is Black, Indigenous and people of colour, while the executive team is 100 per cent female. The studio's founder is Brie Code. Sidebar: how cool is it that Brie's last name is 'Code'? If that's not nominative determinism, I don't know what is. I wonder if she works with someone called Mac.

'The games industry has focused on a narrow subset of human psychology for several years,' Code tells *The Guardian*. 'It is very good at creating experiences that help people feel a sense of achievement or dominance. Game AI created by a diverse workforce will bring life to NPCs (non-player characters) and experiences that represent the breadth and depth of the human experience. We'll see more non-zero-sum experiences, more compassion, more emotional resonance, more insight, more transcendence. We'll see new forms of play that leverage feelings of creativity, love and joy more so than triumph or domination.'[2]

This represents a priceless opportunity to abandon age-old stereotypes by ensuring the algorithms promote fairness and respect. I want to say it's a feminine, rather than masculine, approach, but that's leaning on far too many outdated stereotypes.

Beyond diversity, data mining is a growing issue in gaming. This allows designers to explore what parts people like to play and the factors causing them to stop playing. Then, developers can tweak the gameplay to make more money. If you're wondering who to blame for the sudden dent in your bank account after an errant tween buys too many *Fortnite* skins, it's the developers. This is no accident. The skins, or costumes, make your character more powerful, which is an intoxicating prospect for a hyped-up player keen for a Battle Royale.

MAN-MADE

In *Fortnite*, artificial intelligence is used in the enemy bots and neutral characters. Epic Games delves deep into analytics to make psychological observations about player behaviour. Are they lone wolves or alliance-builders? The AI also monitors what's called 'emergent' gameplay and adapts challenges to suit the players' styles.

Full disclosure: this exploration of artificial intelligence in gaming is somewhat contentious. Many experts bewail the use of the term 'AI' in this field, claiming it isn't about intelligence at all. They say gaming is distinctly different from *academic* artificial intelligence, which they consider to be the 'real AI'. Perhaps they're right: only the academic kind addresses the complexities of machine learning and decision-making from arbitrary input. There's a sniff of 'nasty commercialism getting in the way of robust academic research'.

Game AI is branching away, building its own worlds. Still, I reckon gaming should be considered a sub-branch of artificial intelligence. This is like rock 'n' roll being under the umbrella of classical music, because it uses similar instruments but breaks many of the rules.

Now, let's look at what Tim Sweeney is calling 'the biggest technological revolution in our lifetime'.

21
REALITY CHECK

'Books are the original virtual reality.'
Marsha Dark, author, artist and transhumanist

Artificial intelligence and game development are growing symbiotically. You're about to enjoy a delicious acronym soup as we explore augmented reality and virtual reality. AR and VR are progressively being incorporated into these platforms, making the games as realistic as possible. If data gathered through artificial intelligence is used to build future games, they'll inevitably be skewed towards male players. The Finn brothers from the antipodean band *Split Enz* are dead wrong: history *always* repeats. AI-based voice assistants are coming into the gaming sector too, cementing the bias detailed in previous chapters.

Augmented and virtual reality create bridges between the digital and physical worlds. You're probably aware of VR headsets, which can transport you onto a rollercoaster, beautiful beach or soaring hang glider. They're also used in tours of museums and art galleries. AR is usually used for technical training. For example, you can wear high-tech glasses to look in detail at an aircraft engine. Using voice, images and text, the 'smart glasses' explain the engine's components, and how to fix or replace them. Mixed reality (MR) combines both VR and AR. And they all come under the term, extended reality (XR). Confused yet? I certainly am. So what does it mean in layperson's terms?

In the workplace, this technology is ideal for transferring skills from retiring workers to a new generation. This is timely as baby boomers retire and birth rates continue to fall. We're living through a time of skills shortages. Tech helps to bring people up to speed quickly and efficiently.

The augmented, virtual and mixed reality market is expected to exceed US$250 billion by 2028, according to Statista.[1] This is gobsmacking. Back in 2021, it was only worth US$28 billion. And who are the big players? You guessed it: Google and Facebook.

It takes thousands of hours of programming to design and develop each of these apps. Most of the programmers are white men. What will this mean for police departments, which are using virtual reality to train officers for crisis situations? Will embedded bias in the images – for example, depicting criminals as being Black or Latinx – reinforce existing biases within the minds of these officers?

There are also significant differences between males and females around the sense of immersion in altered reality spaces. Men generally report a greater sense of spatial presence and more perceived realism. This makes gaming less enjoyable for women wearing the headsets, but there are more serious implications. Educators are using augmented and virtual reality to teach students. If the content resonates more deeply with boys and men, women and girls will receive inferior teaching.

What about the myriad privacy complications associated with the smart glasses used with these headsets? The filming and recording function makes it possible to 'broadcast' someone's movements without their knowledge. This represents an unprecedented surveillance of everyday life.

The health care sector is eyeing off these glasses to improve the productivity of clinicians and their staff. Patient data can be captured and stored in real time. But what happens if this information is hacked, or there's a security breach? They're even dangerous to wear in your own home. If hackers gain control of your smart glasses, they could see PIN numbers and passwords.

Still, the tech giants are forging forward: Ray-Ban Stories is a collection of smart glasses as part of a collaboration with Meta. The glasses have an 'indicator light' to show when they're recording, but it's barely visible. Meta needs to be more careful to avoid the fate of Google Glass, which was laughed out of the market.

In mid-2022, Meta releases a report highlighting 'salient risks' with these glasses, including a requirement for 'informed consent from bystanders'. A tiny red light does *not* represent consent. Believe it or not, there are also instances of smart glasses making people feel ill, a phenomenon known as 'cyber sickness'. One research paper reveals four out of five people report cyber sickness after 10–15 minutes of gameplay.

When you think about it, these innovations challenge what it means to be human. The use of altered reality creates a minefield. Not quite as dangerous as the minefields in *Fortnite*, but problematic nonetheless. For example, extended reality enables you to interact with virtual representations of real people. 'Thus, along these lines, is it wrong to perform immoral acts in VR?' asks Distinguished Investigator at the University of Barcelona Mel Slater and co-authors in an article published in the journal *Frontiers* in 2020.[2]

This is further explored in a 2013 play, *The Nether*, by Jennifer Haley: a man commits paedophilia in a fully immersive virtual world. In the play, the man argues to the police this is a safe way to realise his unacceptable drives without harming anyone. Should this be allowed? After all, we're shaped by what we imagine. Or is policing our imaginations the ultimate fascism?

The second episode from Season 2 of the sci-fi comedy series *Red Dwarf* addresses this quandary. 'Better than Life' introduces a total immersion video game which works by inserting electrodes into your frontal lobes and hypothalamus. Players have the ability to indulge all their fantasies. They can command into existence any object, person or environment. However, once the user starts to play, their mind purely perceives the reality of the game. All signals from their real body, except for extreme pain, are ignored. Another spoiler alert: the users have a bad habit of starving to death.

A fundamental moral principle is for humans to treat others with respect. Do virtual characters deserve the same treatment? This reminds me of how we speak to robots. If we treat chatbots poorly, will we end up treating humans badly? Or if we act violently towards virtual characters, are we causing psychological harm to the people those characters represent?

'In XR this is different though – in movies it is other people who treat other people badly whereas in XR it could be ourselves doing so, or other (virtual or online) people may treat us badly,' Slater and co-authors write. 'While this already takes place in video-games, particularly when the character is seen and controlled from a first-person perspective, XR goes a step further in the sense that it can feel more real if the participant is fully embodied as that character.'

Who's legally responsible if a virtual character harms a human? This might seem esoteric, but it can happen. Any adverse feeling is intensified in a virtual or augmented environment. There are many instances of cognitive, emotional and behavioural disturbances after people re-enter the real world.

Soon we'll be able to use extended reality to recreate situations involving dead loved ones. How will we feel after we return to real life without our beloved? Extended reality is controlled by a variety of guidelines and laws around the world, which include respect for the dignity of the people involved, scientific value and social responsibility. But these laws lack the nuance to deal with disputes involving the virtual world.

In Grace Chan's dystopian novel *Every Version of You,* Tao-Yi and her partner, Navin, spend most of their time inside a hyper-immersive, uber-consumerist virtual reality known as Gaia. They go to work, socialise and eat their meals in this digital utopia. At the same time, their ageing bodies are suspended in pods of goo in cramped apartments, the world a wasteland due to the ravages of climate change.

A new technology is developed to upload a human brain to Gaia permanently. Tao-Yi must decide whether to join almost everyone else in this augmented utopia or remain with her dying mother on earth. According to some experts, long-term and frequent use of XR might eventually lead people to prioritise the virtual world over the real one.

Another issue is the large amount of personal data collected during these experiences, in the same way data miners harvest information from gamers. Do governments or third parties have a right to know what we do in virtual places? Pornography and violence will be readily available, and it'll feel more real. This might have grave social consequences.

It's clear we must address these issues now. 'A particular problem set may be caused by what we refer to as "superrealism" where elements and even experiences in virtual or augmented reality may become indistinguishable from reality,' Slater writes in the *Frontiers* article. These devices will become as ubiquitous as smartphones, with people wearing headsets for many hours of the day and night, as in Chan's speculative fiction.

Alternatively, extended reality could be used to *improve* society. The 'golden rule' – known as the ethics of reciprocity – encourages us to treat others the way we'd like to be treated. Already, virtual and augmented reality can put you into the body of another person. Someone with pale skin could temporarily become darker, or an adult could trade places with a child à la the film *Freaky Friday*.

Dubbed the 'ultimate empathy machine', this technology is being used in workplaces to conduct diversity training. First-person experiences can raise awareness and build understanding of others. For example, some devices can manipulate your field of vision, audio output and surroundings to demonstrate what it's like to navigate life with a disability. Other programs put you in a 360-degree video landscape of a refugee camp or a disaster zone.

There's fierce debate among inclusion advocates about whether these interventions are effective. This includes concerns 'they could replace direct engagement with the communities being represented', tech policy analyst Elysse Dick writes for the Information Technology and Innovation Foundation in 2021.[3] Some evidence exists for the capacity for behavioural change. In one study from the Stanford Virtual Human Interaction Lab, participants are presented with exercises designed to elicit empathy for the homeless.

'The results of the study showed that, while short-term emotional responses were similar across VR and non-VR interventions, the immersive experiences "led to more positive, longer-lasting attitudes toward the homeless up to two months after the intervention" than similar, narrative-driven approaches,' Elysse Dick writes. This is replicated in studies showing people who view 360-degree video appeals are more likely to make larger contributions to a charity, than those exposed to traditional advertising.

Could the use of extended reality lead to broader social upheaval? Professor Courtney Cogburn harnesses the technology for racial justice initiatives. The 2018 immersive film *1000 Cut Journey* places the user in the body of a Black man who encounters racism at various stages of his life. 'It's clear to me that – for some people at least – we're definitely hitting the mark that I hoped to hit, which was for White people in particular to come out of the experience feeling like they don't really understand these experiences perhaps in the ways that they thought they did,' Professor Cogburn tells *Yes!* magazine in 2019. 'But feeling bad or connecting to bad feelings that are being experienced by a group is really not sufficient for social change.'[4]

Despite reservations about this tech, it's being fast-tracked in the US to train police officers for high-risk situations, like sieges. But it's also used for empathy training. One series puts officers in the body of a person having a mental health crisis before running a simulated intervention. As the Department of Justice Office of Community Oriented Policing Services notes: 'Through deeply immersive VR experiences, police officers can experience life as a community member in the city they serve.'

In the education sector, virtual reality could reduce implicit bias. Teacher's Lens creates virtual interactions to identify whether the educator has an unconscious preference for people of a certain race or gender. In the psychological sphere, the technology brings phobic people face-to-face with spiders or sharks, by way of exposure therapy. Extended reality systems are often employed for data visualisation in architecture and urban planning, as well as entertainment.

In the 2020s, empathy training is becoming gamified. Digital rights activists are building games to confront our prejudices. *The Choice of the Annotator* is an adventure game that addresses the hidden labour behind machine learning datasets. Taking the perspective of a gig economy worker, the player experiences the appalling conditions imposed by the platforms. Talk about turning the tables on the tech titans!

Another game, *Survival of the Best Fit*, is conceived by people from four different countries, alumnae or students from New York University Abu Dhabi. They want to help people 'better understand how AI works and how it may affect them, so that they can better demand transparency and accountability in systems that make more and more decisions for us'.

Meanwhile, language services provider TransPerfect is shining a light on women behind and in front of the console, many of whom are being erased from history. 'It was generally thought that only men enjoyed playing and creating games, and that they were the only ones who "should" do it, too,' staff write on the TransPerfect website. 'Because of this outdated belief, each aspect of gaming, from design to marketing, was traditionally based around men's tastes, attitudes and interests. This left women out of the conversation entirely but didn't necessarily stop them playing and developing games.'

Some of the women playing pivotal roles include Jade Raymond, who helped create *Assassin's Creed*, and Bonnie Ross, a member of the team behind *Halo*. Women are interested in gaming, but the money's going mainly to the men. This sounds similar to the attitudes to women in computing from its inception.

Female streamers are finding success on Twitch and YouTube, and organisations like I Need Diverse Games are amplifying marginalised voices in the sector. Still, research shows a whopping 84 per cent of board members in the top 20 gaming companies are men. Let that sink in for a moment: more than four out of five. Lawsuits filed against industry giants Activision Blizzard and Ubisoft reveal women suffer from a hostile work environment, including sexual harassment and discrimination.

Aside from being an inclusion issue, sidelining women doesn't make sense financially. The people at the top are effectively setting fire to wads of cash. Diversity and inclusion aren't buzzwords – they transform business performance. And the gaming industry is no exception. 'I think that as more women are in leadership positions and on more boards, it's going to boost everyone's success,' writes Kayla Madsen Lopez, director of sales at TransPerfect Gaming Solutions Europe. 'The pie will just get bigger, for everyone.'

Gaming is one of the newest – and fastest-growing – industries in the world. There's no excuse for its leaders to go down the tired old path of the past. Sadly, one of our oldest industries is still looking backwards instead of forwards. It remains a race to the bottom in the automotive sector.

22
ROAD TO NOWHERE

*'I just see this as a race and we need to win,
second place is first looser [sic].'*
Travis Kalanick, co-founder of Uber

Travis Kalanick is one of the most single-minded developers in Silicon Valley. Watch *Super Pumped: The Battle for Uber* to witness his spectacular fall from grace. Young Travis is cut from the same cloth as Gordon Gekko, the archetypal 1980s businessman with the catchphrase, 'Greed is good'.

After co-founding Uber in 2009, Kalanick works as CEO for seven years building a global ride-sharing brand. Frankly, there aren't enough pages in this book to detail exactly what goes wrong. He acts like a dictator, riding roughshod over government regulations, breaching dozens of workplace laws and engaging in corporate espionage.

Uber ends up in a ditch due to 'bro culture', misogyny and toxic masculinity. 'Tell me more!' I hear you cry. Well, here are a few of the highlights. One day, Kalanick jokes to a journalist at *GQ* magazine that the company should be called 'Boob-er' because of all the female attention he's getting. Executives regularly go to strip clubs on the corporate account, a practice jokingly referred to as 'Tits on Travis'.

Engineer Susan Fowler reveals the extent of sexual harassment and rape at the company, and the CEO's forced to resign. The rise and fall of Travis Kalanick is the quintessential example of the culture in tech companies focusing on self-driving vehicles. This sector sits smack bang at the intersection of three male-dominated industries: transport, manufacturing and technology.

A backlash from Uber drivers, who are living below the minimum wage and sleeping in their vehicles, leads to the dream of self-driving cars. It ticks all the boxes. No more dealing with actual humans and their unrealistic dreams of making ends meet. How dare they expect to be able to put food on the table, or sleep somewhere other than in their vehicles! Of course, Travis has no interest in doing business in the usual way.

The secret to his success is a chap by the name of Anthony Levandowski. According to court documents, Levandowski – a former engineer from Google's self-driving arm, Waymo – transfers thousands of files before leaving the company. He then founds a start-up called Otto, which is bought by Uber. In 2018, Uber and Waymo settle their legal dispute, but in 2020 Levandowski is sentenced to 18 months in prison for stealing trade secrets. He's later pardoned by President Donald Trump, in his dying days in office. You can't make this stuff up.

It's fair to say 'bro culture' continues to play a part in the series of disasters befalling the self-driving vehicle sector since these heady days. *Forbes* magazine calls the hype 'an epidemic of questionable assertions'. There are parallels with the overblown rhetoric about new technology before the AI winter of the late 1970s.

Ford, GM and Tesla are spending billions of dollars and decades in research and development, repeating the mantra that autonomous cars are 'just around the bend'. If that's the case, it's a bloody long bend. A 2022 estimate from consultancy Accenture, reported by *Forbes* magazine, says there's 'no realistic chance that full-on self-driving will be available before 2030'. The road is paved with broken promises, not to mention multiple fatalities.

In 2018, a prototype autonomous vehicle from Uber strikes and kills Elaine Herzberg while she walks her bicycle across an avenue in Arizona. The state's governor suspends Uber's ability to test its technology there; two years on, the company sells its self-driving unit to a start-up called Aurora. Over a period of ten months, Tesla accounts for 273 of nearly 400 crashes involving driver-assist systems, according to the US National Highway Traffic Safety Administration.

Yes, this represents a small percentage of accidents on the road. But surely it's an indication we should wait until the technology is close to foolproof before unleashing it on the general public. In the first trial over a fatal accident involving one of its vehicles, Tesla is held only one per cent responsible for the death of the teenager. The 18-year-old and his father are apparently 99 per cent to blame.

The hype surrounding the creation of the Segway in 1999 bears examination. To say it doesn't end well is the understatement of the year. Engineer and inventor, Dean Kamen, starts the company to produce two-wheeled, self-balancing personal transporters for niche markets. All the Segways sold until 2006 are recalled in order to fix a bug that 'could cause the units to reverse, potentially causing riders to fall off'. Countless people are injured while riding Segways, often admitted to hospital with traumatic wounds to the head and face.

Still, the sales pitch continues: Segway 'will be to the car what the car was to the horse and buggy'. It scooters along before being bought by entrepreneur Jimi Heselden in 2009. Ten months after buying the company, Heselden dies after accidentally driving a Segway off a cliff.

Phil Koopman, an engineering professor at Carnegie Mellon University, says there's no robust research showing that self-driving cars will be any safer than those controlled by accident-prone humans. 'There's nothing I've seen showing whether AVs (autonomous vehicles) will be safer than humans in the short to medium term,' he tells *The Washington Post*.

'Machine learning is brittle, and it struggles with things it hasn't seen before.' For example, there are unusual scenes the computer has never encountered – like a woman chasing a duck with a broom, which a Google car apparently encounters. How does a machine make sense of this? And, importantly, how does the car respond?

It makes me wonder where the industry would be with more women involved from its inception. Fatemeh Janatabadi and Alireza Ermagun are engineering researchers. Their 2021 meta-analysis of 91 peer-reviewed studies on self-driving vehicles is enlightening, to say the least: women and people in minority communities are regularly excluded from the research. People with disabilities and those in racial minorities are only included in 10 and 20 per cent of the studies, respectively.[1]

Much of the research is biased as a result of systematic errors like leading or missing questions, and suggestive information. And an overwhelming 72 per cent suffer from 'sentiment bias': the positive tone of the title and abstract overstate the result. The authors say these flaws lead to 'imprecise findings and unrealistic depictions of acceptance of autonomous vehicles by the public'. To quote the hip hop group Public Enemy: 'Don't believe the hype.'

This lack of diversity means existing bias in car design is being inserted into the transport of the future. The 2022 guidelines 'Autonomous Vehicles through Gender Perspective Glasses', written as part of the Diamond Project by Begoña Mateo from the Valencia Biomechanical Institute in Spain and co-authors, seeks to address this issue. They reiterate that cars are more dangerous for women because they're designed for men.

'The teams of engineers that design both normal and autonomous cars mostly consist of men,' they write. 'While men use the car for what is usually direct travel, like moving from home to workplace, women must make several stops to leave their children at school or day care centers, go shopping, travel to a medical appointment, etc.'

Remember the Swedish snowplough experiment? This highlights the same disparity in driver behaviour. Mateo wants autonomous vehicles to take into account female ergonomics. Things like pregnancy, for example, that directly affect the design of seats and seatbelts, and temperature tailored to the female body.

Research shows women tend to desire cars that allow them to undertake other tasks, like supervising child passengers. As in the home, women are forced to multitask. Men generally aren't interested in this. Oh, to have the privilege of doing only one thing at a time!

Another Spanish study, published by MDPI open access journals in 2022, finds women are more motivated by the promise of greater safety, reduced on-road errors and fewer 'driving demands' than men.[2] Despite men being more likely to have serious crashes, women are less confident in their ability to avoid accidents, so they see this as an advantage of autonomous vehicles: 'In this regard, a reasonably plausible explanation is the fact that, overall, males tend to believe they perform significantly better than others in different tasks including vehicle driving, as well as being more optimistic and perceiving themselves as less prone to get in a crash, particularly when judging their own driving skills.' That's a burn, right there.

Research consistently shows women and non-white people in general are around 1.5 times more likely to be concerned about safety than men and white people overall. In response to these concerns, US consumer organisations are running a campaign to slow the speed of technological advance. These organisations are asking that rather than understanding the public as 'consumers who need to be educated in order to accept the new technology', the car companies should 'develop a view of the public as citizens who are (or should be) engaged in the steering of technological directions and futures'. Yep. Don't act like dictators. And treat consumers like humans. It's really quite simple.

The three most prominent areas of public concern are safety, privacy and data security. Women are more concerned about privacy and data, presumably due to the danger of being tracked by an abusive ex-partner. This poses a conundrum. Women are exposed to sexual harassment, violence and assault in taxis and Ubers. There are thousands of instances each year, many of which are currently before the courts.

Self-driving cars could reduce this risk exponentially. But what happens if autonomous cars are used for ride-share? Governments need to develop appropriate regulations for autonomous vehicles, instead of allowing rampant self-regulation. And it has to happen *now*.

Perhaps the final arbiter will be insurance companies. If they can amortise a lower risk, they'll adjust premiums accordingly; if the risk is deemed too great, the industry will crash and burn. One piece of the puzzle could be using hybrid models in larger vehicles. An autonomous bus could be 'supervised' by a person running a complementary business, like selling water or food. This would be appropriate for school buses, with someone on board monitoring student behaviour. But it still doesn't solve the problem of assault in smaller ride-share vehicles.

Despite its many drawbacks, this technology is an exciting prospect for people with disabilities such as vision impairment. In 2021, a young Pakistani American woman by the name of Sahl Kazi makes a TikTok video about her wish for a self-driving car. Waymo invites her to its facility in Arizona for a test-drive. 'Kazi is candid in her enthusiasm for autonomous cars, as she sees them as an opportunity to eliminate a perceived weakness – namely, that her vision precludes her from driving,' according to Heather Aijian, public affairs manager at Waymo.

'Imagine autonomous driving being the thing that demolishes that feeling of weakness,' Kazi says, 'and instead prompts us to take ownership of the unique ways [we] adapt and advance the world.' Kazi appears at numerous internal Waymo meetings as a guest speaker, becoming a public ambassador for autonomous driving and the disability community.

But the current players still aren't taking full advantage of artificial intelligence. Industry leaders are 'solving very specific sub-problems within the massive software stack – or brain of the self-driving car', machine learning expert Raquel Urtasun tells *U of T News* in 2021. 'This... requires really complex, time-consuming manual tuning.' Her company, Waabi, instead uses 'deep learning, probabilistic inference and complex optimization' to create a new class of algorithms, the likes of which Urtasun says have never been seen before.[3] Enter the idea of robot trucks. And we're not talking about Bumblebee from *Transformers*.

Okay, let's take a step back. There are a lot of tech concepts in Urtasun's statements. I'll endeavour to translate. Waabi's vehicles learn from small amounts of data, instead of 'big data'. It's an elegant solution to a complex and time-consuming problem. The system is also 'interpretable and explainable', which is crucial for safety verification. Urtasun notes: 'women have to do "ten times more" than male counterparts to be recognized.' She learned this firsthand working in the early days of Uber. Now, her hard work is paying off: Waabi is unveiling its first self-driving truck after raising more than US$100 million in initial financing.

Unfortunately, no-one is able to solve the old ethical dilemma in the 'trolley problem' we saw in Chapter 17: should you switch the trolley onto a different track to save five lives at the expense of one?

People in Europe, Australia and the Americas tend to be more willing than those in Eastern countries to switch the track, to save more lives. In China, Japan and Korea, there are far fewer people likely to support this 'morally questionable' view. So what would an algorithm do? Who would be courageous enough to program something like this? And would programmers take into account how local ethics differ across the world?

When we think of smart cities of the future, we visualise robot cars careening down the streets willy-nilly. But in the near term, it'll be much more controlled. Currently, these vehicles are mainly used on closed testing tracks, university and hospital campuses, and big mine sites. The Google subsidiary Waymo is testing robotic driving systems in 25 cities across the US, but they definitely perform better in predictable environments.

Our first sight of fully self-driving vehicles will probably be in the form of smart delivery robots. Serve Robotics, in partnership with Uber Eats, is piloting next-generation bots in Los Angeles. The bots are capable of working entirely without human intervention, but a safety operator will be on board during the pilot. Before you know it, our footpaths will be full of them: annoying, oversized elephant beetles.

The 'last mile delivery' sector is booming, with US company Nuro launching third-generation vehicles with external airbags that deploy if they hit a pedestrian. Hopefully, this doesn't happen too often. Across the Pacific, autonomous robots from the Alibaba Group deliver millions of parcels across China. Dubbed Xiaomanlv – 'little donkeys' in Mandarin – these vehicles can carry 50 packages at a time and travel 100 kilometres on a single charge. The robots can navigate their way 99.9 per cent of the time without human intervention, aided by an algorithm that finds the most efficient routes.

The potential for this type of technology is enormous. During the nursing shortage at the height of the first global Omicron wave in 2021, delivery care robots in Texas are used to alleviate a shortage of nursing staff. This has the added benefit of reducing nurse burnout and high turnover rates. There's always a dark side though, to paraphrase Darth Vader. In future, we'll be dealing with more robots and fewer people: many warehouse, delivery and gig economy workers will lose their jobs. The price of convenience might be too high for society as a whole.

The question of climate change looms large in the self-driving industry. Marketing spin says these vehicles are good for the planet. One experiment proves the much-touted clean energy revolution is a mirage. Around a dozen people in California are given a chauffeur to take them anywhere they want for a week, replicating the experience of an autonomous vehicle.

Freed from the stress of driving, they end up travelling 83 per cent further than when they had to drive themselves. This is called the 'Jevons paradox'. When something becomes cheaper, people find new ways to use it. Self-driving cars reduce the cost and effort of driving, encouraging people to take trips they might not have taken previously.

Over time, people with self-driving cars could opt to move farther from the city, worsening urban sprawl. Whether powered by batteries, petrol or diesel, all cars produce particle pollution from tyre wear. Manufacturing electric vehicles and charging batteries require power and materials, expanding the total carbon footprint.

Corporate consulting giant PwC forecasts that by 2030, 40 per cent of the kilometres travelled by road will be in self-driving vehicles. Without some sort of restrictive policy like decongestion pricing, streets could become gridlocked. You can see it now: owners avoiding parking fees instructing their vehicles to circle the neighbourhood while they meet up with a friend.

By this stage, you're probably wondering: 'If there are so many arguments against self-driving cars, why is there a sense of urgency to produce them?' The answer might surprise you: this industry is being driven by the military. The US Department of Defense is behind the first Grand Challenge in 2004 for the autonomous vehicle, to speed up the technology in order to use it in war zones.[4]

'These challenges helped to create a mindset and research community that a decade later would render fleets of autonomous cars and other ground vehicles a near certainty for the first quarter of the twenty-first century,' according to the Defense Advanced Research Projects Agency website. Instead of safety, ease or convenience, the true motivator behind the advance of artificial intelligence is the military-industrial complex.

23
MILITARY INTELLIGENCE?

>'The US Army wants to turn tanks into
>AI-powered killing machines.'
>**Headline, *Quartz* news site**

In the history of humankind, there's no greater battle than between the military and the English language. Remember 'collateral damage'? 'Friendly fire'? 'Shock and awe'? Humourist P.J. O'Rourke is responsible for describing a staircase at a military headquarters as 'a foot impelled, bi-directional, vertical transport asset' in 2007. But these weasel words have nothing on the contretemps that flare when the US Army rolls out its ATLAS artificial intelligence system.

Stuart Russell, an AI scientist at Berkeley University who's campaigned for a ban on lethal autonomous weapons, is appalled. 'The LA in ATLAS stands for Lethality Automated,' he tells *Breaking Defense* magazine in 2019.[1] This sounds terrifying in anyone's language. No-one wants death to be automated. In reality, ATLAS AI is only a nascent project at the time. Which is why nobody bothers to inform the Pentagon, despite the Defense Department being the organisation that actually funds each branch of the US armed forces. Oops.

Instead, ATLAS creeps into public consciousness through an article on a trade website, before exploding onto the global stage under the headline 'KILLING MACHINES' on the news site *Quartz*. The army does itself a tremendous disservice by worsening the fear and loathing around the use of artificial intelligence in warfare. 'No sympathy for the devil,' to quote gonzo journalist Hunter S. Thompson.

The closest thing to citizen insight into this technology is TV and online footage of a parkour robot and Spot the Dog, created by artificial intelligence giant Boston Dynamics. Scratch the surface of the cute and cuddly spin to see the company's real money-spinner: war.

'Autonomous machines capable of deadly force are increasingly prevalent in modern warfare, despite numerous ethical concerns,' Professor Frank Pasquale writes in his 2020 book *New Laws of Robotics: Defending Human Expertise in the Age of AI*. He refers to a film called *Slaughterbots*, in which college students are killed by drones released into their classroom. It sounds like a schlocky work of science fiction.

But *Slaughterbots* is the work of the Future of Life Institute, an organisation researching existential threats to humanity. *The Terminator* is no longer only a film franchise: Korean engineers are responsible for building a robotic hand strong enough to crush a beef can, yet gentle enough to clutch an egg.

Yes, I'm burying the lede, as we say in the journalism business. The reason I'm writing this book is because artificial intelligence is one of the greatest threats to the continuation of the human race. It's right up there with climate change and bioweapons. And the pace of innovation is increasing exponentially during the pandemic. The US Air Force predicts that by 2040, SWAT teams will be sending mechanical insects equipped with video cameras inside buildings during hostage situations.

Guess who creates the top insect-shaped weapon? Boston Dynamics. 'The US–Mexico border will be monitored by a fleet of robotic birds,' the Air Force claims, 'which may stay aloft for days or weeks without recharging their batteries.' I don't know about you, but I'm getting Alfred Hitchcock flashbacks: 'Birds are not aggressive creatures, Miss. They bring beauty into the world. It is mankind, rather, who insists upon making it difficult for life to exist on this planet.'

MILITARY INTELLIGENCE?

Life-and-death decisions are being made by these machines rather than by humans. It begs the question: When selecting targets, will autonomous weapons distinguish between enemy soldiers and ten-year-olds with toy guns? This is especially difficult when it comes to combatants and civilians in guerrilla or insurgent warfare, which is proliferating across the globe. Ukraine, anyone? Moscow is allegedly deploying Kalashnikovs enabled by artificial intelligence, while Kyiv uses Turkish-made Bayraktar TB2 drones, which are semi-autonomous.

'The problem is not just that when AI systems err, they err in bulk,' the author of *The Novel of Human Rights*, James Dawes, writes. 'It is that when they err, their makers often don't know why they did and, therefore, how to correct them.'

A poet of the Enlightenment, Alexander Pope, once wrote: 'To err is human, to forgive divine.' However, I doubt there'll be much forgiveness when the robots begin killing our children.

Now, couple this with biased facial recognition technology. Data and machine learning models already favour white male faces and bodies. What happens when artificial intelligence becomes 'a rubric for attack and protection?' asks Assistant Professor Katherine Chandler from Georgetown University. 'Facial recognition systems could make men, regardless of their actual combatant or civilian status, hyper-visible as targets,' she writes in *Does Military AI Have Gender?*

On the other hand, badly trained algorithms mean women of colour could be misidentified. A group of individuals including women and children whose faces are partially obscured – say, in Afghanistan or Iraq – may not be identified at all. This has significant implications in search and rescue missions.

Katherine Chandler is calling for the armed forces to disclose how their technologies will interact with gender, race, age and ability. Ethical artificial intelligence expert Dr Catriona Wallace, who's based in Australia, takes this a step further. Dr Wallace is among a group of experts behind the SurvivAI website quoted in the introduction to this book: 'So if we've got bias in warfare, are the drones going to be hunting down the women and children and minorities? Are they going to be avoiding killing white males?' Dr Wallace is also concerned about weaponry being 'targeted at the lowest socio-economic people and favouring the elite'. The message is clear: bias can be deadly.

Then we have the legal quagmire. The Geneva Convention is the thin blue line separating war from massacre. In name, at least. But who's at fault when a robot commits a war crime? James Dawes predicts a future where anyone is able to use unlimited lethal force: 'It is a world where the sort of unavoidable algorithmic errors that plague even tech giants like Amazon and Google can now lead to the elimination of whole cities.' There are parallels with the nuclear arms race. The 1983 movie *War Games* highlights the inability of machines to distinguish between reality and fiction. This is troubling when we're talking about global thermonuclear warfare.

A clue about how this could end is found in Skynet, an artificial general super-intelligence system from the *Terminator* media franchise: 'Defense network computers. New ... powerful ... hooked into everything, trusted to run it all. They say it got smart, a new order of intelligence.' Eventually, Skynet achieves self-awareness and views 'all humans as a threat; not just the ones on the other side' and decides our fate 'in a microsecond: extermination'. Fun fact: the fabulous British actor Matt Smith plays the human version of Skynet. Sure, it's a movie. But the possibility of 'extermination' is terrifying. Put plainly, this will not end well.

Dr Emma Schleiger from CSIRO's Data61 says weaponised robots and privacy concerns are her top two issues with artificial intelligence. However, there are several benefits in bringing technology deeper into the defence space. 'What we hear are worst-case scenarios around *Terminator* and weaponised AI and robots ruling the world,' she tells me over Zoom. 'But when we look at some of the really good things they're doing in the defence space, around the loss of life and being able to reduce conflict, that's really interesting to me.'

Some argue humans also make mistakes during times of war. Like the time the US bombed a hospital in Afghanistan, killing 22 people. As it's happening, hospital workers frantically call their contacts in the US military, begging them to stop. They call it the 'fog of war': once again, wartime weasel words.

But autonomous weapons kill large numbers of people more quickly than human soldiers. Battlefields are complex and ever-changing environments. In the heat of the conflict, artificial intelligence might become overwhelmed. Even if the technology ends up working well, this is the thin edge of the wedge. The robots your government deploys on foreign enemies will one day be used on perceived domestic threats.

We're seeing this in China with the minority Uyghur population. The government hypes up the threat of 'Muslim terrorism' to detain many Uyghurs in 're-education camps' and intimidate others with phone inspections and criminal profiling. In the US, the San Francisco police department wants to be able to use robots with 'deadly force' while responding to incidents, according to a policy draft. These robots would be allowed to kill people 'when risk of loss of life to members of the public or officers is imminent and outweighs any other force option available'. Scary stuff indeed.

This reminds me of the infamous quote by Donald Rumsfeld in 2002 about the 'known knowns', the 'known unknowns', and the 'unknown unknowns'. Rumsfeld is answering a question about the evidence that Saddam Hussein tried to supply weapons of mass destruction to terrorist groups – if you can call it 'answering'. He fails dismally.

But the same could be said for this fraught area. Policymakers must anticipate things they know might go wrong (known knowns), things they can speculate might go wrong (known unknowns) but also things no-one has ever thought of (unknown unknowns). Crikey. I'm quoting Donald Rumsfeld. This is *not* on my 2023 Bingo Card.

One issue is whether combat that reduces human casualties will lead to more frequent and longer wars because politicians won't need to answer to the public for as many dead soldiers. 'Drones have enabled the US to maintain a presence in various occupied zones for far longer than an army would have persisted,' Frank Pasquale writes in *The Guardian* in 2020. 'The constant presence of a robotic watchman, capable of alerting soldiers to any threatening behaviour, is a form of oppression.'[2]

He's right, you know. Will the world end up in a perpetual surveillance state, where oppression is seen as a small price to pay for humanity's survival?

The United Nations recognises that women suffer disproportionately in war through sexual violence and being forced to flee their homes. They're also robbed of educational and work opportunities. Taliban, I'm looking at you. Conflicts and natural disasters 'exacerbate gender inequalities, particularly against women and girls', to quote the UN's Global Humanitarian Overview. Research shows the likelihood of peace is higher if more women are included in peacekeeping forces. However, this isn't happening, despite a Security Council resolution on the matter. Like a lot of aspects of the UN, it works on paper but not in practice.

There are parallels with the self-driving vehicle industry: the people making the decisions in the military, government and technology sectors are predominantly male. Once again, we see decisions about the lives of women and girls being dominated by men in power, because of structural discrimination. Rosa Brooks, a professor at Georgetown Law and former Pentagon official who worked in Defense at the White House under Barack Obama, investigates how this phenomenon affects countries dealing with conflict and threat.

In her 2017 book, *How Everything Became War and the Military Became Everything*, Brooks says US defence experts are slowly realising development, governance and aid are just as important as the projection of force. It makes sense: a world with more real resources has less reason to pursue zero-sum wars. But this is becoming a battle of ideas, one the hawks – those who favour war as the only solution – are winning.

Author and lecturer in human geography Ian G.R. Shaw puts it well, calling the US national security state the 'predator empire': 'Do we not see the ascent of control over compassion, security over support, capital over care, and war over welfare? Stopping that ascent should be the primary goal of contemporary artificial intelligence and robotics policy.' In an attempt at stability, the Pentagon is supporting peace concerts in Africa and anti-extremist materials in Iraq.

But apparently, this soft diplomacy infuriates those in the military, who resent peacekeeping efforts. 'You've got these *kids*, these 30-year-old captains who've spent their lives learning to drive tanks and shoot people, and they think they know how to end poverty in Afghanistan, in six months,' a staff member for the Agency for International Development tells Rosa Brooks, according to a 2016 *New York Times* review of her book.[3]

An obvious solution would be prioritising human life above machines. A missile could be programmed to move slower than optimum speed to collect more data on the target. It could avert or disengage if civilians are under threat. But – you guessed it – this would cost more money. And what do we know, above all else? Uber-capitalism wins the day.

Instead of retrospectively fitting ethics into killing machines (or humans) perhaps we should try to create a world without wars. Call me a Pollyanna. It wouldn't be the first time. The way forward is to improve diversity in military decision-making and peacekeeping. With the election of Joe Biden as US President in 2020, Rosa Brooks – in her role as co-founder of the Leadership Council for Women in National Security – advocates for a woman to become his Secretary of Defense. Biden instead chooses retired General Lloyd Austin.

Part of the problem lies in the pipeline: women in the US have only been allowed to serve in combat roles since 2015. This is one of the reasons there are so few females in senior military positions. Australia lifted the 'combat bar' in 2013.[4] Which is remarkable, given the attitude of the likes of former SAS Commander Brigadier Jim Wallace, who in 2011 explained to ABC Radio his objection to allowing women on the frontline. And it's a well-considered argument, indeed. 'I'm sitting here at breakfast, my wife just handed me a jar that she couldn't open and I opened it,' he tells the ABC. 'You know, I rest my case.'

It seems critical thinking is not a prerequisite for reaching the senior ranks of the Australian armed forces. Brigadier Jim Wallace continues to shove his foot further into his mouth. 'They've got to be able to carry specific weights . . . women are not designed to carry these weights. They've got a lot of other strengths. I'd hate to give birth to a child.' Apparently, we're all just breeders; characters in *The Handmaid's Tale*.

A similar attitude exists in the US. 'If it took decades for a sizeable pool of highly qualified women to emerge as potential senior Pentagon leaders, that's no accident,' Rosa Brooks writes in the *Times* in 2020.[5] These laws and policies aren't only unfair to women: they diminish the ability to develop smart, effective security policies. Organisations with gender-diverse teams outperform those under male-dominated leadership. Surely it would be wise to have more collaboration, less groupthink, and fewer acts of recklessness in military policy.

Brooks nails it towards the end of her searing piece: 'The United States faces national security problems ranging from the pandemic to climate change, refugee crises and the rise of near-peer competitors such as China. These complex and interconnected issues require fresh approaches, not a reversion to old modes of thinking about defense policy.'

However, one piece of old thinking turns out to be right. In 1961, Dwight Eisenhower, a Republican president and former general, warns against the rise of the 'Military-Industrial Complex'. His comments show how far the so-called Grand Old Party has since moved to the Right. This debate is now moving beyond political ideology. Autonomous weapon systems may have killed people earlier than the war in Ukraine, according to a United Nations Security Council report on the civil war in Libya. An incident in 2020 might have marked the beginning of a new arms race.

So what does the UN do in response? Well, at the next Convention on Certain Conventional Weapons, member states fail to reach consensus on a ban, due to opposition from several countries including the US and Russia. The next meeting? 2026. Apparently, there's no urgent need to try to save the human race.

'Much of global capitalism has invested a lot in the industrial-military complex, so the incentives to ban killer robots are actually limited for those who benefit the most,' AI futurist Michael Spencer writes. He warns the period leading up to 2040 will be 'one of the most dangerous in the history of humanity'. It makes sense: no-one is overseeing the robots being unleashed onto battlefields. Spencer doesn't mince his words. 'Men with their toys and the relentless pressure for greater profits could end us as a civilization.' Boom! A big boom that could kill us all.

Some of the arguments heard at these forums in support of autonomous weapons are spurious. It's claimed violence perpetrated by machines could be less lethal and more controlled. This relies on machines being trained to make 'rational' decisions. For the sake of amusement, let's break this down. Robots are being fed data by biased humans. They continue to learn in the same way as chatbot Tay did on Twitter. Suddenly, they're expected to become rational? Give me a break! Frankly, this argument sounds like one from the

1997 Australian film *The Castle*: 'It's the vibe of the thing, your Honour.'

Suffice it to say, there are practical difficulties in coding ethics into killer robots, not least of which is the 'trolley problem' mentioned in chapters 17 and 22. There are also concerns about how a machine calculates what is a 'proportional' response. It's not proportional for a machine to kill the human attacking it, because the robot can't die. In this David and Goliath battle, we're fighting with our hands tied behind our backs.

Ethics are being sacrificed as world powers endeavour to keep pace with one another. Microsoft and Amazon work closely with the Pentagon. What's their primary motive? Profit.

To find out about the kind of world we're leaving for the next generation, we need to follow the money.

24
WORKER BEES

'Radical for capitalism.'
Ayn Rand

The denizens of Silicon Valley are beholden to a cult. It's not Jonestown, although they're definitely drinking the Kool-Aid. The pervasive ideology is often attributed to writer Ayn Rand. She described Objectivism as 'the concept of man as a heroic being, with his own happiness as the moral purpose of his life, with productive achievement as his noblest activity, and reason as his only absolute'. Seems selfish, I reckon. Despite being classified as a conservative, Rand denounced libertarianism.

But this memo must've got lost on its way to the Valley, because Rand is still one of its most popular philosophers. Tech-heads embrace extreme libertarianism in their feverish race for wealth. 'Disruption of any kind is seen as good; government on the whole as bad,' Toby Walsh explains in his 2018 book, *2062: The World that AI Made*. Walsh, who's based in Sydney, is one of the world's leading researchers on artificial intelligence.

The pandemic destroys my dreams of travelling to Silicon Valley itself. Instead, I speak to Toby and others who are privy to the inner circle to get a sense of the culture of the place. (In case you're wondering, the translation software otter.ai gets his name right.)

'You know, white male people like me are the masters of those machines, and the machine does everything perfectly for you,' Toby tells me. 'I think for many years I was seduced by this idea that I knew I had this perfect, perfect world that I can manipulate.'

I can understand the lure of a world in which you have ultimate control over all you create. The otherworldly profit margins are merely a bonus. The only businesses with wider margins are illegal. So who's making all this money? Principally, it's men from wealthy parts of the US and Asia. *Forbes* magazine reports in 2022 that tech is the third-most lucrative industry for billionaires in the world.

At the time of writing, Elon Musk is the richest individual in the world with a net worth of US$196.5 billion. This is the guy who spends almost a million dollars on a 'submarine' car: 'It was amazing as a little kid in South Africa to watch James Bond in *The Spy Who Loved Me* drive his Lotus Esprit off a pier, press a button and have it transform into a submarine underwater,' Musk says in a statement to the car website Jalopnik. 'I was disappointed to learn that it can't actually transform.'

Seriously, a person with that much money could use it to address climate change or reduce global poverty. But the big baby wants a car he can drive underwater. Truly, I despair. And don't get me started on his 2022 acquisition of Twitter.

I dive into The Real-Time Billionaires List on the *Forbes* magazine website.[1] Wannabe astronaut and founder of Amazon Jeff Bezos is the second-richest person in the world with US$122.9 billion. Larry Ellison, of Oracle, rakes in a tidy US$114.3 billion. Bill Gates of Microsoft follows closely behind, worth US$106.7 billion. Computer scientist Larry Page of Alphabet – Google's parent company – is sitting at US$82.3 billion. Michael Dell of Dell Technologies languishes at US$52.4 billion. Ma Huateng, CEO of Tencent, is next, with US$39.6 billion derived from the instant messaging company. William Lei Ding from Netease has a net worth of US$27.8 billion. Shiv Nadar, the founder and chair of HCL Technologies, is worth US$25.6 billion. The only woman in the Top 15 is L'Oreal's Francoise Bettencourt

Meyers and her family with a combined net worth of US$82.9 billion. The first individual female tech billionaire on the list is Mackenzie Scott of Amazon, ranking 54th with a fortune valued at US$26.8 billion – tens of billions below her male contemporaries.

For context, Croesus is famed as the richest man in ancient Rome, worth an estimated US$13.7 billion in today's money. In 1913, J.D. Rockefeller topped out at US$24.7 billion, in 2021 dollars adjusted for inflation. So these tech dudes are really rocking some coin. Or, as Toby Walsh puts it, 'Most of them sit on huge cash mountains'.

It's clear inequality worsens during the pandemic: the ten richest people on earth double their wealth between March 2020 and November 2021. Everyone else *loses* money over the same period. This figure is from an Oxfam report aptly named 'Inequality Kills': 'A new billionaire was created every 26 hours since the beginning of the pandemic – with those in tech leading the way.'

The worldwide market for artificial intelligence, valued at US$68.8 billion in 2022, is projected to reach US$459.3 billion by 2030, according to the International Trade Authority's Global Artificial Intelligence Industry Report.[2] For maths-minded readers, that's a compound annual growth rate of 26.8 per cent. China is forecast to grow at around 31.1 per cent for the same period. These are very large numbers. My head's starting to spin. Let's examine what this means for people living outside Silicon Valley: i.e., the rest of us poor suckers.

Artificial intelligence may eliminate 85 million jobs and create 97 million new ones by 2025, if forecasts by the World Economic Forum are correct. This is good, right? Wrong. There's no evidence they'll be equivalent, well-paid or secure jobs. Which groups will miss out? Human Resources and middle management roles will become automated at some stage during the 2030s. This means most of us will be managed by an algorithm, without any recourse to complain to a human. Even if there is human oversight, this leaves us in an endless loop of filling out automated forms in order to continue working. We all know how frustrating this is.

Writing in the *Harvard Business Review*, futurist Mike Walsh imagines what lies ahead: 'There are a million ways that algorithms in the hands of bad managers could do more harm than good: How about using an algorithm to set your work rosters so that the number of hours is just below the legal threshold for full-time employment? Or automatically sending emails to people when they are more than five minutes late to work?' Walsh also details dystopian measures, like using sensors to make sure warehouse workers are moving quickly enough, and changing the office lighting so employees think the afternoon is actually the morning.

Workplace surveillance using artificial intelligence is increasing around the world. Amazon has patents to manufacture wristbands, designed to guide the movements of warehouse workers. Vibrations nudge them into working harder and faster, like hamsters on a perpetually spinning wheel. According to Mike Walsh, IBM is applying for a patent for devices that track workers' pupil dilation and facial expressions. Data on employees' sleep quality prompts the deployment of drones to deliver caffeinated liquid, so productivity isn't disturbed by coffee breaks. While I'd love a drone to deliver me a cuppa, this level of oversight is, frankly, terrifying. What's next? Catheters operated by artificial intelligence, so we don't leave the desk for a toilet break?

In 2019 the International Monetary Fund projects 11 per cent of jobs held by women are 'at risk of elimination as a result of AI and other digital technologies'.[3] Smaller subsequent studies suggest the risk of job transformation for women may be as high as 44–50 per cent. The three occupations with the largest projected declines in employment are cashiers, administrative assistants and executive secretaries, according to the Bureau of Labor Statistics in the US. Here's one example, provided by co-founder of the Women

Leading in AI Network, Ivana Bartoletti, writing in *The Guardian* in 2018: three out of four shop cashiers are female; 97 per cent are expected to lose their roles due to automation.

Overall, the biggest losers will be women, countries in the global south, and workers who do menial jobs – effectively human computers, doing what machines can't do. Yet.

'Computers' is the original term for people doing mathematical calculations in scientific fields including astronomy, meteorology and naval navigation. Women are 'allowed' to perform this work during World War I, while the fellas are away. But once money comes into the sector, women are pushed aside. We're only viewed as worthy of menial work.

The racist, misogynistic and colonial structures of the first Industrial Revolution are being scaled up in the fourth. Like the early weavers, coders and kilo-girls, the 'piecework' of women and migrant workers is hidden, their backbreaking labour unrecognised and poorly compensated. The overwhelming majority of them are gig workers, who are exposed to mental stress and vicarious trauma. It's being said we're witnessing the rise of a 'cyber-proletariat'.

People living in developing countries are structurally and systemically excluded from the top levels of the tech sector because of a lack of educational pathways. As a consequence, these workers will only be able to do unskilled jobs with no road to promotion, and little input in decision-making. For many of them, it's the only way out of poverty. Worsening this situation is the deep disparity between metropolitan and rural areas. In Peru, for example, one-third of women in the cities complete their higher education; in the regions, the percentage drops to just 6.2 per cent, according to the not-for-profit organisation Laboratoria.

In 2014, three rookie entrepreneurs try to start a web development agency in Lima. But they hit an unexpected hurdle. 'Technology builders were apparently a rare breed, and women in the tech space seemed to be on their way to extinction,' Mariana Costa Checa tells me. She's the co-founder of Laboratoria, which teaches women aged 18 to 28 to code before connecting them with quality jobs in the tech sector.

'We foster a community of alumnae where they support each other's growth as future leaders in the technology sector,' Costa Checa says. One success story is Denisse Peralta from the third cohort in Guadalajara, who works as a software engineer at AstraZeneca. Laboratoria has now expanded to Chile, Mexico, Brazil and Colombia, with more than 2000 female graduates.

But these examples are few and far between. Overwhelmingly, the tech sector is built on unpaid labour, which is often female. There's an old saying: if you're not paying for a product, you *are* the product. Every time you play a game online, post a photo on social media, or fill out a survey, you're supplying a valuable commodity to these companies. But do we get a pat on the back? A small sum in compensation? Or even a 'thank you'?

We're feeding this insatiable beast, creating millions of underpaid jobs. In her 2020 book *An Artificial Revolution: On Power Politics and AI*, Ivana Bartoletti writes about a new 'category' of work. People are being paid pennies to go through piles of our data, labelling it for use in algorithms. Dangerous 'asymmetries of power' underpin this digital ecosystem.

An allegory can be found in the tragic tale of Tian Yu. At the age of 17, she's hired as an Apple iPad assembly worker at Foxconn in Shenzhen. Thirty-seven days after taking the job, Yu tries to take her own life by jumping from the fourth floor of her factory dormitory. In the same year, 2010, 15 workers attempt suicide at the facility and 10 die. Yu survives but spends 12 days in a coma: she's now paralysed from the waist down.

At Foxconn, the employee handbook urges: 'Hurry towards your finest dream, pursue a magnificent life.' Yu tells interviewers about the working conditions: 12 hours a day, six days a week; toilet breaks restricted; no training whatsoever. However, if you make a mistake, you're loudly reprimanded.

Foxconn eventually pays Yu a one-off 'humanitarian payment' of A$32,000 to help her go home. 'It was as if they were buying and selling a thing,' her father says. In the same year Apple CEO, Tim Cook, is paid US$4 million. Foxconn tries to handle the crisis by requiring employees to sign a waiver absolving the company of responsibility if they kill themselves.

Following a backlash, they retract this document. Instead, the company decides to string nets under the dorm windows, according to an article in *The Guardian*. 'Workers of the world, unite!' indeed. I guess they ignore that bit of *The Communist Manifesto*. Marx would be rolling in his grave.

The culture fuelling the extraordinary rise of China's tech factories is known by the number 996. This means most employees work from 9 am to 9 pm six days a week, according to *Quartz* magazine. In 2019, Chinese tech workers launch the online project 996.ICU, to protest against their working hours and conditions. ICU is a reference to the intensive care unit they expect to end up in as a result of the long hours. The *Quartz* article reports 'souring public sentiment' toward Chinese tech companies, and some are changing their operating practices. However, while employees would clearly benefit from fewer hours, many depend on the overtime payments to survive.

There's another term used for the work done by Yu and her downtrodden colleagues: ghost work. This is reminiscent of the work done by women over the centuries, particularly the 'ghosts in the machine' in the early days of computing. In the 2013 movie *Snowpiercer*, a post-apocalyptic world is circumnavigated by a never-stopping train. The engine is powered by kidnapped child slaves in the 'poor' section, separated from the wealthy passengers. Humanity has a long history of hiding inconvenient truths. If this is the first time you're reading about such exploitation, it's not your fault. The human labour powering digital software is hidden deliberately.

In their 2019 book, *Ghost Work: How to Stop Silicon Valley from Building a New Global Underclass*, anthropologist Mary L. Gray and computer scientist Siddharth Suri write: 'From labeling data to transcribing audio to content moderation, ghost work happens when tech companies assign tasks to an unseen and unacknowledged workforce (that has few, if any, labor protections), rather than full-time workers.'

During every automation throughout history, from textiles to coding, 'finishing tasks' are done by hand. Computer automation requires 'algorithmic piecework', in which payment is set by the amount of work rather than the hours. Ghost work is thriving as tech companies outsource labour around the world to reduce costs. This is called the 'paradox of the automation's last mile' – the 'automation' is never fully automated.

Developers use on-demand labour platforms to hire casual workers, who are required to perform repetitive tasks. Many are women seeking flexible hours at home to combine with caring responsibilities. Others are immigrants, people with disabilities or low-skilled workers who can't afford to pay for courses, instead seeking out experience. Moderators are required to monitor pornographic, violent, racist, homophobic, transphobic and misogynistic content which creates an 'ecosystem of harm', in the words of Mary L. Gray and Siddharth Suri.

Of course, this work is rarely unionised or insured. Increasingly, shifts are also *assigned* by artificial intelligence: the robots become the masters. AI decides who gets a shift and who doesn't. Workers feel the need to be on-call 24/7 so they don't miss out. People around the world bid for job opportunities, driving down wages and conditions in a race to the bottom.

Tech companies alienate content moderators from one another, to prevent organising and whistleblowing. The industry is hostile to organised labour. Some of the worst conditions are found in machine learning, which is particularly data-hungry. 'Manually labelling each image, text, audio, etc., in large datasets is tedious and a labour-intensive process,' Meeta Ramnani writes in *Analytics India Magazine* in 2022. 'Hence, many companies choose not to handle data labelling and use specialised software.'[4]

But the pre-built solutions don't often meet the tech companies' needs. So they turn to labour-hire platforms to outsource this work. 'But companies fail to focus on the ethical considerations around the processes,' Ramnani writes. Yep. It's the salt mines again.

The market for data collection and labelling is likely to grow to US$8.2 billion by 2028, according to market research company Grand View Research. Consequently, more 'crowd workers' will be exploited. Around 94 per cent of them have work rejected or aren't paid for work already done. 'But the requesters retain full rights over the data they receive,' Ramnani says. The workers end up with nothing. This is wage theft, writ large.

Most countries don't have regulations around crowd work, and the minimum wage doesn't apply because they're independent contractors. This is exacerbated by geography. Overly developed countries are in the best positions to profit from artificial intelligence, while those in sub-Saharan Africa and Southeast Asia provide cheap labour. Appallingly, technology companies use the inclusion of underpaid workers to claim their workforce is diverse. This is called 'participation-washing': using a person of colour to lend an organisation moral legitimacy. What a disgraceful practice.

'While data labeling is not as physically intensive as traditional factory labor, workers report the pace and volume of their tasks as 'mentally exhausting' and 'monotonous' due to the strict requirements needed for labeling images, videos, and audio to client specifications,'

Chan and co-authors point out in their 2021 paper, 'The Limits of Global Inclusion in AI Development'.[5] Sure, they're not digging ditches. But this is tough work.

People who label data are detached from the rest of the machine learning workforce. They have scant idea about the purpose of their labour – only building 'parts' of a product – and rarely get the satisfaction of seeing it created. Nor do they share in the obscene profits. In a way, they're being treated like mere machines with no heart or soul. Think of Winston Smith in George Orwell's *1984*: working away at the Ministry of Truth in a never-ending cycle of 'corrections' with no ability to question the end result.

The philosophy underpinning this entire industry is white supremacy. The development of artificial intelligence has happened in the global north because of readily available capital, cashed-up research institutions and technical infrastructure. It's impossible to unpick this from the history of colonial exploitation of the global south, when European states plundered labour.

AI companies further exploit those from the global south when compiling their databases. People either aren't paid – or are paid a pittance – for agreeing to share information, images or videos. This data is interpreted by people unfamiliar with, and perhaps insensitive to, these cultures. The result? Racial stereotypes continue to be codified. It's a vicious cycle. This is an ugly problem at the intersection of radical capitalism, colonialism and the technological revolution.

At the very least, these companies should provide grassroots resources and education to Indigenous groups in developing countries, so they can participate fully in the sector. They should also offer compensation. 'As the development of artificial intelligence continues to progress across the world, the exclusion of those from communities most likely to bear the brunt of algorithmic inequity only stands to worsen,' Chan and co-authors contend.

WORKER BEES

Over the centuries, automation moves compensation from worker bees to business owners, who enjoy higher profits with lower-cost labour. Regardless of the relative wealth of one hemisphere over the other, there's one consistent factor that determines who rises to the top of the pile, and who remains at the bottom. It raises the same question we ask almost every time we see a panel discussion at a conference about technology: where are all the women?

25
CRACKING THE CODE

*'It's not really about asking for the raise but knowing
and having faith that the system will actually give
you the right raises as you go along.'*
Satya Nadella, former CEO of Microsoft

It's 2014 and Satya Nadella is flying high as head of Microsoft. During an event, he's asked what women should do if they feel uncomfortable about requesting a pay increase. Bear in mind the question comes during the Grace Hopper Conference, which celebrates women in computing. His answer about having faith in the system – which seems aimed at deterring women from daring to ask for a raise – sparks a global outcry.

'That's good karma. It will come back,' Nadella says. 'That's the kind of person that I want to trust.' So sit back, ladies, and wait for a billionaire to deign to reward you for your toil! Like the generations of women before you, crawling in and out of computers for a pittance.

As a middle-aged woman in employment since the age of 15, I can tell you this is not the way to get ahead in the workplace. Being the 'good girl' only ends in tears. 'Faith', 'karma' and 'trust' won't overcome entrenched bias and discrimination within hierarchical structures. It's called the patriarchy. To be fair, Satya Nadella later apologises, admitting he got it 'completely wrong'. But it makes you wonder: if a woman talks about unconscious bias in a forest, does anybody hear? Calling out this stuff all the time is exhausting.

The problem isn't a lack of qualifications: women in artificial intelligence generally have higher levels of formal education than men. The 'achievement gap' is even greater in the senior ranks. There's evidence of 'persistent structural inequality in the data science and AI fields, with the career trajectories of data and AI professionals differentiated by gender', postdoctoral research fellow Dr Erin Lorelie Young writes for the Heinrich Böll Foundation in Israel in 2021. 'Women are more likely than men to occupy a job associated with less status and pay in the data and AI talent pool, usually within analytics, data preparation and exploration, rather than the more prestigious jobs in engineering and machine learning.'

In a 2020 report, the World Economic Forum estimates women make up roughly a quarter of the workforce in artificial intelligence.[1] Other studies reveal only 10 to 15 per cent of machine learning researchers in the main technology companies are female. While the percentage of women in the US labour force is almost half, it's notably lower in the tech sector: female employees make up between 29 and 45 per cent of employees at the largest companies. Looking at actual technical jobs, the figure drops to one in four. This matters because tech roles are the highest paid, with an added bonus: there's a clear path to management.

Google's glossy Diversity Annual Report 2022 contains inspiring images of 'Black+ and Latinx+' employees. The headline boasts: 'Our best year yet for hiring women globally.' But the increases are incremental, within the margin for error. Currently, only around 9 per cent of Google workers are Black, with a similar percentage Latinx. Let's interrogate this for a moment.

Despite being aware of the systemic bias existing within software, such as the COMPAS program profiling and incarcerating innocent Black people since 2016, tech firms are *still* failing to seriously address the issue of bias within their own organisations. Frankly, this is negligent to the point of being criminal.

'We know we have a long road ahead', the Google report says. That's the understatement of the century. Men outnumber women almost two to one in Google workplaces across the globe.

Maybe I'm being snarky. After all, in one year alone this company invests US$50 million in historically Black colleges and universities. In another year, it ploughs US$55 million into economic empowerment programs for women and girls around the world. But this smells like spin.

You only have to look at the balance sheet to see the true story: Google records a net worth of US$1853 billion in 2022. Yep – *billion*. Diversity initiatives are barely a drop in this vast ocean. Disappointingly, it takes until 2019 for this supposedly progressive organisation to include 'LGBTQI+, people with disabilities, military and veterans, and non-binary Googlers' in the Diversity Annual Report.

Where do we sit in Australia? 'Aboriginal people have been consciously and preconsciously told they can't do science, that science isn't for them, and predominantly women have as well, and all minorities,' Corey Tutt, founder of DeadlyScience, tells me during our Zoom interview. 'And the thing for us is that we need to decolonise the lab coat. It's silly to think middle-aged white fellas are the only people that can wear lab coats. Lab coats can be worn by anyone.' DeadlyScience provides early reading materials to remote schools to try to redress this imbalance.

'If the only books we're sending are of Albert Einstein and Thomas Edison, and not a great woman in science, or great Black people in science, or people of colour, then where do they fit in the picture?' Tutt asks.

This reminds me of the tremendous breakthrough the late actor Nichelle Nichols made by appearing as the first Black woman in a lead role on TV in the series *Star Trek*.

'In Romania nobody told me I wasn't meant to be a scientist,' Doina Precup from Google DeepMind tells the 2021 Canadian Celebration of Women in Science. 'My grandmother was a mathematician and my mother was a computer scientist. I didn't know I shouldn't do computer science until I came to the US.'[2]

Our Chief Scientist, Dr Cathy Foley, makes a salient point about the subjects women choose to study in Australia, during her 2021 Helen Williams Oration. 'The latest STEM Equity Monitor shows that more than a third of men in tertiary education are studying STEM qualifications; areas related to maths, or the sciences or engineering – excluding health,' Dr Foley says. Women are overwhelmingly represented in the caring streams, studying health, veterinary and environmental science.

Overall, women comprise almost 30 per cent of employment in technology in Australia. Based on current trends, it'll take 66 years for technology occupations to reach a level of female participation close to parity, according to Deloitte Access Economics' report, 'Australia's Digital Pulse 2021'. This is a national disgrace.

Modelling for the report finds increasing diversity '. . . would grow Australia's economy by $1.8 billion each year on average, over the next 20 years. This amounts to an $11 billion opportunity for Australia's economy in net present value (NPV) terms. In employment terms, it could create almost 5000 full-time equivalent (FTE) jobs on average each year.' Reports like this tend to motivate government ministers, who love having money waved in their faces. It aligns with the mantra of 'jobs and growth'. In 2021, the response from the Morrison federal government is to lower university fees for STEM subjects and offer grants to entice women into the sector.

But an investigation by the *Australian Financial Review* uncovers many deterrents, including job insecurity, sexism, low workplace morale, fatigue, the gaping gender pay gap, dissatisfaction with remuneration rates, and deprofessionalisation within the industry. It seems the tech sector has a similar culture to the media in the 1980s and 90s.

In my memoir, *The Good Girl Stripped Bare*, I write about the exodus of women from TV, radio and newspaper jobs because of the relentless sexism and discrimination.

In 2022, the federal Minister for Industry and Science Ed Husic announces a review to improve the pathways for women and girls. 'Women remain chronically underrepresented in STEM, making up only 16% of people with STEM qualifications,' the minister says. 'Of First Nations people, only half a per cent hold university-level STEM qualifications.' Change can't come soon enough.

Around 90 per cent of coding and engineering in artificial intelligence is *still* done by men. Remember how much of the coding in the 1940s–60s was done by women? Well, it appears we're going backwards. This nugget of information comes from the founder of Flamingo AI – and the brains behind SurvivAI – Dr Catriona Wallace. She tells me about her path to a career in technology, after working as a police officer in Kings Cross.

'I developed an interest in Organisational Behaviour,' she says. 'My thesis was on the role technology plays in substituting for human leadership.' In the AI sector, she soon becomes aware of unconscionable behaviour: 'Because we were dealing with large Fortune 100 financial services companies, we started analysing some of the data that they were using to train algorithms. And we started to see that the data was all historical data. And it wasn't transformed. It wasn't cleaned. It wasn't analysed in order to see whether there were skews or biases in there.'

The responsibility comes back to the companies selling these large datasets. Dr Wallace shares an example from schools in the UK. 'During COVID, the equivalent of Year 12 students couldn't be sitting their exams in the normal way, so they used an algorithm to determine the grades that the students would get,' she says. 'Traditional historical data was used to train the algorithms, and they gave grades to students which were all way off. Again, those students from lower socio-economic groups had much poorer grades than what they expected, and those from higher socio-economic groups had much higher grades. And it was a big outcry, the whole thing got shut down.'

Another example involves teachers rather than students. Over a period of four years, teachers in Houston are evaluated by a data-driven algorithm called the Educational Value-Added Assessment System. This decides which teachers get bonuses, are sanctioned for poor scores or are actually fired. 'Obviously, something like that is going to really affect low socio-economic groups,' Dr Emma Schleiger from CSIRO's Data61 tells me. 'Schoolteachers with classrooms of students that don't have all of those opportunities at other schools could do poorly on a standardised test. But that doesn't mean the teacher is doing poorly.'

If you think this is unfair, it gets worse: there's no recourse. Teachers are unable to challenge the decisions or ask for an explanation. The algorithm's codes are trade secrets owned by a third party. Following a lengthy lawsuit, a federal judge rules this denies teachers their constitutional rights. We'll see more of these cases as workers and unions take action over the use of impenetrable artificial intelligence.

Regardless of these systemic failures, Dr Wallace says artificial intelligence will continue to flourish because it's cost-effective. This means bias will become further entrenched. From there, it becomes a chain of events: fewer than 2.8 per cent of all venture capital goes into women-led businesses. 'And so even a very small fraction of the fraction would go to women-led AI businesses,' according to Dr Wallace.

How we're going to improve this situation remains a challenge. 'A riddle, wrapped in a mystery, inside an enigma,' to quote Winston Churchill. Repeated analyses of the pipeline show blockages from start to finish, like a backed-up portaloo at a barbecue meat festival.

It begins with children from wealthier families attending fancy-pants private schools. 'There's this term that I think was coined a few years ago about how Silicon Valley tech companies are not meritocracies, but "mirrortocracies", so you're hiring people who have similar credentials to you, had the same sort of schooling,' Dr Joy Lisi Rankin from the AI Now Institute tells *Yahoo!Finance* in 2021. 'But that doesn't necessarily mean they're more qualified.' In Australia, we call it the 'old school tie'.[3]

When women are employed in technology organisations, structural inequity leads to high turnover and attrition rates. Even after #MeToo, around one in two women are sexually harassed, based on figures from the not-for-profit organisation Women Who Tech. A startling 44 per cent of these are founders. It's no wonder women and people from marginalised communities leave to pursue other careers.

'I have certainly been the only woman on my team before, and the scrutiny of how that feels, and the microaggressions really grate on you, where you find your colleague is making substantially more than you,' the founder of Women in Voice, Dr Joan Palmiter Bajorek, says via Zoom. 'It's the near constant barrage of frustration, and potentially feeling alone.' She evokes the Beatles to explain how this eats away at women in the industry: 'I've actually thought about this climate like the "Eleanor Rigby" effect, or something. It's like all the lonely people.'

Australia's Chief Scientist, Dr Cathy Foley, expands on this theme in the Helen Williams Oration. 'I remember trying to fit in when I studied physics at university, and just be one of the boys in what was a pretty male-dominated environment,' Dr Foley says. After wearing a dress on her first day at CSIRO as the only female research scientist, she quickly reverts to trousers to be part of the team. Dr Foley's formula for removing 'blockages from the pipeline' includes encouraging girls into STEM subjects, improving the visibility of science careers and raising the profile of female role models.

There's a suite of wonderful programs around the world including Girls Who Code, AI4All, Girls in AI, Black Girls Code, Young Women Leaders in Artificial Intelligence and Girl Geek Academy.

These certainly give women a leg-up. But the trick is to *keep* them in the sector by supporting their progression through to leadership. Many early- and mid-career researchers leave because of the lack of flexible and part-time work, and plateauing due to non-linear career paths. These qualified, experienced and highly intelligent women often choose more family-friendly roles. It's devastating to witness this brain drain. Whatever happened to Australia being the 'clever country'?

One of the leading national research centres – the Walter and Eliza Hall Institute – is proactive on equity. It boasts comprehensive measures to support promotions and career breaks, including a childcare centre adjacent to its laboratories.

Gemaker is another example of a progressive company. Since 2011, every staff member has been able to work remotely and flexibly at the technology commercialisation firm. Gemaker has also provided career pathways for many of the female researchers axed from universities during the years of the Morrison government.

On a broader scale, Australia's STEM Returners program mentors skilled women back into the workforce. At the time of writing, women are heading the Australian Research Council, the National Health and Medical Research Council and Science & Technology Australia, and both the CSIRO Chief Scientist and the Defence Chief Scientist are female.

One of the many light-bulb moments in Dr Foley's speech is a lesser-discussed form of discrimination, against women aged beyond their mid-forties. We tend to become invisible. Or in my case, the late thirties, when I'm deemed to be 'too long in the tooth' for television. To quote the boss, 'Maybe you should consider radio?' I must have a 'good head for it', to quote an old joke.

I'm reminded of comedian Amy Schumer's Last Fuckable Day sketch, starring Tina Fey, Julia Louis-Dreyfus and Patricia Arquette. Schumer stumbles upon these doyennes of film and TV enjoying a picnic. They're commiserating about reaching an age at which women are no longer cast in bankable Hollywood roles. This hilarious clip targets the entertainment industry for its blatant disregard for older women, but it also acts as a metaphor for other industries.

Women in this age group could become powerful leaders in STEM, a 'valuable pool' to draw from during the current skills shortage. Dr Foley distils the major issue as menopause: 'Half the population goes through menopause. And it's not a moment in time – it's a process that takes some years. But there is surprisingly little research relating to the impact of menopause on women's careers in Australia.' A British parliamentary inquiry notes more than a million women in the UK leave employment because of the symptoms. Many are in the process of launching employment discrimination cases.

Speaking of 'the change', it's a-comin'. Although women make up only 20 per cent of Silicon Valley's workforce, they're shaping the future. Stanford professor and artificial intelligence entrepreneur Daphne Koller tells *Vogue* magazine in 2019: 'A lot of people think that technical fields and especially computing are this kind of geeky thing where people go off and do these obscure mathematical formulas that have no relevance to anything . . . [but] you can help fishermen in South Africa figure out where to sell their fish or use computing as we're doing to discover new drugs. There are just so many ways now to have a tremendous impact on society.'

During a panel discussion I facilitate for International Women's Day 2022, doctoral researcher Manika Saha from Monash University speaks eloquently about the intersection with climate change, known as the 'eco-gender gap'. For example, underpaid women farmers in Bangladesh suffer an added penalty, because every natural disaster worsens the incidence of domestic violence and sexual assault.

'A rich body of literature shows Information and Communication Technologies can contribute to improving women's condition in developing countries,' Saha and co-authors write in their 2020 paper 'Building Sustainable Digital Communities: A Five-Pronged

Social-Informatics Research Approach in Bangladesh'. In a project with Oxfam, her team is working with women in this region to design sustainable mobile apps based on their community's values. If this isn't a virtuous circle, I don't know what is.

Artificial intelligence has the potential to change the lives of women in agriculture. But there remains a digital literacy gap. This is the subject of a 2022 UNESCO (and partners) report entitled 'The Effects of AI on the Working Lives of Women'.[4] The gap is clearly evident among 'older, less educated and poorer women, and those in rural areas'.

The report reveals women could benefit from agricultural AI but 'those in a better financial position i.e. mainly men, are best placed to adopt the technology, implying that AI adoption will worsen existing gender inequalities'.

How do we fix this? The UN is calling for equality to be built into both the AI workforce and the design of the technology.

Positive moves are afoot. At the 2021 Generation Equality Forum, world leaders, philanthropists and the private sector pledge US$40 billion towards upending structural inequity. Dr Joan Palmiter Bajorek's global organisation Women in Voice is growing exponentially. At the time of writing, there are 20 chapters in 14 countries with more than 100 ambassadors. 'I meet young Latinas, who see Latinas on stage and they're like, "Oh, I could join this field. I could belong here, this seems of interest",' she tells me.

Let's look at the multitude of ways we can work together to create lasting change – before it's too late.

26
EMBRACING EQUITY

'If we don't get women and people of color at the table – real technologists doing the real work – we will bias systems. Trying to reverse that a decade or two from now will be so much more difficult, if not close to impossible.'
Fei-Fei Li, co-director, Stanford Institute for Human-Centered Artificial Intelligence; co-founder, AI4ALL

Born in China, Fei-Fei Li and her family move to the US when she's 16. While studying physics at Princeton, Li works every weekend in her parents' dry cleaning store. For a long time, she's the only woman in her faculty – a 'lonely process' she tells the CNBC website in 2019, echoing Dr Bajorek's line about Eleanor Rigby.

In 2015, Li launches a summer outreach program for Stanford's Artificial Intelligence Laboratory. This evolves into AI4ALL, a free online program for high school students. 'Women, underrepresented, racial minority, low income family students and geographically diverse students. And we're seeing this message spreading. We're seeing their leadership spreading. And I think they're going to become a powerful force in AI's future,' she says.

Programs like this are popping up everywhere, from the global group Women in AI to Australia's Young Women Leaders in AI, TechDiversity, Queensland's Women in Technology (WiT) – which was established back in 1997 – and the Yielding Accomplished African

Women organisation. The latter is responsible for the largest digital academy for African women in STEM.

Based in Sydney, Dr Nicky Ringland describes herself as a recovering computer linguist. This Superstar of STEM is the brains behind the Girls' Programming Network in Australia. Tens of thousands of students and teachers benefit from her programs.

Activists, advocates and scientists are generating opportunities for greater diversity and inclusion in the tech sector. By golly, we need it. A report by Deloitte Access Economics in late 2022 reveals a retrograde nation: almost one in three Australian men think gender inequality doesn't exist. This is second only to Saudi Arabia.

Education and training, role modelling and mentoring, and leadership programs are terrific, but they only go so far. They don't address historical data, which is poisoning machine learning. When this happens, we 'breathe our own exhaust', in the words of Loren Goodman, Chief Technology Officer at InRule Technology.

Goodman suggests a human solution to this man-made problem: 'Put people at the helm of deciding when to take or not take real-world actions based on a machine learning prediction,' he writes on the website VentureBeat in 2022. 'Explainability and transparency are critical for allowing people to understand AI and why technology makes certain decisions and predictions.'[1]

Oversight is crucial. But people are fallible. Also, on occasion, venal. So should we also hold a big stick?

'Quality marks need to be introduced to showcase that an algorithm has undergone due process,' Ivana Bartoletti, Global Chief Privacy Officer at Indian technology company Wipro, tells me during our Zoom interview. 'Risky algorithms need a licensing mechanism. In the case of breaches, stark fines should be issued, as well as redress mechanisms.'

Antitrust reform in the US would go a long way towards fixing this, by breaking up the cabal that is Big Tech. This is legislation that prevents or controls trusts or other monopolies.

Other researchers are looking at the root of the problem. How can we create more diverse datasets to erase the mistakes of the past? Artificial intelligence services could be rated for 'most accurate' or 'freshest dataset'. This would improve the transparency of the tech companies' processes. Of course, ratings would have to be decided by unbiased experts, rather than crowdsourced.

In medtech, more diverse populations could be enrolled in clinical trials. This has the benefit of opening up the trials to people from marginalised communities. Their data is added to the body of research used by the machines. Another virtuous loop!

However, these are long-term salves to festering wounds. Legal action seems to be a faster pathway. Many companies and software sellers are worried about being sued, because their automated systems discriminate against 'protected classes of individuals' under employment law. This is fuelling an industry of consultants who recommend tools to eliminate bias.

Organisations need to use more diverse datasets. And they need to test rigorously to ensure historical bias isn't replicated by artificial intelligence. But this isn't as easy as it seems.

Let's look at research into AI bias in a system classifying brain activity from MRI scans. This is front of mind for me – literally and figuratively – after undergoing several scans during long COVID. Incidentally, one uncovers an aneurysm. The neurologist breaks the news by saying, 'Oh, you have an incidental aneurysm', then starts talking about something else. Quite the bedside manner!

My doctors are uncertain about whether the inflammation from COVID-19 contributed to the creation or growth of this aneurysm because the pandemic is relatively new. And – you guessed it – aneurysms in this position are predominantly experienced by women, particularly those who are postmenopausal. Researchers haven't spent enough time studying why older women are predisposed to this condition.

In a similar way, there isn't much historical data from Black populations, so artificial intelligence performs poorly on this cohort. In 2022, researchers decide to do an experiment, curating a dataset containing *only* images from Black people and comparing the results with a dataset dominated by white people. The results are astonishing: the AI system is *still* less accurate for Black patients than it is when using a majority white dataset. The question is why. The answer is, we don't know. But it could lie in the past. Our understanding of how blood flows through the brain may be racially biased.

Jingwei Li, who co-authors the paper 'Cross-ethnicity/race generalization failure of behavioral prediction from resting-state functional connectivity', explains it like this: '. . . during preprocessing, a convention is to align individuals' brains to a standard brain template so that individual brains can be comparable. But these brain templates were usually created from the White population.'[2] Li stresses the research *doesn't* confirm there are neurobiological or psychometric measures that differ in populations due to their ethnicities. The history of eugenics casts a long shadow.

The question remains: do we need legislation, regulation or more consternation? There's no one-size-fits-all solution. In 2022, New York City Council passes a bill about artificial intelligence in employment. This requires managers to engage an independent auditor to evaluate their algorithms. If in breach, companies face fines of up to – wait for it – US$1500. Talk about being slapped with a wet lettuce leaf.

Groups like the Centre for Democracy and Technology are further concerned about the design of audits 'based solely on race and gender, and not other variables like disability, age and other factors'. Deb Raji from the Algorithmic Justice League reckons there should be an external audit oversight board and a national reporting system to flag potential violations. Otherwise, in-house audits would be prone to bias, with a low likelihood of anyone belling the cat. We know how well self-regulation works – cue eye-rolling emoji. *Quis custodiet ipsos custodes*, to quote the Roman poet, Juvenal. Who's watching the watchers?

Perhaps answers exist within other industries. Writing for the website Swiss Cognitive, ethics researcher Lorenzo Belenguer calls for 'a transnational independent body with enough power to guarantee the implementation of [AI bias] solutions'. In particular, Belenguer is looking to the pharmaceutical industry.

Any new drug goes through four stages in order to be released onto the market. Once it's on sale, regulators do follow-ups. Before being introduced into another country, the drug is assessed by an independent body, such as the Therapeutic Goods Administration in Australia. If any harm is caused, there's a scheme for compensation. Other academics argue artificial intelligence companies should be regulated like architects, who learn to work with city planners, certification schemes and licences to make buildings safe.

I love the idea of a 'dignity lens' being put on artificial intelligence. What does this mean? Well, it comes from a collaboration between the Australian National University and the Centre for Public Impact. In 2022, Lorenn Ruster, a PhD candidate in the School of Cybernetics at ANU, examines the extent to which dignity is a driving force behind AI ethics in the governments of Australia, Canada and the UK. She discovers the ecosystem is 'off-balance' because governments take action to protect citizens reactively rather than proactively. In other words, the horse has bolted; the damage is already done. Governments tend to act at a glacial pace: asbestos, anyone?

Manisha Amin, CEO at the Centre for Inclusive Design, points to a fundamental misunderstanding in the way we think about artificial intelligence. According to Amin, we tend to assume that rational decisions, like those made by Spock on *Star Trek*, are the gold standard. '. . . as such,' she tells me by email, '[we] will veer on the side of an AI decision rather than our own.' Amin cites examples in the US in which judges with AI support are more likely to change their verdicts if the technology's results differ from their own.

'It's true,' says Amin, 'we aren't like Spock but more rounded and emotional – like Captain Kirk – and that's a good thing.' Humans often make decisions by weighing up the social implications. AI simply doesn't have our 'evolutionary advantage'. Australia is fortunate to have great thinkers like Manisha Amin, and the scientists at CSIRO.

CSIRO's Data61 made an early attempt at grappling with this issue in its 2019 discussion paper 'Artificial Intelligence: Australia's Ethics Framework', insisting that: 'AI systems must also be contestable, and the people and organisations behind algorithms must be held accountable for their impacts.' But by the time it gets to government, the paper is replete with weasel words. Under the AI Action Plan developed by the Department of Industry, the ethics framework is entirely voluntary. Someone should send the department a dictionary so staffers can learn the definition of 'action'.

Anyone who understands human behaviour knows we're motivated by sticks as well as carrots. Personally, I prefer dark chocolate. But seriously, intimidation works every time. Regulators need to turn up the threat level to 11, to quote the rockumentary *This is Spinal Tap*.

Unsurprisingly, some of the best solutions are contained in a 2021 report written by my mate Ed Santow, the former Human Rights Commissioner.[3] It's an opus: a three-year report into the 'unprecedented opportunities and threats' posed by artificial intelligence. This is the most extensive consultation on artificial intelligence and human rights conducted anywhere in the world.

'We then need to make sure we put in place the protections that ensure we don't have a dystopian reality that we wake up to,' Santow says. Damn right.

He's concerned the gains we've made around equality in recent decades will go backwards. With ropey connectivity on Zoom due to his children schooling from home, Santow traverses the international landscape.

While China is pursuing artificial intelligence untethered from liberal democratic values and America is letting the market decide, Australia has the opportunity to forge its own road.

'Responsible innovation is precisely what citizens of countries like Australia, Canada, France and so on want,' Santow says. 'There's a competitive edge there. And so I think that it's not just the right thing to do. It's a smart thing to do.'

There are parallels in renewable energy. Progressive solar, wind and hydro companies are at the forefront of responsible innovation: good for the planet and the bottom line.

Multinationals often use Australia as a testbed, particularly for new technology. This represents another opportunity. The tech giants could pilot innovations here, following a proper human rights assessment. Ed Santow refers to the concept of a regulatory sandbox. This means companies creating devices must reach a certain threshold of safety before they're tested in the real world. Use of the devices would be monitored closely by authorities to ensure people are protected. If not, the rules are tweaked. 'It provides a bridge from the lab to the real world,' he says.

Santow's report calls for Australia to establish the world's first AI Safety Commissioner. But the role wouldn't be that of a regulator. The commissioner would lead an organisation providing advice to the government and the private sector about inserting fairness and accountability into artificial intelligence. Santow says he's 'optimistic' the federal government will take action on the report but is urging haste.

'My hope is that it doesn't take the next kind of catastrophic failure in AI for the government to really prioritise this,' Santow says. 'I hope, rather, that Australians will be very clear with the government that this should be prioritised.'

How many people will be wounded – or killed – before proper protections are put in place?

What I'm learning is there are plenty of well-intentioned statements on this topic, and very little real-world action. Australia is one of 42 countries committed to developing standards for AI based on principles developed by the OECD. For example, artificial intelligence should benefit 'people and the planet by driving inclusive growth, sustainable development, and wellbeing'; and 'respect the rule of law, human rights, democratic values and diversity'.

There should be transparency and responsible disclosure around AI systems, which must function in a 'robust, secure and safe way', and 'organisations and individuals developing, deploying or operating AI systems should be held accountable for their proper functioning in line with the above principles'. Well, who wouldn't want that?

The World Economic Forum is strengthening the governance of artificial intelligence through its aptly named Centre for the Fourth Industrial Revolution. This includes high-level guidance, workbooks and frameworks to assist in decision-making, in collaboration with national governments.

Meanwhile, the European Union is explicitly highlighting the ethical development of artificial intelligence as a source of competitive advantage. Maybe waving cash at parliamentarians and business leaders will work after all? If appealing to our leaders' basic humanity fails, we can always rely upon bribery. Gotta have carrots as well as sticks, remember.

The EU Parliament is currently debating a wide-ranging AI Act that would categorise technologies depending on the risks they pose to social wellbeing, with stringent obligations on those that could substantially disrupt society. About time! Germany is tapping the brakes on automated vehicles, rolling out ethical guidance on their development. And back home, the Office of the Australian Information Commissioner is investigating Kmart and Bunnings over the use of facial recognition technology in their stores.

Frankly, the stakes couldn't be higher. Our lives hang in the balance.

27

THE EXISTENTIAL THREAT

> 'If AI has a goal and humanity just happens to be in the way, it will destroy humanity as a matter of course without even thinking about it . . . It's just like, if we're building a road and an anthill just happens to be in the way, we don't hate ants, we're just building a road.'
> **Elon Musk**

Terrorism, pandemics, seatbelts, cigarettes and mesothelioma have one thing in common. And it's not the letter 'e'. Nor 's'. But thanks for playing, fellow Scrabble nerds. We don't think too deeply about these subjects until calamities occur on a global scale, like September 11 or COVID-19. Or until we lose a loved one to a car accident or cancer.

Humans are reluctant to act with haste, even when presented with compelling evidence. Research warning of the dangers of driving, smoking and asbestos was published many decades before it was taken seriously. The question now is: will we act to restrict rampant artificial intelligence before it imperils us all?

In mid-2022, US Republican senator Rob Portman and Democrat Gary Peters introduce the *Global Catastrophic Risk Management Act*. A bipartisan bill is quite a feat in these polarised times. The name says it all: the risk of malfunctioning AI is on par with novel diseases, biotechnology accidents, super volcanoes and solar flares. There's a far higher risk of artificial intelligence destroying humanity by the end of the century than climate change or nuclear war.

Elon Musk has claimed that artificial intelligence is our 'biggest existential threat': 'Mark my words, AI is far more dangerous than nukes . . . why do we have no regulatory oversight?'

These are strong words for someone who expresses a libertarian philosophy. But no-one is ready for this technology to go rogue.

The usual 'risk versus reward' levers aren't working. We're viewing this issue through a microscope instead of a fisheye lens. Perhaps it's time to rethink how entire organisations are structured. During one of the COVID-19 lockdowns, I do a company director's course. I'm a devotee of lifelong learning. And I've run out of Nordic Noir to watch on Netflix.

Fun fact: a company is its own entity with rights – just like a person. As a director, your foremost obligation is to the survival of this entity. Therefore, the profit motive is enshrined in legislation above all else: ethics, morals or humanity. If you ignore this, it's a breach of the law. By definition, this system values the almighty dollar above human life.

At an individual company level, there should be shorter terms for directors and increased diversity on boards to eliminate dangerous 'group think'. Back in 2013, all seven Twitter board members were male. This partly explains the culture of toxic masculinity on the platform. At the time of writing, three of the nine directors are female. In 2022, Meta's board is 40 per cent female.

Google has an external advisory council on artificial intelligence while Meta has co-founded an AI ethics research centre. Does this mean they're finally taking ethics seriously? Probably not. Experts say these bodies have little or no impact.

Could our great thinkers get us out of this mess? Universities are bastions of progressive thought. Stanford University has an Institute for Human-Centered Artificial Intelligence with this mission:

'The creators and designers of AI must be broadly representative of humanity.' However, the majority of the 121 faculty members are white and male. The AI Now Institute, based at New York University, does a better job. Co-founded by Meredith Whittaker from Google and Kate Crawford at Microsoft, the organisation is fiercely independent, refusing to accept corporate donations.

One of its funders, the not-for-profit Luminate, is spending US$27 million to create the Ethics and Governance of AI Initiative. Indian billionaire Romesh Wadhwani, with his brother Sunil, is putting a similar amount towards the Wadhwani Institute for Artificial Intelligence. They're among a handful of tech giants forging a new frontier in philanthropy because they're so perturbed by artificial intelligence. But when you compare it with the net worth of tech billionaires, you realise these numbers are small change.

A lateral approach comes in the form of copyright law. Data used to build artificial intelligence systems might violate copyright. But a case hasn't yet been contested at law. Until this happens, tech companies will continue to use easily accessible and biased datasets, while their inner processes remain opaque. In the battle between ethics and economics, the latter always comes out on top.

AI expert Dr Catriona Wallace says nothing will change while the tech gurus are raking in the big bucks. 'Having strong ethics and responsible AI frameworks, and a diverse team, etc, makes that process much slower, much more expensive, and much more difficult to do,' she says. 'And so the model of profit trumps anything ethical or any real investment in diversity at this point in time.' Only eight per cent of Australian-based organisations are 'regarded as mature in their use of the responsible AI principles and have acted on them'. She cites Telstra as one company building decent ethical frameworks.

This is no surprise. Former CEO of Telstra David Thodey is an early adopter of 'all roles flex', with the policy of employees choosing how, when and where they work implemented across every business unit during 2013–14. Yes, telcos piss us off from time to time. I'm a frequent visitor to the complaints line. But large organisations need to lead the way in transforming culture.

Known as Australia's Godfather of Innovation, Thodey is a tech leader who studied Anthropology and English at university. He's a big picture thinker who's still walking the walk as a Champion of Change (a member of the coalition striving for gender equality). 'We have so many wonderful people, we just need to give them opportunities, and capability is not defined by gender,' he tells the EY *Change Happens* podcast in 2022.

Thodey and Genevieve Bell of ANU's School of Cybernetics have been pushing for an AI ethics body for years.

Of course, the problem is broader than gender. Fortunately, there are more opportunities for people from marginalised communities during this time in history. Dr Wallace issues a strong call to action in her speeches: 'Those of you who are sitting there and you might be female, or you might be from a minority group, or you might be transgender, or you may come from the disability sector. You might think this is a challenge to your career. But it will be your asset, because what we know going forward is the big tech companies, and all of us investing in AI, are desperately after diversity. So I would say particularly women of colour, you've got it made. Just know it, own it, be confident, and use it.'

'The Frontiers of AI', a panel discussion hosted by the Australian National University in 2022, features the founder of the country's first Indigenous edu-tech company. 'So bringing our people along on the journey, allowing us space to dream and think and do in AI, is going to be really important,' Indigital's Mikaela Jade says. The way for artificial intelligence to benefit all of humanity is to 'bring it back to country and bring it back to my people who have 80,000 years of science, technology, engineering, and mathematics in our DNA'. What an eloquent point. Journalists, take note.

Still, Associate Professor Yolande Strengers of Monash University isn't confident things will shift 'within the institutional supertankers of the "big five" in terms of their dominant trajectories'.

She's only optimistic about progress on the margins: 'It's in the startups. It's in the novelty kind of voices and personalities. So it's on the fringes.' The regulatory environment around technology is incredibly far behind. 'It's going to be extremely difficult to retrospectively impose any kind of regulatory, ethical, or environmental or other kinds of codes and practices onto this industry, particularly given how powerful it now is,' she says. That horse is out of the paddock and galloping towards the horizon.

Perhaps a grassroots approach is required – led by all of us. We need to value the kind of things we want embedded in these devices. 'Now, it's a bit of a chicken and egg scenario, which comes first,' Strengers says. 'I think the technology industry can bring society along that path, if it wants to, and if that's part of its goals and missions, and hopefully, ideally, it would be. But it can also work the other way. Society can put pressure on those companies, and we can help them see that we value that diversity.' (You can find some suggestions about how to apply this pressure in the Epilogue.)

Part of the answer lies in the history of artificial intelligence, and the failure of the Dartmouth Conference: a multidisciplinary approach. A unique Australian organisation is working on this now. The ARC Centre of Excellence for Automated Decision-Making and Society brings together researchers in the humanities, social and technological sciences. Director Julian Thomas says his 'central gravity' is the humanities.

'When we're dealing with something like Robodebt, for instance, we're not just dealing with a little bit of code,' he tells me. 'That kind of system is the result of not just the code, but the kind of data that people have fed into that system. It's a product of the political and economic context in which it's been generated. And of course, we'd say it's also a creature of the sort of institutions that have produced it.' Unfortunately, most universities don't teach artificial intelligence beyond the Computing and Engineering schools.

Thomas cites blockchain and smart contracts as two areas of rapidly emerging technology to be watched closely. Blockchain is a system in which transactions are recorded across computers linked in a peer-to-peer network. It's used a lot for cryptocurrency. Smart contracts are scripts on a blockchain that execute an agreement between a seller and a buyer. 'You see some amazing successes, but you also see great failures,' he explains. 'There's also that risk of significant failure, which can have very damaging consequences for people.'

It seems the entire institutional system in government, the legal and business sector, and the media is being replaced by machines. Humans are overwhelmingly being sidelined from making important decisions.

Robodebt is a classic case, involving recovery notices creating debts based on a mismatch between two pieces of data. In the past, people would oversee such processes. Not anymore. The ARC wants citizens and consumers to play bigger roles. In Australia, organisations like CHOICE could educate the users of these services to avoid the pitfalls while concurrently influencing change in government and business.

In the future, artificial intelligence will be the lynchpin in how we communicate and interact with others in the world. It's incumbent upon us to understand the basic building blocks; to make informed choices. Yes, it's hard to understand, but this is short-term pain for long-term gain.

To automate equality instead of inequality, Associate Professor Virginia Eubanks says we should interrogate the past. 'I think we can make much better decisions about the ways these technologies will impact our communities if we look to our history,' she says. 'We can also see how struggle has succeeded in the past, and how we can make it succeed again in the future.' Eubanks, from the University at

Albany, cites the civil rights movement as a template. The ability to transform society is within our hands. We should view this as a once-in-a-lifetime opportunity.

The tech companies care about cash, so hit them where it hurts: in the hip pocket. Boycott brands selling biased devices. Lobby power-brokers to regulate and legislate, and support innovative organisations led by women and people of colour.

Dr Joan Palmiter Bajorek, of the advocacy group Women in Voice, gives a terrific example in the area of speech recognition. 'Remember that women and minorities have huge purchasing power,' she says. 'This is absolutely a matter of social injustice. But if that alone doesn't convince companies to fix the problem, they should consider that the accuracy of speech recognition also affects customer purchasing decisions. I have affluent English-Spanish bilingual friends who have chosen not to buy smart fridges because they know that the fridges will not understand them.'

Philanthropist Melinda Gates frequently discusses financial 'blind spots'. 'Women are [responsible for] 85 per cent of consumer dollars spent. Women control 70 per cent of financial decisions in the house. So, you're missing an opportunity . . . you're leaving money on the table,' she tells *Bloomberg*.

While applying financial pressure, we can also change the narrative. Storytelling moves hearts and minds. There's a lovely article on the website of the United Nations Conference on Trade and Development penned by Director Shamika N. Sirimanne. She's determined to use global storytelling to reposition women in STEM. Like the story of Anna Ekeledo, executive director of AfriLabs Foundation, who by early 2023 runs a network of 400 technology and innovation hubs across 52 African countries assisting entrepreneurs to create jobs.

'Unless we get more women working on technology and innovation and have more stories to tell, women will not have a say in how we communicate, work, produce food, provide health care and educate the world for future generations,' Sirimanne writes. 'That's not the future we need.'

Indeed.

Machines representing *all* races and genders should serve us equally, as we face an uncertain future. In 1972 political philosopher John Rawls speaks of lifting the 'veil of ignorance'. He suggests the best way for leaders to make decisions with far-reaching impact is to put themselves in the shoes of the people directly affected. Yes, it's the 'golden rule' again. A little bit of empathy goes a long way. The behemoths of tech should take a leaf out of Rawls's book: the future of humanity is in their hands.

28

DYSTOPIA?

'Seek success but prepare for vegetables.'
Inspirobot

Sentient machines could be running the world within our lifetimes. This is why we secretly like it when they stuff up. Inspirobot is an artificial intelligence designed to create inspirational quotes. This should be quite easy: take some positive mantras and pop them over a pretty backdrop. The results? Well, see for yourself. 'Before inspiration comes the slaughter'; 'Keep panicking'; 'If you want to get somewhere in life you have to try to be dead'. Yep. Another epic fail. What's not so funny is the result when the stakes are somewhat higher.

'The development of full artificial intelligence could spell the end of the human race,' Stephen Hawking tells the BBC in 2014.[1] 'It would take off on its own, and re-design itself at an ever-increasing rate. Humans, who are limited by slow biological evolution, couldn't compete, and would be superseded.' Gee, that's cheery. Thanks, Steve. The fourth Industrial Revolution will alter everything. But the question is, will it be for better or worse? For richer or poorer? In sickness and in health? After all, we'll become wedded to this technology.

Transhumanism is no longer a scene from a B-grade science fiction movie. The World Economic Forum (WEF) predicts the first implantable mobile phone will be commercially available soon. If you're recoiling and thinking, 'Not this little black duck!', remember this: our smartphones are already attached to our hands. We're wearing mini-computers on our wrists. And many of us have medtech devices implanted in our bodies. Frankly, we're becoming the monsters we're fighting.

Taking an optimistic view, artificial intelligence and machine learning could contribute to a healthier, more equitable and less environmentally destructive society. Woo hoo! I'm sure we'd pick this option, given the choice. But make no mistake: there's a clear and present danger that we're heading towards a dystopian future marked by authoritarian governments, mass unemployment and poverty, and digitally-entrenched injustice. That spot you're standing on, right now, is at the crossroads to one of these futures. If we don't act quickly, we'll be so far down the track there may be no way back. And I'm not the only Chicken Little.

Klaus Schwab, German engineer, economist and founder of the World Economic Forum, sounds a warning bell back in 2016: 'The speed of current breakthroughs has no historical precedent.'[2] This global revolution is evolving exponentially and disrupting every industry: 'The breadth and depth of these changes herald the transformation of entire systems of production, management, and governance.' Schwab is convinced the pay gap between high- and low-skilled workers will widen, intensifying the racial and gender tensions causing fault lines across the globe. Social, economic and political instability will likely lead to war.

So what do the futurists see? In the same year as the comments from Klaus Schwab, a chap by the name of Robin Hanson releases his book *The Age of Em*. Hanson envisages human work becoming obsolete and an elite class of humanoid robots ruling the world. They have a choice to put people out to pasture or exterminate us. Like the Daleks from *Doctor Who*: 'Exterminate! Exterminate!' I beseech you to be nice to the robots; you may be spared by our overlords.

DYSTOPIA?

If you consider this far-fetched, think again. Robin Hanson isn't a fantasist. He's a graduate of one of the world's top research universities, Caltech. You might know of this institution as the alma mater of the characters in *The Big Bang Theory*. Hanson now works as an economist at George Mason University. 'You should expect whatever change is going to happen, it's going to happen pretty fast,' he says in a 2017 TED Talk. 'Like, five years from nothing different that you'd notice to a completely different world. What I want is to have people understand how urgent it is, when this thing shows up, to have made a plan.'

This monster is already wreaking havoc in the workplace and taking unsteady steps into our households. A single Twitter exchange exemplifies the relentless march of technology: 'Wait. I've just seen a touchscreen toaster,' to which someone responds, 'A friend told me recently he had to upgrade the firmware in his kettle.' Firmware. In a kettle. I need another cup of tea and a good lie-down. The speed at which artificial intelligence is developing is alarming. Today, scientists are less worried about smart robots than the errors we're coding into the not-so-smart machines proliferating around the globe. Like Google Nest, which left people freezing in their homes due to an unfixable error.

Perhaps we're looking at this upside-down. Australia's Gradient Institute is dedicated to building ethics, accountability and transparency into artificial intelligence systems. In 2022, the institute makes a submission to a government task force about the role of regulation in allowing automated decision-making to reach its full potential. But the scientists warn the government it's asking the wrong question: the danger is not that *regulation* will prevent AI from reaching its full potential, but that *lack* of regulation won't prevent AI from reaching its 'great potential for harm'.

The institute warns about so-called 'tail risks'. These occur in complex networked systems because mistakes multiply exponentially; so fast they can reach crisis point before there's time to avert a disaster.

What we know is this: inequitable, flawed and potentially lethal technology is coming at us like an out-of-control freight train. Soon, it'll be unstoppable. It's almost impossible to retrofit solutions.

At the Dartmouth Conference in 1956, the 'Founding Fathers' have no idea this technology could revolutionise the world. In that heady North American summer, as Senje the dog plays about their feet and Mrs Minsky makes coffee, the fellas contemplate artificial intelligence solely in terms of cost savings for business. They give no thought to the possibilities for social improvement or any negative consequences.

Narrowly focused, this hodgepodge group has no consideration for the capacity for harm, should their vision be realised.

Before and after Dartmouth, the members of AI's famed patriarchy build their fortunes on the backs of others, including many women. This gender imbalance is endemic within the field of artificial intelligence research and development. They're not only responsible for a man-made future; it's a future made for men.

Let me be clear: The men of Dartmouth are not the owners of this intellectual property. It's Ada Lovelace who takes a broader view of computing; Hedy Lamarr who pioneers technology leading to wi-fi, GPS, and Bluetooth; and Grace Hopper who discovers a way for us to 'talk' to machines. Almost entirely unrecognised, the kilo-girls and ENIAC girls of the 1940s – and the 'stable of secretaries' in the 1980s – do thousands of hours of tedious, repetitive and underpaid work to create the 'computer age'. In the 1950s and 60s, as 'man' begins to look to the stars, women like Hilda Carpenter and the 'Little Old Ladies' at NASA hand-weave memory into the computers that take Apollo 11 to the moon.

Without Digital Equipment Corporation's commitment to affirmative action, we might not have STP or TRILL, brought to us by the 'mother of the internet', Radia Perlman. Tim Berners-Lee is credited with 'inventing' the internet, 20 years after Pam Hardt-English developed a computerised bulletin board linking libraries and bookstores in the San Francisco Bay area. This history proves women do much of the physical, creative and intellectual work in the technology sector, but men set the parameters and maintain control, taking the credit *and* the profits. It remains the same to this very day.

Where do women and people in marginalised groups fit into this man-made utopia? Who will access the new technology? Whose interests will it serve? Whose pockets will it line? Who will it empower? Who will it disempower? Who will decide what innovations are helpful and which are harmful – and will they actually care?

There's an existing 'digital divide' with women, older folk, those from low socio-economic backgrounds, people with disabilities, and anyone living in developing nations being less likely to have smartphones or the internet. If artificial intelligence is to become the new global 'means of production', are we content for it to be principally owned and operated by wealthy white men?

A 2019 report by consultants, McKinsey & Company, details how quickly workers will have to adapt. The authors say by 2030, as many as five million Australians may be forced to change their occupations because of automation.[3]

Jobs once thought of as immune to displacement, in the creative industries and visual arts scene, are being shaken to their foundations. Copyright law is insufficient to protect artists and designers. Machine learning systems DALL·E and Midjourney use massive data banks to generate images within seconds. The name of the former is a clever combination of the Pixar character WALL-E and artist Salvador Dalí.

A case in point: the publishers of this book use Midjourney to create the cover. The idea has been suggested by designer Meng Koach to show the impact of AI on his profession. To construct this image, we feed phrases into the machine. This is not a fringe practice: esteemed magazines like *The Economist* and *The Atlantic* are doing it, too.

In fact, Midjourney is winning art prizes, to the consternation of actual artists. There are accusations of cheating, plagiarism and the death of artistry. Certainly, there are worrying copyright issues. But I tend to agree with the head of CSIRO's Data61 Institute, Professor Jon Whittle. 'Even things like DALL·E I don't necessarily see as replacing human creativity but rather augmenting human creativity,' he tells the ABC.

Image generators remain controversial, epitomised by an experiment unveiled in August 2022 involving Stable Diffusion, a deep-learning text-to-image model. AI researcher Sasha Luccioni decides to build a tool to expose the biases behind the model. Using the Stable Diffusion Explorer, if you type 'ambitious CEO' the machine will generate pictures of men in black or blue suits. At least there's diversity in their attire. 'Supportive CEO' displays an equal number of women and men. Try asking Stable Diffusion to show pictures of an engineer: all of them are men. It seems no women work in engineering in the robot world. And if you want an image of a male nurse? Forget about it. They don't exist, either.

Models like Stable Diffusion consume an enormous amount of energy. As these companies use larger and larger datasets, their requirements go through the roof. What are the implications for our climate?

First, the good news: artificial intelligence can be utilised to design more energy-efficient buildings, optimise recycling systems and monitor emissions. For example, AI could reduce greenhouse gas emissions by 5–10 per cent, according to Boston Consulting Group.

But US computer scientist Kate Saenko brings us back to earth: artificial intelligence has a skyrocketing carbon footprint. Training a single AI model generates as many carbon emissions as building and driving five cars over their lifetimes. One. Single. Model. What will happen when the world is powered by artificial intelligence? 'Unless we switch to 100 per cent renewable energy sources, AI progress may stand at odds with the goals of cutting greenhouse emissions and slowing down climate change,' Saenko writes in *The Conversation* in 2020.

DYSTOPIA?

I decide to email one of my clients about this thorny topic. Natalie Kyriacou is an environmentalist, board advisor and CEO of My Green World. Kyriacou is concerned about AI's ability to accelerate fossil fuel exploration. Imagine a planet where coal and oil barons can extract outdated power sources more easily, using modern technologies. It's frightening. She also points to 'more systemic consequences in which AI applications – particularly through advertising – may affect society more broadly by encouraging unsustainable consumer behaviours'. This is happening in a host of ways. Businesses use big data to micro-target people in particular demographics in order to sell them stuff. Generally, it's stuff we don't need.

Like me, Kyriacou is a glass half-full kinda gal. I ask whether she predicts a future utopia or dystopia: 'I imagine a utopian future where AI augments our human ingenuity, creativity and empathy to assist us in protecting and restoring natural resources; a future where the people and communities impacted by technology transition play a critical role in reasserting their culture, their voice and their right to determine their own future through AI.' But there's a caveat. 'Whether or not we choose to harness this technology for the betterment of the planet, however, is up to us,' Kyriacou says.

We must act quickly. Climate change is escalating the incidence and intensity of natural disasters. Women and girls – particularly in developing nations – are disproportionately affected. If artificial intelligence worsens this crisis, guess who'll pay the price? Women, too, are affected in the aftermath of war, while men make up most of the casualties in the heat of battle.

But modern warfare is evolving. Scientists, academics, geopolitical analysts, the United Nations and even China are alarmed at the implications of killing machines driven by artificial intelligence. Our inability to regulate AI could cause World War III. It'd be over within minutes. Staying silent could mean the end of humanity. The time to raise our voices is *now*.

29
UTOPIA?

'The future is a choice between Utopia and oblivion.'
R. Buckminster Fuller, inventor and visionary

We don't need a crystal ball. To predict the future, we must look to the past. The rise of new, urban manufacturing industries in the late nineteenth century fundamentally altered the nature of work. During the second Industrial Revolution, concerns were raised about child labour, working hours, pay and conditions. Most workers repetitively constructed components, deriving none of the creative pleasure that comes with producing a complete object.

As artificial intelligence becomes ubiquitous, alarm bells are ringing about the rise of the gig economy fuelled by underpaid, overworked and invisible 'ghost workers'. A twin threat is the huge potential for job losses in both blue and white collar work. Stanford University researcher, Andrew Ng, reckons the fear-mongering about a dystopia caused by 'Evil AI' – sentient robots intent on world domination – is diverting us from a much more likely outcome of this fourth Industrial Revolution: mass unemployment and its inevitable social and political impacts.

'AI is expected to be better equipped than humans to write a high school essay by 2026, drive a truck by 2027, work in retail by 2031, write a bestselling book by 2049, and perform surgery by 2053,' Darrell West, vice-president of the Brookings Institute, explains in his 2019 book, *The Future of Work: Robotics, AI, and Automation*. 'There is a 50 per cent chance AI will outperform all human tasks in 45 years and automate all human jobs in 120 years.'

If you want to write a book, you'd better get cracking! Before ChatGPT takes all of our jobs.

Once again, people in low-status jobs – mainly young folks, people of colour and women – will be the most vulnerable. Governments will have to reskill workers and pay the unemployed to study. Education, the economy and welfare systems will have to be restructured. A Universal Basic Income would be a robust solution: a government program providing every adult with an income to meet their basic needs. Historically, governments move too slowly to adjust to tectonic societal shifts.

The first Industrial Revolution gave rise to capitalism. The second deepened the gap between rich and poor. The third enabled the transition to an inter-connected economy. This works well when everyone's playing together nicely. It falls apart when the US housing market sneezes and we all get colds during a Global Financial Crisis, or Russia invades Ukraine and Europe suddenly runs out of gas.

Mass unemployment would create a larger underclass. This is always a catalyst for social unrest, creating an environment in which extreme forms of populism flourish. Imagine a future full of Donald Trumps. Brrrrrrrrrr! I don't know about you, but this is making my blood run cold.

On 6 January 2021, the world watches aghast as a mob fired up by Trumpian rhetoric storms the Capitol Building, intent on overturning the result of the election. It's an assault on democracy itself. In a global economy, the rise of more populist leaders could have dire ramifications. Darrell West warns we could end up with 'Trumpism on steroids'.

Proto-fascism is creeping into politics, emboldened by white, middle-class people complaining they're getting a raw deal. As we see in the US – and, at the risk of invoking Godwin's Law, in Germany under Hitler – certain groups do not fare well in these circumstances. If artificial intelligence turbocharges populism in politics, we face an apocalyptic future.

People living in the global south will suffer the most. Simon Greenman, who's a member of the Global AI Council at the World Economic Forum, predicts artificial intelligence is only going to profit the big corporations and countries where research and development is centred: specifically China, the US, Japan, Germany, the UK and France.

The AI economy is looking a lot like a colonial economy, in which people in poorer nations work long hours in low-paid menial jobs to provide profits for their Western masters. Women and children are already working in sweatshops to keep the West supplied with fast fashion. Will artificial intelligence entrench this kind of economic colonialism?

The tech industry is not known for its equitable distribution of wealth. The bulk of the benefits flow to tech billionaires – almost all of them male, mostly in the US. When wealth is distributed inequitably, it destabilises geopolitics.

Of course, artificial intelligence is not, of itself, evil; nor are the men who dominate the industry. This isn't about individuals.

At issue is the lack of diversity, the disparity in power and profits, and the structures continuing to exclude women and people in marginalised communities. An industry that loves to see itself as 'disruptive' is reluctant to disrupt the male-centric, capitalist and colonialist structures that threaten technology's potential to create a kinder, smarter and healthier world. Ironic much?

When I speak to Dr Calvin Lai, Assistant Professor of Psychological and Brain Sciences at Washington University in St Louis, he expresses some optimism about the future, but concedes dystopian outcomes are likely if we continue on this trajectory. Dr Lai's silver lining lies in the actual coding of bias into artificial intelligence. He describes it as 'a kind of paper trail that makes it visible and fixable in a way it wasn't before'. Essentially, Lai says bias may be easier to control in algorithms than in human interactions.

The question is, will artificial intelligence programs be sufficiently transparent for us to identify these biases? Will companies and governments take on the cost and responsibility of fixing the problem? And will they do it as a priority before the systems become unfixable?

In his 2019 article 'The Good Life After Work', economic historian Robert Skidelsky suggests if AI is built with human wellbeing rather than profit in mind, this might 'offer an emancipation from work, opening up a vista of active leisure – a theme going back to the ancient Greeks'.

Skidelsky's views echo those of Oscar Wilde writing in response to the massive changes occurring in the nineteenth century. Most utopian thought at that time saw socialism as the dominant form of government. Wilde's essay 'The Soul of Man Under Socialism' predicts a world where machinery does all the 'ugly, horrible, uninteresting work'. Humans have 'delightful leisure in which to devise wonderful and marvellous things for their own joy and the joy of everyone else'. That sounds wonderful!

Amid the upheaval of the second Industrial Revolution, British textile designer and social activist William Morris and American author and journalist William Bellamy have vastly different concepts of how the future might unfold.

In his utopian novel *Looking Backward,* Bellamy envisions a world embracing technology, with a universal basic income, shorter working hours and early retirement.

Responding to Bellamy's work, Morris writes *News from Nowhere.* In Morris's utopia, the people revolt against the dystopia of industrialised society and return to a rural way of life. According to Morris, the simplicity of their lifestyle requires only voluntary labour, most of it pleasurable and rewarding. Money effectively becomes redundant.

UTOPIA?

Mass unemployment doesn't have to be a disaster, Sami Mahroum from the not-for-profit business school INSEAD writes in *The Jordan Times* in 2019. According to Mahroum, some unemployed people don't necessarily want work: they seek financial security, a comfortable lifestyle and the opportunity to pursue fulfilling interests.[1]

The belief that the only way to achieve this is by working 9 to 5 isn't shared by every culture. Mahroum notes that Arab societies, which generally 'work to live' rather than 'live to work', may provide a template. But how does this sit within an economy obsessed with productivity?

These attitudes are 'not particularly compatible with economic systems that require squeezing ever more productivity out of labor, but they are well suited for an age of AI and automation', Mahroum writes. 'With the right mindset, all societies could start to forge a new AI-driven social contract, wherein the state would capture a larger share of the return on assets, and distribute the surplus generated by AI and automation to residents. Publicly-owned machines would produce a wide range of goods and services, from generic drugs, food, clothes, and housing, to basic research, security, and transportation.'

Governments around the world have the capacity to make such structural changes. It's their role, after all. But this would mean a major redistribution of wealth. Vested interests would fight tooth and nail to maintain the status quo. Mega-companies like Amazon, Facebook and Google – which are involved in a digital arms race – would have to be broken up. Tech billionaires would have to decentralise systems which currently funnel AI profits to individuals.

This isn't some lefty, commie utopia: in 2017, Bill Gates tells *Quartz News* that governments should tax companies' use of artificial intelligence robots to temporarily slow the speed of automation. Gates rejects self-regulation, insisting governments must oversee programs of wealth redistribution. We all know the dark side to the 'boy genius', but this idea is brilliant. Believe it or not, it's even considered by the

European Union. Sadly, European legislators ultimately reject the proposition.

Let's take a deep breath: dystopia is far from inevitable. But almost without exception, the experts I consult are very worried about the road we're travelling. So how can we move towards a more utopian vision? First, we must ensure our AI future is humanistic, collaborative and intersectional. Women, people of colour, the LGBTQI+ community, those with disabilities and older folk need quite a few seats at an awful lot of tables. Seismic changes are required at schools, within industries and at the local community level to support more inclusion in STEMM and STEAM.

People from disciplines beyond STEM will have to be involved in planning and developing artificial intelligence systems, especially in terms of identifying and managing risks. 'AI is a bit like maths in a way, it's going to be required in every discipline, and so we need to be training up future workers not just to be experts in health or law or manufacturing, or whatever it is, but to have those underlying digital AI skills as well,' Data61's Professor Whittle tells the ABC in 2022. 'There's a wonderful quote . . . in the past jobs were about muscles, currently they're about brains and in the future about the heart.'

But what does this mean for specific sectors?

The ability of artificial intelligence to mitigate climate change should be explored, but the industry must take steps to reduce its own footprint. This technology can be a boon for women's health and safety, but devices need to be designed in consultation with diverse groups. Health care of the future will be predictive and preventative, rather than reactive. But it has to be accessible to everyone – not just white people in wealthy countries. AI could change the lives of people who use social services. But the users must be included from the outset.

Innovation has the potential to smooth every aspect of our lives, from shopping to transport, employment and household duties. Machines that gestate human life could free women from reproductive obligations and biological restraints. A step too far for many, but something to think about, nevertheless. If developed sensibly, artificial intelligence could take part of the burden of caring for children, people with disabilities, and elderly relatives away from women.

Currently, Indigenous people are looking into how artificial intelligence can help conserve traditional lands, revitalise lost languages and preserve ancient knowledge. This is through something called artificial-intelligence-enabled cyber-physical systems (AI-CPS). Jeez. What on earth is that? Communications professionals really need to simplify the tech-talk. Put simply, these systems could monitor wildlife, reduce poaching and simulate ecological interventions.

Nowadays, Indigenous peoples manage around a quarter of the world's land surface. Imagine the impact of combining old and new knowledge. It could sustain the land and its inhabitants for future generations. In Australia, artificial intelligence is already being used to care for Country.

During his Master of Applied Cybernetics at the Australian National University, Rodolfo Ocampo works on the CSIRO Healthy Country AI project. Developed in collaboration with Bininj Traditional Owners and Indigenous rangers, the project manages invasive weeds, which are decimating biodiversity in Kakadu.

'The Healthy Country AI-CPS uses drones to survey the land, machine learning algorithms to classify aerial images and cloud technology to visualise infestation maps,' Ocampo writes on the Australian National University website in 2021. 'Algorithms and data management were trained integrating traditional knowledge. For example, the Bininj six-season calendar is used to classify drone footage.'

I've said it before. I'll say it again. We have so much to learn from Indigenous culture, including in the area of artificial intelligence.

Distinguished Professor Genevieve Bell from the ANU echoes this thought. She recommends taking inspiration from First Nations peoples when designing the future. 'The concept of "always was, always will be" offers a through line from past to present to future and makes clear both persistence and responsibility,' she says in the 2021 Garran Oration. She calls it 'a meditation on the shape of the future, and the tools and approaches we might need to cultivate in order to succeed in it'.[2]

We need to work together to create a utopia. This begins with words and ends with actions.

'I tend to think we have an obligation to tell stories about a future that is more just and fair and equitable and sustainable, and thus also more optimistic,' Bell tells me. 'And I think we also have an obligation to actively disrupt the present to make those stories possible.'

This time in history is nothing short of transformative. However, it's painful and exhausting because we're evolving from one stage to the next. 'Are we in the process of giving birth to a whole new world?' social commentator Jane Caro writes in the *Sydney Morning Herald*. 'Hopefully a fairer, less hierarchical world, where we will live in greater harmony with one another and with the natural environment? Is that why we are in such an uncomfortable and panicky place right now? Just like mother and child, we know the world we are leaving but we do not know the one we are going to.'

Maybe we should all go with the flow, confident of soon holding new life in our hands. But it takes more than one party to create life. That's why the future must be made *by* all of us, *for* all of us: human-made, not man-made.

EPILOGUE:
RAGE AGAINST THE MACHINE

'Next time, ask: What's the worst that will happen?
Then push yourself a little further than you dare.
Once you start to speak, people will yell at you.
They will interrupt you, put you down and suggest
it's personal. And the world won't end.'
Audre Lorde, poet, activist, and radical feminist

It's 7.47 pm on a Monday in late 2022 and I'm lying in bed, reflecting upon my hypocrisy. Two torn paper bags decorate the sheets: Uber Eats and CHEMIST2U. After almost a year of chronic illness, I'm accustomed to needing help for day-to-day activities like cooking, shopping and personal care. But I still struggle with relying on Big Tech to deliver food and medicine.

Yes, I want you to rage against the machine. However, I understand – viscerally – it's not possible to banish technology from our lives entirely. Herein lies the conundrum: how can we change the machines when they're becoming our carers, feeders and shoppers? Our substitute family? And our masters?

My latest mission is to switch from Uber to female-run transport in the form of Shebah. The drivers are women, many of whom pick up a few extra dollars during school hours. On paper, this business ticks all the boxes. But there are simply not enough people using the service. It's tough to get a car when you need it, especially at the last minute. Still, it's incumbent upon us to support these efforts, to break the stranglehold of the homogenised tech titans. If not us, then who? And if not now, when? Put your money where your mouth is: collective action is the only way forward.

It's well and truly time to bankroll tech companies run by women and people from marginalised populations. Australian tech company Canva – a global goliath – is led by co-founder and CEO Melanie Perkins. Entrepreneur Shivani Gopal is the brains behind the app ELLADEX, which mentors, educates and guides women to grow their wealth. A proponent of 'tech for good', Gopal plans to start her own cryptocurrency.

Cheryl Bailey leads Indigenous Technology, an IT company 100 per cent owned and operated by Aboriginal and Torres Strait Islander people. Take a look at the Superstars of STEM website to find women like Natalie Chapman from gemaker, a trailblazer in the sciences who's been fighting the good fight for decades.

Despite announcing a review into diversity in STEM, the federal government has committed no new funding for women in tech programs, according to co-founder of the Girl Geek Academy, Sarah Moran. Let's support organisations like the Academy, which offer workshops, courses and scholarships to 'girl geeks'.

Obviously, targeting individuals isn't enough to create lasting change. Sometimes I yearn for a return to the consciousness-raising days of the 1960s, 70s and 80s. During that era, discrimination was endemic: a wallpaper of misogyny. Women often attributed their circumstances to personal failings rather than wider structural issues. Gathering in groups in homes, parks and halls, they realised they were not alone.

A similar truth-telling occurred during the Me Too movement, started by Tarana Burke in 2006 before being popularised as a hashtag in 2017. Joining together is an effective way to lobby for lasting change. Grassroots protest and legislative reform are responsible for the great achievements of the civil rights movement, action on climate change and every wave of feminism since the nineteenth century.

Dealing with big hairy issues like intersectional discrimination in artificial intelligence can seem overwhelming. This is frontier feminism. After reading this book, your consciousness is raised. You have the information, motivation and language to craft a short but powerful message: 'Enough!'

Talk to your family, friends and co-workers. Are you a member of a business organisation, women's professional body, political party, parents' group or not-for-profit? Start a conversation or create an event centred on AI bias. Write emails to your local politicians. Call talkback radio whenever the topic is discussed, and pitch stories to the media. We're always seeking interesting, future-focused content.

There are simple things you can do in your home, car, or workplace. Change the voices of servile assistants to male instead of female. Better still, find a 'gender-neutral' option. Siri now has a non-binary voice. Open the 'Settings' app on your iPhone or iPad and go to 'Siri & Search'. Choose 'Siri Voice' then select 'Voice 5' to switch to gender-neutral.

When buying a new vehicle, ask questions about the voice controls. What's the accuracy rate for female voices? For people whose first language isn't English? Or those with an accent? Take it a step further and ask about the composition of the upper echelons of the company manufacturing the car. Most are still stuck in the 1950s.

Perhaps you're realising your absent partner knows where you are, what you're doing and the conversations you're having. Ask yourself these questions: why are they so keen for me to use the Alexa? Are the lights, air conditioning and/or heating being turned on and off? What about the time heavy metal music screamed from the smart speaker for no apparent reason? You could be experiencing high-tech gaslighting.

If you work in a women's shelter or law enforcement, be on alert for men using tracking devices like Apple AirTag. As small as a coin, this can be attached to keys and handbags or slipped into a woman's pocket. Of course, you're probably all too aware of the latest methods being used to stalk women and girls.

Are you reeling after being rejected for a job, credit card or home loan? Don't take it lying down. Ask follow-up questions. Was this decision made by a human or software? If it's the latter, are the algorithms audited regularly for bias? Does the software use historical data to make decisions? Is machine learning involved in this process? What recourse do I have to lodge a complaint, or reapply?

It might be worthwhile contacting the Australian Human Rights Commission or the Banking Ombudsman. Or consider taking legal action. This book is a reminder that we live in a democracy and you have rights. Know where you stand, take a deep breath and push back.

When you receive the results of your medical tests, maybe they don't seem quite right. Ask your doctor whether the diagnostic machine is as accurate for women as it is for men. Or people with disabilities, Indigenous communities, or transgender populations.

If a clinician recommends a new drug, device or treatment, ask about the science. Are there peer-reviewed studies? If so, what's the gender/race/age make-up of the cohort? For example, much of the international long COVID research is based on a male experience, through the US Department of Veterans Affairs.

With mass automation occurring in the workplace, join a union and agitate to retain people – or at least retain human oversight. Seek legal recourse if you're sidelined or sacked by the machines. Ask your boss whether these robots will be as accurate, effective and productive. Play devil's advocate: what happens if something goes wrong?

Managers, executives and board members, I hope this book gives you some ideas about the questions you should be asking. Who are our technology suppliers? What's their record on diversity and inclusion? Where does the data come from? What auditing are we going to do in-house? Should bias-testing be done externally for a more robust result? How can we continuously monitor our algorithms to ensure they're up-to-date with society's mores?

In an era in which employers use workplace surveillance to monitor our productivity, we often forget that we can turn the tables. Futurists predict workers will soon be monitoring their bosses using the same tools. For example, employees can check and record stress levels on their Garmin, Fitbit or iWatch.

Perhaps there's a place for a website to publish the results of smartwatch data from employees at particular companies. Kinda like a high-tech Glassdoor, the website where employees anonymously review companies. It'd be fascinating to see the results from the likes of Apple, Google and Facebook. Talk about turning the tables on the tech titans. Solidarity forever!

Nowadays, male allies are refusing to speak at conventions where there's an unequal representation of genders. Advocates are highlighting this on social media using the hashtag #Whereareallthewomen. If you work in tech and are slated to present at a conference, ask yourself: is there someone I can nominate instead? It might be a woman, a person of colour, or a colleague with a disability.

Ethical investors should be putting a gender lens over tech stocks. 'What's the composition of the executive team and board?' 'How many women are involved in research and development?' 'Does this company invest in organisations with a history of gender or racial bias?' Talk to your bank, superannuation fund or financial advisor about your concerns. By the end of this decade, women will control US$30 trillion in financial assets. Yep – trillion.

Do you work in the university sector? Lecturers should be aware of the pitfalls of using machine learning to evaluate assessments. There needs to be human oversight. Sophisticated algorithms can pinpoint struggling students and organise assistance. However, they can also exacerbate existing bias, further sidelining these students.

It might be time for your uni to create a department dedicated to AI bias. The Human Technology Institute at the University of Technology Sydney is hitting the ground running with a world-leading report recommending reform on facial recognition, based on international human rights law. The report urges the federal attorney-general to lead this 'pressing' process.

Maybe you're a lawyer working in the technology field, or a judge who'll be presiding over cases of alleged algorithmic bias. It's your job to decide what 'fair' means as it pertains to the use of artificial intelligence and machine learning. So too, insurers must adopt robust fairness criteria. One test being developed centres on something called 'counterfactual fairness'. Yikes! What the heck is that? Apparently, it asks AI systems this question: if attributes such as race, gender or sexual orientation are changed, do the model's decisions remain the same?

Where can you look for more details? The Alan Turing Institute's website is an excellent source for information on fairness, transparency and privacy. Google AI and Fairness 360 provide open-source toolkits to check for bias in datasets and machine learning models. IBM's Watson OpenScale performs bias-checking and mitigation in real time. Read the 2021 book co-authored by Dr Catriona Wallace, *Checkmate Humanity: The how and why of Responsible AI*.

One easy suggestion is to include a human in the loop: an actual person double-checking everything. The World Economic Forum wants businesses to be aware of the three main forms of machine bias. (Yes, there are more than three, but these are often evident in the workplace.) These are:

1. *Implicit bias*: A system that discriminates against a person or group on the grounds of gender, race, disability, sexuality or social class.

2. *Sampling bias*: This occurs when the data used to train the machine isn't representative of the population the machine will be servicing. For example, we know about the problem with data from white middle-class hospitals failing to represent non-white populations from poorer neighbourhoods.
3. *Temporal bias*: Even if the AI produces fair results today, it may not do so in the future, as circumstances change.

Put simply, we should all be aware of the 'red flags', as my teenage daughter would say. Although she says it at the slightest provocation. I'll try to give her a kiss on the cheek before bedtime: 'Red flag, Mum!' Gotta love Generation Alpha. These kids really know their boundaries!

If you think speaking out about red flags will make little difference, think again. Research by the Brookings Institution reveals public opinion is hugely influential in relation to legislation on AI fairness, privacy and safety in the US. Here in Australia, we're at the beginning of the conversation. We can exert enormous influence in the coming years.

Follow the international change-makers and donate to their foundations. Hop onto ajl.org to give money to the Algorithmic Justice League, which is fighting for equitable and accountable artificial intelligence.

Maybe you work in voice software. Anyone who identifies as 'a female, non-binary, genderqueer, genderfluid, gender non conforming, agender, and all minority genders' can be part of the community at womeninvoice.org.

Bias in artificial intelligence is seen as a technical issue. But it stems from existing biases within society. If you're uncomfortable talking about tech, bring the dialogue back to historical inequity. Intersectional discrimination pervades every aspect of society. If we can change the culture from the ground up, we'll solve the problem.

When I take a television network to court for maternity discrimination, present documentaries about the rights of women and girls, and work on investigative stories as part of the #MeToo movement, these are not solo efforts. It may seem like a pebble in a pond, but one person can embolden others to speak out. This creates a ripple effect that can change the world.

During filming for the documentary *Silent No More*, I learn about bystander training at Queensland's Griffith University. The MATE program teaches people how to safely call out unacceptable behaviour. This empowers victim-survivors and puts perpetrators on notice. What does this have to do with data, algorithms and machine learning?

Creating environments where discrimination is not tolerated is *crucial* to shifting the mindset of blithe acceptance of biased bots. Have a quiet chat with like-minded colleagues about how you can question AI bias at the next team meeting. Standing up for yourself is like building a muscle at the gym: the more you do it, the stronger you become.

Hopefully, you have enough ammunition to counter the inevitable backlash: 'Now you think even the *robots* are biased? Crazy, hairy-legged, woke, left-wing feminazi!' When trolls say this, my latest response is to treat is as a compliment. Well, on the days when I have the energy to bother responding. 'Why, thank you for noticing! Yes, I support equality in all forms. How about we sit down for a nice cup of tea to discuss this?' Of course, they never get back to me.

If they don't believe feminists, maybe they'll listen to big business. As early as 2018, business insights giant Gartner was predicting that by the year 2030, 85 per cent of artificial intelligence projects will provide false results caused by bias. But it doesn't have to be this way. I invite you to join a movement with its sights set on a fairer future. A future for all of us; a future made for humans. Collectively, we have the power to determine our destiny.

GLOSSARY

'By far the greatest danger of Artificial Intelligence is that people conclude too early that they understand it.'
Eliezer Yudkowsky, autodidact and artificial intelligence researcher

Algorithm: A set of rules a machine can follow to learn how to do a task or solve a problem. We use algorithmic thinking every single day of our lives. Examples include using a recipe to make a meal, working out how to sort a pile of papers or following a step-by-step process in order to tie our shoelaces.

Artificial intelligence: This refers to the concept of machines acting in a way that simulates human intelligence. Fun fact: there is no such thing as 'one' AI; there are many types of artificial intelligence. AI can have a variety of features, including communication or decision-making.

Autonomous: When a machine can perform tasks without human intervention, it's described as 'autonomy'. Think self-driving cars, smart assistants and manufacturing robots. While autonomy is enabled by artificial intelligence, not all uses of AI are necessarily autonomous.

Backward chaining: A method in which the model starts with the desired output and works in reverse to find data that might support it. You start by breaking the task into small steps. Then you do the last step first, working backwards from your goal.

Bias: I cover this at length in the book. Machine bias is caused by a combination of human bias, and assumptions made by a model that simplifies the process of learning. These biases are exacerbated as the machine continues to stereotype different pieces of information.

Big data: These are datasets that are too big or complex to be managed by traditional processing software. But they are extremely valuable. Big data can be used to address business problems that are unsolvable using any other method.

Chatbot: From Siri to Alexa and beyond, these programs are designed to communicate with people using text or voice commands. Chatbots are supposed to mimic human-to-human conversation, but often fall far short.

Data science: Drawing from statistics, and computer and information science, this interdisciplinary field uses modern techniques to sift through volumes of data. This is aimed at finding unseen patterns. Machine learning algorithms are used to make predictive models.

Dataset: This is a collection of numbers or values relating to a specific subject. It could be students' test scores from a particular class or patients' medical results from a hospital department. Categories of datasets include record data, graph-based data and ordered data.

Deep learning: Strap yourself in! This is a type of machine learning based on artificial neural networks. These neural networks try to simulate the human brain. Many layers of processing are used to extract high-level features from raw data. Facial recognition, vision for driverless cars and virtual assistants are examples of deep learning.

Entity annotation: Annotators label unstructured sentences with information, so a machine can read them. This can involve labelling all people, organisations, and locations in a document. AI systems then learn to make sense of these images, videos, and text. As you can probably guess, annotation is open to all sorts of bias.

General AI: Also called 'artificial general intelligence'. This is a theoretical form of AI that could do sophisticated cognitive tasks of similar breadth and diversity to human capabilities. It's sometimes referred to as *'strong AI'*, although they aren't entirely equivalent terms. General AI is likely to emerge between 2030 and 2100.

Machine learning: This subset of artificial intelligence is particularly focused on developing algorithms that will help machines to learn and change in response to new data without the help of a human being. The autonomous aspect of machine learning has many people concerned.

Narrow AI: This is artificial intelligence that is capable of specific tasks, such as searching the internet, diagnosing illness, screening applicants for a position, or operating a vehicle. Machine learning is a subset of this category.

Neural network: Also called a neural net. This is a computer system designed to function like the human brain. Current neural networks can perform a variety of tasks involving speech, vision and game strategy.

Python: No, this is not a type of snake. Python is a popular computer programming language. This is the first programming language my son, Taj, learned, as it's often taught to beginners. It's also one of the most widely used in the world.

Turing test: Named after computer scientist and mathematician Alan Turing, this tests a machine's ability to pass for a human. This is especially relevant in the areas of language and behaviour. A person 'passes' the machine if its output is unable to be distinguished from that of a human.

ENDNOTES

INTRODUCTION
1   Long COVID is experienced by twice as many women as men taken from the *Financial Times*: https://www.ft.com/content/ea2d58c5-ae62-442c-b721-364c95852209. However *The Guardian* says it's actually four to one, yikes: https://www.theguardian.com/society/2021/jun/13/why-are-women-more-prone-to-long-covid

CHAPTER 1
1   Claims against Minsky via: https://www.theverge.com/2019/8/9/20798900/marvin-minsky-jeffrey-epstein-sex-trafficking-island-court-records-unsealed

CHAPTER 3
1   Women outnumber men four to one as psychologists in Australia: https://www.statista.com/statistics/806623/australia-registered-psychologists-by-gender/
2   Funding reduced after Lighthill report as referenced in *Forbes*: https://www.forbes.com/sites/gilpress/2016/12/30/a-very-short-history-of-artificial-intelligence-ai/?sh=2ee4f40d6fba

CHAPTER 4
1   John Sims interview: http://www.maynardlifeoutdoors.com/2020/03/digital-equipment-corporation-diversity.html
2   Ellen Broad on invisibility from *Inside Story*: https://insidestory.org.au/computer-says-no/

CHAPTER 5
1   First female crash dummy arrives in 2022 via BBC: https://www.bbc.com/news/technology-62877930

CHAPTER 6

1. *TIME* magazine on ChatGPT: https://time.com/6238781/chatbot-chatgpt-ai-interview/
2. Microsoft Cybersecurity Field Chief Technical Officer Diana Kelley speaking on the Tay catastrophe via: https://www.zdnet.com/article/microsoft-and-the-learnings-from-its-failed-tay-artificial-intelligence-bot/
3. Edward Santow in the *AFR*: https://www.afr.com/companies/financial-services/banks-warned-using-ai-in-loan-assessments-could-awaken-a-zombie-20210615-p5814i

CHAPTER 7

1. Anonymous software engineer tells the BBC: https://www.bbc.com/news/technology-57101248
2. Clearview AI fined over £7.5 million as per BBC: https://www.bbc.com/news/technology-61550776

CHAPTER 9

1. Researchers estimate the number of digital voice assistants worldwide will reach 8.4 billion by 2024: https://www.statista.com/statistics/973815/worldwide-digital-voice-assistant-in-use/

CHAPTER 10

1. The number of virtual voice assistants in the world set to exceed the number of people by 2024 via Statista: https://www.statista.com/statistics/973815/worldwide-digital-voice-assistant-in-use/
2. According to TechJury, 97 per cent of people with mobile phones use the AI-powered voice assistant and two-out-of-five people use the voice search function at least once a day: https://techjury.net/blog/ai-statistics/#gref

CHAPTER 11

1. Algorithmic recommendations account for 80 per cent of the content we watch on Netflix: https://www.lighthouselabs.ca/en/blog/how-netflix-uses-data-to-optimize-their-product

ENDNOTES

CHAPTER 12

1. Your smart fridge might kill you: https://www.infoworld.com/article/3176673/your-smart-fridge-may-kill-you-the-dark-side-of-iot.html
2. Hod Fleishman on whether companies should continue going into the home tech space in *Forbes*: https://www.forbes.com/sites/hodfleishman/2019/09/01/how-to-determine-if-your-company-should-go-into-the-smart-home-space/?sh=633ba022da73
3. The global robotic vacuum cleaner market is expected to reach US$15.4 billion by 2028: https://www.meticulousresearch.com/pressrelease/400/robotic-vacuum-cleaner-market-2028
4. Helen Greiner on girls entering STEM: https://techcrunch.com/2017/07/06/flux-robot-queen-helen-greiner-on-robots-drones-and-the-self-aware-roomba/
5. 2021 Australian report from the Australian Housing and Urban Research Institute: https://www.ahuri.edu.au/sites/default/files/documents/2021-12/AHURI-Final-Report-372-Impacts-of-new-and-emerging-assistive-technologies-for-ageing-and-disabled-housing.pdf

CHAPTER 14

1. Academics claim to be able to predict family violence in Bangladesh with 62–77 per cent degree accuracy: https://www.mdpi.com/2571-5577/4/4/77
2. Ten leading startups brainstorming industry response to domestic violence in *Wired*: https://www.wired.com/story/israeli-hackathon-domestic-violence/

CHAPTER 15

1. Robots, Rape and Representation paper: https://research.monash.edu/en/publications/robots-rape-and-representation

CHAPTER 16

1. Dr Claire Benn on consent and deepfakes: https://law.anu.edu.au/event/anu-law-and-philosophy-forum/deepfakes-pornography-and-consent
2. Poem extracts from *Deepfake: a pornographic ekphrastic* by Helen Mort accessed via: https://nowthenmagazine.com/articles/helen-mort-behind-every-image-is-a-person-violence-against-women-deepfakes

CHAPTER 17

1. Dr Ayanna Howard recounts a story of a child and robot interacting: https://au.mathworks.com/company/mathworks-stories/machine-learning-robots-vr-help-children-with-disabilities.html

CHAPTER 18

1. The World Health Organization on eliminating ageism in AI usage: https://www.who.int/news/item/09-02-2022-ensuring-artificial-intelligence-(ai)-technologies-for-health-benefit-older-people
2. Three out of four people over 65 use the internet in the US from Pew: https://www.pewresearch.org/fact-tank/2022/01/13/share-of-those-65-and-older-who-are-tech-users-has-grown-in-the-past-decade/
3. Daniel Allen on how data will be used on the aged care residents in Japan: https://emag.medicalexpo.com/from-ai-to-robots-japans-advancing-agetech/
4. Cost of a PARO from their website: https://www.paroseal.co.uk/purchase
5. Kate Loveys and co-authors' findings: Loveys K, Prina M, Axford C, Domènec ÒR, Weng W, Broadbent E, Pujari S, Jang H, Han ZA, Thiyagarajan JA. Artificial intelligence for older people receiving long-term care: a systematic review of acceptability and effectiveness studies. Lancet Healthy Longev. 2022 Apr;3(4):e286-e297. doi: 10.1016/S2666-7568(22)00034-4. PMID: 35515814; PMCID: PMC8979827

CHAPTER 19

1. Emily Pfaff on the difficulty in building an algorithm to identify long COVID: https://www.statnews.com/2022/04/29/long-covid-machine-learning-n3c/
2. Angelica Marotta on what happens on when algorithms get it wrong: https://www.tandfonline.com/doi/full/10.1080/08874417.2022.2089773
3. The European Union's latest General Data Protection Regulation coming into effect in mid-2018, via their website: https://gdpr.eu/what-is-gdpr/

CHAPTER 20

1. Uma Jayaram quoted in *The Guardian*: https://www.theguardian.com/games/2021/jul/19/video-gaming-artificial-intelligence-ai-is-evolving
2. Brie Code quoted from the same *Guardian* article.

ENDNOTES

CHAPTER 21

1   The augmented, virtual and mixed reality market is expected to exceed US$250 billion by 2028: https://www.statista.com/statistics/591181/global-augmented-virtual-reality-market-size/
2   Is it wrong to perform immoral acts in virtual reality? From *Frontiers*: https://www.frontiersin.org/articles/10.3389/frvir.2020.00001
3   Concerns that technological experiences will replace direct community engagement: https://itif.org/publications/2021/06/01/current-and-potential-uses-arvr-equity-and-inclusion/
4   Professor Courtney Cogburn in *Yes!* magazine: https://www.yesmagazine.org/health-happiness/2019/01/15/using-virtual-reality-to-teach-empathy

CHAPTER 22

1   Minorities excluded from research into self-driving cars: https://www.sciencedirect.com/science/article/abs/pii/S1369847821002837
2   Spanish Study in MDPI finds women are more motivated by the promise of greater safety, reduced on-road errors and fewer driving demands than men: https://www.mdpi.com/2076-3417/12/1/103
3   Machine learning expert Raquel Urtasun: https://entrepreneurs.utoronto.ca/the-road-ahead-raquel-urtasuns-startup-to-unleash-full-power-of-ai-on-self-driving-cars/
4   The US Department of Defense is behind the bid to speed up autonomous vehicle technology in order to use it in war zones: https://www.darpa.mil/about-us/timeline/-grand-challenge-for-autonomous-vehicles

CHAPTER 23

1   The LA in ATLAS stands for Lethality Automated: https://breakingdefense.com/2019/03/atlas-killer-robot-no-virtual-crewman-yes/
2   Frank Pasquale in *The Guardian*: https://www.theguardian.com/news/2020/oct/15/dangerous-rise-of-military-ai-drone-swarm-autonomous-weapons
3   *The New York Times* review: https://www.nytimes.com/2016/08/04/books/review-how-everything-became-war-and-the-military-became-everything.html

4   Australia lifted the 'combat bar' in 2013 in *The Guardian*: https://www.theguardian.com/world/2014/jun/03/women-in-combat-63-sign-up-for-frontline-military-roles
5   Rosa Brooks in *The New York Times* regarding women in the Pentagon: https://www.nytimes.com/2020/11/30/opinion/defense-department-woman-secretary-biden.html

CHAPTER 24

1   The Forbes Real-Time Billionaires List: https://www.forbes.com/real-time-billionaires/#2a56565f3d78
2   The worldwide market for artificial intelligence is projected to reach US$459.3 billion by 2030: https://www.marketresearch.com/Global-Industry-Analysts-v1039/Artificial-Intelligence-AI-32280864/
3   The International Monetary Fund projects 11 per cent of jobs held by women are at risk of elimination as a result of AI and other digital technologies: https://www.bcg.com/publications/2019/artificial-intelligence-ai-help-hinder-women-workforce
4   Conditions around data handling in India: https://analyticsindiamag.com/is-ai-fast-becoming-a-technology-built-on-worker-exploitation-from-global-south/
5   'The Limits of Global Inclusion in AI Development': https://arxiv.org/abs/2102.01265

CHAPTER 25

1   The World Economic Forum estimates women make up roughly a quarter of the workforce in artificial intelligence: https://www.weforum.org/agenda/2021/08/5-ways-increase-women-working-ai/
2   Doina Precup's story referred to in: https://medium.com/element-ai-research-lab/women-in-machine-learning-negar-rostamzadeh-dbb58dc75e81
3   'Mirrortocracies' as reported in Yahoo Finance: https://finance.yahoo.com/news/examining-pipeline-problem-173021399.html
4   UNESCO report found here: https://unesdoc.unesco.org/ark:/48223/pf0000380861

ENDNOTES

CHAPTER 26

1. Loren Goodman on whether to take or not take real-world actions based on a machine learning prediction from: https://venturebeat.com/data decisionmakers/bias-in-ai-is-spreading-and-its-time-to-fix-the-problem/
2. Jingwei Li et al explain that brain templates come from White populations: https://www.science.org/doi/10.1126/sciadv.abj1812
3. 2021 report by Edward Santow: https://humanrights.gov.au/our-work/rights-and-freedoms/publications/human-rights-and-technology-final-report-2021

CHAPTER 28

1. 'The development of full artificial intelligence could spell the end of the human race,' Stephen Hawking tells the BBC: https://www.bbc.com/news/av/science-environment-30289705
2. 'The speed of current breakthroughs has no historical precedent.': https://www.weforum.org/agenda/2016/01/the-fourth-industrial-revolution-what-it-means-and-how-to-respond/
3. By 2030, as many as five million Australians may be forced to change their occupations because of automation, via McKinsey: https://www.mckinsey.com/featured-insights/future-of-work/australias-automation-opportunity-reigniting-productivity-and-inclusive-income-growth

CHAPTER 29

1. Quotes from Sami Mahroum in the *Jordan Times* in this chapter: https://jordantimes.com/opinion/sami-mahroum/how-ai-utopia-would-work
2. Professor Genevieve Bell at the 2021 Garran Oration: https://www.ipaa.org.au/wp-content/uploads/2022/03/Garran-Oration-2021_publish.pdf

ACKNOWLEDGEMENTS

It takes a village to write a book. I'm fortunate to be surrounded by kind, clever and diligent people, who've helped me every step of the way.

Chrys Stevenson is one of the best researchers in the country. Without her tenacity, intellect and global view, this book would have remained a mess of ideas in my head. I am eternally grateful for her work and friendship.

Speaking of friendship, there are few better buddies than the legendary Selina Day. Early readers are priceless, especially ones who are excellent subs. Thanks to Selina's hours of toil, I was able to submit 'a lovely "clean", well-written' manuscript, according to Simon & Schuster. Phew!

James McIlwain is a boon companion to have when you're grappling with complex technical concepts. A solution architect with a development background, Jim shares a similar sense of humour, which is priceless when dissecting the absurdity of this brave new world. A thousand thanks.

My clever publisher, Emma Nolan, was one of the first people to see the potential for this book. Her enthusiasm, hard work and big picture thinking brought this project to fruition. The publishing deal wouldn't have happened without the chutzpah of literary agent, Jacinta di Mase. I am forever indebted to Jacinta for supporting my dream.

Managing Editor Michelle Swainson is an absolute gun for keeping us on schedule during a global pandemic. I'm especially thankful for

Michelle's wit and wisdom during the editing process. Her instincts are bang on.

If you look up 'forensic' in the dictionary, there's a photo of copy-editor Katie Stackhouse. Katie has an incredible eye for detail, and the patience of a saint. If there are any mistakes in *Man-Made* they are surely mine, not Katie's!

The cover designer, Meng Koach, is an utterly delightful fella. His idea to create the image using artificial intelligence was genius. It was a joy immersing ourselves for hours in the digital space.

Special thanks to everyone who kindly agreed to be interviewed for this book, and the countless academics and technologists who I've quoted throughout its pages. You are the experts in this area. It's a privilege to be able to platform your powerful work.

I'm not gonna lie: this was the 'difficult second book'. During the first two years of the researching and interviewing process, I was struggling with a major depressive disorder due to vicarious trauma. While writing the final chapters and going through the rounds of editing, I was living with long COVID. Wholehearted thanks to my loyal clients, who moved heaven and earth so I could keep working during this time, albeit in a severely reduced capacity.

To the family, friends and fellow travellers who came to stay, cooked meals, sent care packs, supported long COVID advocacy, or simply called to make me laugh, how can I ever thank you? You kept me sane! I'm blessed to have a beautiful sister, Suzanne, who flew interstate several times to nurse me back to health. She is a rare gem, indeed.

Mostly, I'd like to thank my lovely hubby Jason, our terrific teens Taj and Grace, and border collie, Arabella. For almost a year they did pretty much everything around the house, while I languished in bed. They put my broken body back together again. Put simply, they are my everything.

ABOUT THE AUTHOR

Tracey Spicer AM is a multiple Walkley Award-winning author, journalist and broadcaster who has anchored national programs for ABC TV and radio, Network Ten and Sky News.

The inaugural national convenor of Women in Media, Tracey is one of the most sought-after keynote speakers and emcees in the region.

In 2019 she was named the NSW Premier's Woman of the Year, accepted the Sydney Peace Prize alongside Tarana Burke for the 'Me Too' movement, and won the national award for Excellence in Women's Leadership through Women & Leadership Australia.

In 2018, Tracey was chosen as one of the *Australian Financial Review*'s 100 Women of Influence, winning the Social Enterprise and Not-For-Profit category. She was also named Agenda Setter of the Year by the website Women's Agenda.

For her 30 years of media and charity work, Tracey has been awarded the Order of Australia.

Made in United States
North Haven, CT
13 May 2024